TELL ME THE NAMES
OF YOUR FRIENDS
AND
I WILL TELL YOU
WHO YOU ARE
Arab Proverb

"*Gramma said when you come on something good, first thing to do is share it with whoever you can find; that way, the good spreads out where no telling it will go. Which is right.*"
The Education of Little Tree. Forrest Carter

In gratitude to all who created this book with me and for all the friendships in my life.

This edition published by
Dog Ear Publishing
4010 W. 86th Street, Ste H
Indianapolis, IN 46268

www.dogearpublishing.net

ISBN: 978-160844-407-6
This book is printed on acid-free paper.

Printed in the United States of America

CONTENTS.

Introduction

INTRODUCTION.

"Look back in your life and pay less attention to what interests you in your own respectable person and much more to those figures that have come into contact with you, educating you, befriending you, assisting you, perhaps also injuring you - often injuring you in a helpful way. One thing will then become evident to you and that is how little reason a person really has to ascribe to himself what he has become."
Rudolf Steiner.

When I read about people surviving genocide, rescuing folk from burning buildings, dedicating their lives to healing humanity or the earth in some way, I feel humbled and wonder why I think this little story might interest others. I didn't suffer deeply, or lose that much, and I am now, a year later, on the road to some sort of recovery. However, we aren't all major league players, and all our stories matter, so I thought of three good reasons for writing this book.
First, I love to talk, and I couldn't for a year, so this was the next best thing. Second, it was a way of sharing my friends – with each other, maybe even with a wider circle of people. And *thanking* them. I do not know how I could have gone through these times without them. Third, famous people have their "Collected Letters" published posthumously. Why not infamous, and unknown folk during their lifetimes? Everyone's life is extraordinary. Everyone's story deserves to be told and heard. So, those are, in my view, good reasons. There may be some bad ones too, like my still being unable to learn to keep my mouth shut!!
The fact that some friends and I had fairly lengthy and frequent exchanges and others barely appear does not indicated a hierarchy of my preferences for one person over another, or their care for me. Some expressed this in other ways: visits, messages left on my phone etc. But I hope I have managed (or each person has managed) to convey something of him or herself through what appears here. Some people entered at key moments and then vanished again, like some angelic visitation. Some, like my son, have been stalwart travelers beside me throughout. I have also curbed my enthusiasm for all the exchanges we had, and excluded at least 75% of them!
For all of us our group of friends are "insider traders" so to speak. We have our particular interests and connections that may be gobbledygook to others. Many of us have been students of Anthroposophy (Rudolf Steiner's work) and involved in Waldorf education. Google all that, if interested. Some may have to snap the book shut and burn it quickly. Pity, but we can't please everyone, can we! What I hope is that this "mini memoir" illustrates the deepest truth of all our existences: that we are nothing without others, each other human being shapes our destiny, is a color, a thread in the tapestry. I hope others will be inspired to share their tales, their friendships. Yes: **Tell Me The Names of *Your* Friends** and - maybe - we can tell you who *you* are!

Lee Sturgeon Day. April 2008

CHAPTER ONE. PRELUDE

"Each of us bears the imprint of a friend met along the way. In each the trace of each."
Primo Levi

This story begins in the winter of 2006. I had been working in New York and San Francisco when I realized I am losing my voice. Always pretty low and husky (both depth and tone compounded by 40 years of smoking and talking) it reached a subterranean level where it had been hard to project across a room when I was teaching, or facilitating large groups.
"It feels like a prolapsed womb." I told a concerned student. I have never had a prolapsed womb, but this analogy seemed to fit the sagging exhaustion, the effort to lift my words across space. A couple of days before leaving San Francisco, I make an appointment with a dear doctor friend.

This friend is, variously, an MD, psychiatrist, homeopath, acupuncturist, cranial sacral therapist, anthroposophic doctor, art therapist, and is also known as The Patron Saint of Lost Causes, having turned around major illnesses and disabilities in some I know, and even more in those that I have never met. I think of her as the "one touch cures all", as I always leave her office renewed and revivified.
I make my way over on MUNI, the marvelous bus service, and clamber up a few flights of stairs to her warm little flat. After she has touched me tenderly in a few places, so that I feel I am breathing easily again, and the dull ache in my throat has vanished, she asks:
"Would you consider seeing an ENT doctor while you are here? My friend, Dr. B. is one of the best I've ever met: old school, intuitive, you know what I mean. I can see if he can make time for you tomorrow." Because I'm fantastically squeamish, she assures me the procedure is simple, he will shine lights down my throat, to see what he can see, and it will probably only take 15 minutes or so, which may well be all the time he can spare. He's a very busy man, works down in the Mission, and has trained several laryngeal surgeons in the Bay Area.
"I don't think I've ever met a better one," she adds. So I agree, before we plunge out together in pouring rain to the nearest sushi bar. Then she gives me a piano concert, and drives me home. How's that for good medical attention!
The next day she calls me.
"I asked Dr. B. if he could spare 15 minutes to see a patient of mine. He said: 'For you, I will spare 16 minutes'. Your appointment is at 1 o'clock." I promise I will be punctual, suspecting I am fitted into his lunch break.
Another bus ride down to the Mission, arriving in time to sit in a park full of fascinating folk, before sliding in between two storefronts and climbing stairs to Dr. B's office.
How much you can tell from a doctor's waiting room! Here, as I half imagined, the reception is warm, the room is warm, the sofas and chairs are

deep, slightly shabby and comfy, the lighting is soft, and the other folk, mostly Hispanic, waiting there with me, look very much at ease. Nothing fancy, nothing pricey, a home from home. Just as I like it.

Dr. B. is ready for me on the dot, together with another doctor, an Indian woman I would guess, in her 40's, who is probably interning with him. He explains the procedure, numbing my throat and going in through my nose to take a good look.

" I must give you a thorough examination." Which gently, and a little too slowly for my liking, he proceeds to do, pointing out the various features of my anatomy to the other doctor who takes notes. I am almost on the verge of a panic attack when he finally withdraws his fishing rods.

"Well, dear lady," he tells me. "You are fine except for some smokers' polyps on your vocal cords. Like Frank Sinatra," he adds. "Many singers and speakers also get these. Now you must stop smoking and have total voice rest for one month. No talking, no telephone. Your husband will be very happy with me."

I tell him I have no husband, but I will follow his instructions. I ask if that can, in itself, heal this.

"I have known this to happen," he replied. "But you must promise me that you stop smoking now, for ever. And when you return to Arizona, you must find another ENT doctor to work with." I promise I will do both things.

Then he leans forward, taking my hands in his own warm ones, and looks me in the eye.

"Dear lady, I want to assure you of one thing. You do not have cancer." Although I am a "cancer survivor" it had actually never occurred to me that I might have it now. I thank him.

"Did you know I have been treating people with cancer for fifty years?" he asks. " I assure you, everything is fine except for these polyps of yours. I want you to leave my office knowing that." I look back into those kind old eyes, and promise him that too.

There is one more appointment before I go home: this to a curative eurythmist. My doctor friend had prescribed some exercises to begin the healing process. I spend a lovely hour with Maria in a room at the San Francisco Waldorf School. If anything can heal my voice it must be this form of movement, based as it is on the movements our larynx creates in the air as we speak, but that – in eurythmy - we project in space, moving our whole bodies instead. She gives me a sequence of consonants this time round. The curative eurythmy works very deeply into our organs, you can often feel liver, womb or lung actually responding as we move. Yet it is all so subtle and quiet and beautiful as is Maria herself that I come, as always, close to tears. At the end of the hour, Maria and I take our last bus ride home and – I confess – I decide tomorrow is the day to quit smoking. I definitely need a few last puffs after the challenges of today!!

Next day I pack my bags and leave for Sacramento for my "Biography Research Group". These people are very precious to me, never more so than now. We spend lovely hours together where I just listen, and drink in all this fine company, knowing they will be supporting me long-distance (there are no distances for the human soul). A day later I fly home.

          *   *   *

Of all the incredible friendships of this lifetime, I count first and foremost my son, Adam. I had called him in Berkeley (he is in his last semester of Law School) before taking my Trappist vows. He was, as ever, upbeat, sympathetic, supportive in every way. I seem to have lost our earlier emails, so rather than make them up (as he suggested), I just need everyone to know he was there from the start, and still is. We went through my cancer when he was nine, so we are old hands at taking some challenges together.

Jane is the first friend to write. I realize a signature of our friendship is she brings "firsts" into my life..

Jane met my future husband, Bill, when he was teaching at Santa Clara University. Neither of them had yet encountered the work of Rudolf Steiner or Waldorf Education. 14 years later, they met again at a biography workshop Bill led in Los Angeles at the Highland Hall Waldorf School where Jane was then teaching.. When he told her he had married and I was pregnant, she had a dream of me and my son!
Another 14 years passed, and she moved with her three children, to teach at the Detroit Waldorf School, where Adam was enrolled. Only then did we meet, and become firm friends.
When she returned to California, she invited me to give another Biography workshop at Highland Hall (the first since Bill's all those years earlier!).
Later I moved to California, where she works as an Educational Psychologist. We had been together for our group in Sacramento.

March 24th
Dear Lee,
Well, when you do Lent, you really do it. I am so sorry. I have been thinking of you and hope you are happier, (as happy as anyone can be while not smoking or talking) now that you are back home. It was lovely seeing you, albeit briefly, in Sacramento. Much love, Jane

Thanks, my friend.
Yes, a pretty Lenten experience. Let's hope there is an Easter!!! I apologize for my "distance" last Sunday – in my own wilderness!! To crown it, our shuttle driver nearly took four of us into the grave late on Tuesday night, skidding (in a blizzard) into a car, across the freeway into a deep ditch and up the other side, uprooting a tree before slithering to a stop. Worst was waiting

in freezing cold for an hour outside a closing Dairy Queen. But I'm still on this side of the threshold. Love you, Lee

Hi, Lee,
I hope there's an Easter too. I was amazed to hear you had to endure an accident plus freezing cold – on top of everything else. I am presently doing a paper on PTSD and have a whole book on the unrecognized trauma of traffic accidents – even minor ones. Warmth and body work, as you know are very important. Not the greatest time to give up smoking. You are in my thoughts and prayers. I have had a wrenching week - teen suicides and one young girl raped. She was developmentally disabled too! Love Jane

Dearest Jane,
Well, your teenagers certainly put my little ordeal in perspective. What agonizing things are done in this world! As for the accident, you would have had a chuckle. There was a rather saucy fellow on his way home from New Zealand. In other circumstances, I might not have minded exchanging a little "warmth and body work"!!! Thanks for prayers, I'll gratefully receive any and all. Love Lee

Hi Lee,
Here is a poem I was sharing with my dear high schoolers yesterday. Thought you would appreciate it: Love, Jane.

Refuse.

Refuse to fall down,
If you cannot refuse to fall down,
Refuse to stay down.
If you cannot refuse to stay down,
Lift your heart toward heaven
And like a hungry beggar
Ask that it be filled.
It will be filled.
You may be pushed down.
You may be kept from rising.
But no-one can keep you
From lifting your heart toward heaven.

Clarissa Pinkola Estes from **The Faithful Gardener.**

      Although I have been pretty scathing of email as a means of communication, in the next days I begin to see its value as I try to locate a local ENT doctor through my various friends. No one seems to know one. I make an appointment with Dr. Z., another homeopathic/anthroposophic doctor and friend. He is equally unknowing, and says something about mainstream medicine and its practitioners that I will not commit to print. So that doesn't help. But he prescribes a couple of remedies that I need to order from the Hahnemann Pharmacy in San Rafael, before he leaves town, and suggests some ozone treatments when he returns from a trip. The remedies arrive with double bold capitalized instructions: **DO NOT DRINK COFFEE WHILE ON THESE REMEDIES. IT WILL ANTIDOTE THEM.**

The next three days may well be the worst in my long life. I have woken myself with a cup of coffee, the stronger the better, since I was 15 or so. Actually, I've begun each day with more like three cups of coffee. For over four decades, I have accompanied this delightful, irreplaceable beverage and "start-me-up" with a cigarette. But I am desperate. I need my voice. So this is what I do. I don't smoke and I don't drink coffee, and I think death would be a great and welcome relief, and when I arrive in Dr. Z's office three days later and he asks how I am doing, I tell him in my harshest whisper that I am frankly ready to wring his neck. Sensibly, his first prescription is to go home immediately and make and drink a huge pot of my preferred Organic Shade Grown French Roast Fair Trade coffee from Trader Joe's and then come back later!

"They should never have put those instructions in with those remedies," he assures me. And he adds a lovely anthroposophical remedy *Larynx Levisticum*, which he tells me will strengthen my larynx and was very effective in healing another patient's paralyzed vocal cords. I feel in good hands. Ozone therapy is one of many that he prescribes for me, shooting ozone up my sinuses and down my throat. Apparently there have been great successes in dissolving colon polyps this way. I must say that after three or four treatments my nose and sinuses are clear as newly installed piping. On good days I even believe my voice is stronger. This is fairly easy to believe because I am not using it!!

Then, out of the blue, Barbara emails me. When she left Prescott a year or so ago, she moved to San Antonio, and now writes that she is returning to Phoenix and will call me soon. I write back telling her of my plight, and ask if she knows a good ENT doctor in her neck of woods. She promptly replies that she does – a top of the line guy in Scottsdale no less (Scottsdale being a top of the line sort of place, if annual income is a determining factor. It is often referred to as Snottsdale, but who's fussing now?) I get his name and make an appointment for the following week.

Dr. Ws office is somewhat different from Dr. B's: i.e. the chairs are elegant and uncomfortable, there is no drinking water that I can see, the faucets in the bathroom are the automatic kind that refuse to respond to my particular hands, but, other than that, folk are generally welcoming, and Dr. W's examination of me is so speedy I don't even have time to panic (a great point in his favor.) He explains the procedure known as vocal cord stripping, removing the polyps in a jiffy, and recommends this. When I ask what risks there might be, he assures me none. When I ask if he knows about reducing them by natural methods (voice rest, no smoking, a few "*woo woo*" i.e. natural/unorthodox treatments) he says he supposes it could be possible but could take 5 yrs, whereas he can clean me up and get me going again in a matter of weeks. He passes me on to his assistant and dashes off to the next patient.

His very nice assistant explains the procedure, together with everything I would need to do before surgery and what to expect after it. No voice use for the first week to 10 days, then the voice would begin to return, at first hoarsely, but 3-6 weeks after surgery in full working order. We look at possible dates, with my son's graduation coming up soon, and a teaching engagement in Honolulu soon after. I tell her I'll get back to them.

Dr. Z. and I meet again. Neither of us are in favor of invasive medicine of any kind, surgical or pharmaceutical. However, as he points out, in a straight choice between a longish time to shrink the polyps, or 3 weeks to recover full vocal capacity, this may well be a time for strong measures.

"Your voice is your life, and livelihood," says Robert. "In your case, it is probably best to go ahead. Then you can work again."

On that happy note, I arrange the surgery, get half my blood taken and examined, an EKG, and sign a waiver giving Dr. W permission to cut my throat if he feels like it. "Just a formality," his assistant assures me, "Nothing terrible like that will happen."

Barbara will be my caretaker. I'm all set. I return to Prescott, pack bags, and drive back down the mountain for supper, a walk in a desert sunset that even the suburbs cannot wholly despoil, and tuck in at the condo Barbara only moved into that day. How's that for true friendship? I doubt I'd be so generous spirited!

The following morning she drives me to the Scottsdale Health Center. When Dr. W. comes (late as most surgeons are prone to do) I ask for a last time: "Tell me now what could go wrong. After this I won't be able to ask questions."

"What do you mean, go wrong?" he enquires raising his eyebrows and probably thinking, "sooner we get her anaesthetized, sooner I won't have to allay this mad British woman's fears."

"This is a very simple procedure," he reiterates. "You're going to be fine. Just don't talk for a week." On that happy note, I submit to the lethal injections and go under the knife.

Five days later, feeling fine, I drive myself home, vaguely wondering what I would do in an emergency, living alone and unable to make a sound, but consoling myself with the thought that I've lived alone for years, and, hey, I only have another five days or so, and my voice will begin to come back.

CHAPTER TWO. NOISES OFF.

"Silence is the clay from which we shape our world, the marble at which we chip away with our words."
The Beggar King and the Secret of Happiness. Joel ben Izzy.

Five days pass. My friend, Joan, despite her incredible schedule of remedial work with children, plus taking care of the rest of the world, has driven over to put a message on my phone, telling people why I won't be answering. Although I am not speaking, I have a subliminal sense that, should I try, nothing would still come out. When the ten days have passed, and I'm almost due to leave for Adam's graduation, I drive to her house and ask if she could call Dr. W's office. They tell me not to worry, but to call again at the three week mark if I am still experiencing problems. I'm just taking a little longer, they say! And now it is almost time to head out with my pencil and pad.

Date: Sat, 6 May 2006
Subject: Deep Throat.

Darling Adam,
Hope finals went "as well as can be expected". (I'm getting very British now, but not quite prepared to say of my condition "can't complain"!) Being still utterly mute - now 8th day and was supposed to begin to sound again - I do feel a little complaining. Doc says if I'm still silent after 2 weeks I have to call them again. If that isn't a Catch 22, I don't know what is. Maybe we can call together. Thought we should fix a meeting point for next Thursday? Some coffee shop convenient to Bart Berkeley exit? Around 4pm? Longing to see you - at least my eyesight is unimpaired. Love you, Mum

Dear Mum,
There's a coffee shop right outside the Bart exit. I'll be waiting. Longing to see you too, Love Adam.

After a few wonderful days in Berkeley, in my son's tender care, he insists on calling the doctor's office and making an appointment. Somehow we both knew deep down something was really wrong and healing was not occurring as promised.

Subject: Further revelations from Deep Throat.
Date: Wed, 17 May 2006

Darling Adam,
Hope the Fletcher graduation went well. Just in the door from my trip to Snottsdale. Doc said not to worry, he did a very deep and thorough and all round job (makes me think of someone carving a vast joint of beef, slicing

huge bloody slabs!) I'll see him in 3 weeks. I asked when he would begin to worry and he said if I still couldn't talk in 6 months. Well, so would I! Julie Andrews sued when her recovery was delayed! Anyhow, I'm still mute, still sore, but now able to relax somewhat, (oh gosh I'll have to begin memoirs, won't I!) Thanks so much for your tremendous support, I felt so cared for through those days, and loved being with you, and your friends.   Much love, Mum

Dear Mum,
I'll be sure to beef up on medical malpractice. Just hoping, though, you'll get to feel better - and sound better - soon. Love, A.

One of my next friends to kick in is **Steph** from Honolulu, where she administers the Waldorf Teacher Training program. I had already asked her if I might postpone my teaching there till the fall.

Rudolf Steiner describes wonderfully how we often enter a group of people in order to meet just one or two, with whom our destiny is deeply connected. Some figures stand out like mountains, others appearing like "molehills" beside them, and reveal their true significance quietly over time. Steph is definitely a favorite "molehill",as we have slowly come to know one another over the decade that I have been teaching in this program. She is now one of my dearest and truest friends, and staying with her and her husband Sam one of the highlights of my Hawaiian trips.

May 18th

Dearest Steph,
Just to report the doc was not worried, I'm just taking a long long time. (Thank God, I'm not flying to you today, I still have no sound, bar a whisper!) I reminded him that Julie Andrews sued her surgeon. That got his attention! Anyhow, I should at least be able to produce a husky tone by October, probably like my old one!! It really is enough to drive me back to the Marlboros. In fact, I think they would probably sort the whole thing out in no time! Love Lee

Dear Lee,
Well, I'm glad the doc's not worried. Go for a Julie Andrews sound-alike or sue!! How was Adam's graduation? Chris says Oct 21 in Kona sounds good. Trying to reign (rein?) in threatened panic mode. I thought I'd lived in "busy" mode before. But wedding planning, house painting, house addition plans, one job crisis after another are threatening to do me in. But I'll "muddle through". Must confess that I agree – the Marlboros would probably sort it all out. X0X0. Steph

Dearest Steph,

You'll do more than muddle through, I'm sure, but I'm sorry you have so much on your plate, when you deserve lots of relaxation. I do hope you are anticipating a break after the wedding. So much love. Wish I were there to give you a foot rub but you probably wouldn't put your feet up for me!! Lee

It is now close to a month since my surgery. I still have no sound whatsoever. I take my little notepad about with me. I try not to panic at night, wondering how I could call for help. I buy a dog whistle and wear it round my neck. At least another week passes before someone points out that only dogs will respond. Well, I'm getting to know a lot of great dogs. My social life is confined to a brief walk twice a day round my little local park. Folk hail me with a cheery "Good morning," I raise a regal hand, point to my throat, and cross my lips to indicate my vow of silence. The dogs bound over and I actually feel more connected to these lovely "dumb" animals than my vocal fellow humans.

Meanwhile, more healers are stepping up to my plate. One friend, commissioned by Joan, comes over and uses a sort of cross between a riding whip and a cocktail twizzle stick to try to remove all inflammation (in "woo-woo' parlance I guess that is "negative energies") She also calls **Dr. Kelly,** an anthroposophic doctor in Sacramento, whom I've known for many years.

Kelly responds with warmth, practical advice and encouragement typical of her as a talented and loving healer. She points out that sometimes people over 63 take on some physical challenge or illness as a sacrifice. I hadn't heard that before. Not entirely certain what that might mean, but it is uplifting to be told this might not all be wasted!

Her prescriptions include various homeopathic remedies, a number of compresses: yarrow, mustard, lemon, for throat, tummy, calves and feet: these mainly to reduce inflammation, and diet which (from Kelly) always includes sauerkraut, her "heal-all". Well, she is a great healer, no doubt of that, and as much for her warmth and compassion as any remedy she suggests. Perhaps the yarrow compress recipe she sent to my friend Lana (the twizzle stick lady) to perform on me gives you the flavor of such treatments.

"The patient should be lying comfortably in bed. Pay attention that extremities are warm and the room is quiet and has fresh air. The yarrow compress can be done after each meal, to improve digestion....
Method.
Add a handful of yarrow (organic preferred) to about 1 pint of water (preferably non chlorinated). Boil and let stand for ten minutes.
Use a cotton cloth about six inches square for the compress over the liver (right front lower rib cage).
Strain the tea. Put the compress cloth into the tea, and wring it out thoroughly but carefully so you don't burn your fingers. The cloth should be damp not drippy, and hot to the touch.

Put the compress cloth on the lower right front rib cage, touching the skin briefly first to let the person know heat is coming, and this will also let you know if it is too hot, and you can briefly fan the cloth in the air to cool it. Apply the hot compress quickly and immediately secure it with a cotton or linen cloth tightly round the body. Cover with a woolen cloth. The cloths should be much bigger than the compress to prevent cold areas arising along the edge. Place a loosely filled hot water bottle on top, perhaps tucked inside pajamas. Let the compress stay in place for 20-60 minutes, or as long as it is warm. If the patient falls asleep, simply cover him or her warmly and do not disturb...."

Anthroposophic healing approaches every aspect of the person and his or her life. I wrote so fully about my experience of this in my previous book **A Slice of Life,** I won't dwell on it again. There are many websites and publications so anyone interested can discover more for themselves. I just ask any reader to imagine how it might feel, lying in bed, toasty warm, with a light breeze blowing through the open window, no sounds but birds and the wind in Ponderosa pines, with loving hands tucking a yarrow compress round your tummy and the owner quietly tiptoeing away to let you sleep? Does it matter, you think, as you drift off, if you ever speak again?

My friend **Esther,** who had been in Sacramento when I was diagnosed, now writes from Europe, where she has been travelling with her eurythmy troupe.

Esther and I go back 35 years. We met at Emerson College in England, as Foundation Year Students, being introduced to Rudolf Steiner's work, Anthroposophy. She is Australian. We lived in each other's pockets even after her marriage and move to Vancouver, where she and her husband (an architect) built a house with a basement designed, they both claimed, to house me. I never moved, and we spent many years apart and almost out of contact. However, Esther arrived in Sacramento to do her eurythmy training, and get strength to face the breakdown of her marriage and subsequent divorce.

Hello darling!
Where are you? Have you seen the Dr. yet? And what did he say? How shall I keep your spirits up? Describe myself at 55 being a dancing loaf of bread....or a Greek zephyr??
Sunday we went to see a gorgeous old village....old mediaeval buildings...I do love Europe. And so I literally go from heights to depths. (B. is moving my things into the new apartment. Very 'helpful' of course, but unbelievably painful.) And, there is all that goes on in the world...so it makes one feel so selfish and self-centered to be wailing about such things in the context of world tragedies. The only thing that makes sense is having friends to share all the nonsense with. Hugs, and much much love, Esther. P.S. Saw constellation of Taurus (Taurus rules the larynx) in my dreams last night. I have said all along, and will say again: *"the world needs you to speak!"*

Darling Esther,
I agree. Thank God we can moan and groan to friends. Except I still can't moan or groan. Oh, I wish you were here, preferably for ever! But we will have to weather our individual storms of grief and rage and misery and look forward to snuggling into that little apartment and painting it, or Vancouver, red. Thanks for cheering words and prayers and dreams of Taurus. Keep in touch. Enjoy Europe. I'm hoping it can only get better for both of us. At least we have each other. Love you, Lee

And now the Dutch arrive! The moment I hear that wonderful "hochhhy" sound, I am instantly cheered. My dear friend, **Marion**, a music therapist, who left Prescott for Portland last year, has been sending messages of love and cheer from the beginning. Then I read in some newsletter that she and another Dutch friend, Jannebeth, are offering a conference in August – drawing plants, making music. Now doesn't that sound like something for someone who can't talk? (Of course, my predicament will be over by then, but how lovely that could be.) So I begin by contacting Jannebeth,whom I haven't seen for many years.

Jannebeth is a healer. Wherever she goes, whomever she touches, is healed in some way. She does this through nursing (the anthroposophic kind), art therapy, and her own being. When I first met her in Sacramento, she was dashing to San Francisco to be with dying AIDS patients. It doesn't matter what the problem is, Jannebeth has something for us all. Her presence alone heals me! Somehow she sends me a description of a "lemon collar", another compress to reduce the inflammation, that I could prepare and wear. "It is good to do this for 42 nights. But only if you want to."!! (I think I actually managed 35 nights, and only because the suggestion came from her!)

Dear Lee, I am so happy to hear from you. I wrote sort of tentatively just in case I connected with some oddball. How have you been? You are this light house in my life through connecting me with Rhoda, Fred and Sally. That time was an incredible learning curve for me and an essential preparation for what came later.. Without you this episode in my life would have been different and therefore the course that followed.
Anyhow, lots to catch up with. Marion told me that you are going through quite an ordeal with your voice. Come for the week! For the beginning part of the week I have a guestroom for you, the second part Marion has a place. As to the activity that I do, I will be focusing on shapes of leaves and shapes of flowers., we look and draw and share experiences. In my experience this plant work has not made me smarter but brought me closer to the wonders of the world of the Father . I hope this will seduce you enough to come. Love Jannebeth.

Dearest Jannebeth.
Glad to have found you too. You were the first person in Fair Oaks prepared
to stop and have a cup of coffee with me! And do you remember that
amazing concert we went to with Maria Guinand (I think) from Venezuela
and those High School choirs? You are a very big destiny connection for me
too. No seduction needed, I'll book my flight. How lovely to stay with you
both. I get dimmer and dimmer as the years go by, but I know what you mean
about the wonders of the Father Ground. I first felt this in the desert. And
then, oh, then, the resurrecting power of the Son. Well, I'd hoped to resurrect
a bit at Easter - no luck there so now I'm focused on Whitsun – my favorite
festival – when, maybe even if I can't speak, people will still understand me?
Love Lee

Then at the one month mark, I hear from Cynthia, of whom you may read in
A Slice of Life.

*Cynthia and I go back a long long way! Like a few others, I met her at
Emerson College in the early 70's. She was cooking there. Later, we found
ourselves together in Detroit and she came to live with Adam and myself.
There are not enough words to describe someone so stalwart, faithful and
true, such an amazing support to me through so much. She just digs in and
does the practical things! She is now a Waldorf teacher in Chicago..*

May 30th

Hi, I hear life has been difficult for you recently, to say the least. I am, of
course, in the processes of writing those ##***## reports (I hate it), but I am
also looking for poems and verses for the children for next year and I came
across this. Thinking of you always.

FRIENDS (Anon)
*We do not make our friends, we find them only
Where they have waited for us many years:
One day we wander forth when feeling lonely
And lo! A comrade at our side appears.
'Tis not discovery, 'tis recognition –
A smile, a glance, and then we grasp the hand –
No explanation needed, no condition
That we are friends is all we understand.*

Dearest Cynthia,
I'll always thank the angels for our friendship and often think what a miracle
that you appeared at my side - like now "out of the blue" (what a lovely, true
expression!) Yes, it's a real ordeal. Way worse than the cancer business
actually. I have a team of healers, not quite certain yet what they are
supposed to be healing: inflammation, severed nerves, trauma, vocal cord
paralysis...? Today I decided to stay in bed – why not?? I can't speak or

smoke!! Best thing – as always – is the support system I have, old and new. Thanks for the lovely poem, and good luck with the #***ing reports. Love you, Lee

What a way to conclude this first month, hearing from **Teri**. I think her words say everything you need to know about her, but she deserves a little bio too.

Teri is a *singer, married to John, a retired Christian Community Priest. From a Grammy award for folk singing to teaching the Werbeck Method, (an abstruse and beautiful way of working with the voice) Teri can make the stones sing. I picture her standing in her cowboy boots, hair tousled and eyes bright with passion as she conducts 6th, 7th and 8th graders. I watch them almost levitate from their hunched, laconic stances, and hear their young and beautiful voices soar in harmonies. I only met her a few years ago, when she and John moved to Arizona. It always amazes me how long we sometimes need to live, and wait, before meeting up again with someone we have clearly known forever. People so often appear just at the very moment we need them most. Sometimes they vanish again soon after. When I am given what Teri gives me now, I have to wonder how I too might be there for another at a critical moment. I do hope I don't miss too many of those opportunities. Our destinies are woven of such convergences. Here is her voice calling to mine.*

May 30th.
Subject: Teri is thinking of you.

Dear Lee,
This morning as I was organizing my papers for the move, I ran across this quote from Doris Lessing. I remember we had discussed her.

"It seems that any battle must win more than the territory that is being fought over. She had done more than she had set out to do... Pain had become, not something which engulfed, but a landscape she could move into and out again. The hatreds and resentments were places or regions in her mind which she could visit, test, - as one might dip a hand into water to see if it is too hot to bear."

So then: I am truly sorry that I have not written. I thought I did send an email to you either right before your surgery or directly after. I don't know. Life has been overwhelming. That is certainly no excuse. I can only say to you that I care deeply about who you are, and all your marvelous gifts and graces. I hope you are recovering well. I heard recovery was slower than hoped for. I also heard that you have quit smoking.
I would love to hear from you before we leave. I haven't called because I heard you are still having difficulty speaking. Is this really so? John and I are leaving (Tucson)Tuesday the 6th. We will move into our new house (in Germany) on July 23rd. I hope you are recovering and finally have the time to do the writing I know you have wanted to do. Much love to you, Teri

Dearest Teri,

I had been meaning to get in touch with you, and I am so so sad and sorry that we can't actually SEE each other before you leave. Had been thinking so much about you, will miss you both hugely and horribly. What another year of letting go!!

Yes, this ordeal is horrible. Only way I'm getting through is with friends (astonishing) and hearing about/seeing those poor kids coming back from Iraq with no limbs, half their brains etc., and reminding myself (how often do I hear my mother's voice "remember those less fortunate than you…") that my little challenges are negligible and it honestly isn't the end of the world, or of me, if I never speak again. (Though if that's the case, I might have another ciggie! 2 months without smokes and I'm still frantic!) So, no, I haven't recovered my voice since surgery, now 5 weeks ago, and I should have done, and no one knows why not. I go to the surgeon next week and he will plunge down my throat with mirrors and hopefully be honest about what he finds. Well, Docs R., and Kelly, are all kicking in big time, to try to heal this, and we can take further steps, hopefully, after next week when we have a clearer picture of what needs healing. I've so often thought of crying out to you (metaphorically of course) as you know what voice, larynx means. I'd hoped I might wind up singing arias after this, not being silenced utterly. Oh, I'm sure you barely have time to read this with packing and leaving, which is always such a wrench, even if one is doing what one wants. So much love to you and John. And thanks for your presence in my life. Lee

Dear Lee,

Damn. I can't find your phone number. Please do what I tell you to do. I don't believe your nerves are severed. I believe your organism is severely traumatized. You must make a regime of this. Sit down. Meditate for a few minutes until you feel free of fear and self judgment. Then very peacefully imagine a sung tone, a pitch low in the breast area. A pitch you can theoretically very easily reach. You never wanted to sing. Ironically, I think it will heal and transform your voice, which is still very much there. Now imagine how it would sound coming out of the spiritual world, how beautiful it is. Try very calmly to give it a space in your body, in your thoughts, in your mouth. Desire to house it, to infuse it with your I. You must really desire this and think of it as an act of sacrifice. Form the speech sound – start with **m** – then when you feel as if the one has entered you, simply take it up with your lips, almost like tasting it – and sing it. Not long. Just long enough to experience it. Probably nothing will come out. But do it anyway and imagine the sound. You will undoubtedly become emotional and may sob. Sob. Sorrow, all these things will appear. This is good. Try to nonetheless enjoy the experience, because what you are doing is good, and forgive yourself that you cannot physically achieve it. Accept the trauma. Befriend it, because it is a messenger from the spiritual world.

Remember the more your imagination can grasp the tone – the logos - the more you will experience Christ's healing power. Here is the sequence – **m,** n, ng, rolled r, v, s. Repeat each sung tone, three times before you move on to the next consonant. Don't sing vowels at this time. Your physical organism needs to unite again with your incarnation. When you do this exercise, wait between the three attempts and listen very deeply to the *"nach-klang"* or after-effect. Don't concentrate on the rasp or air which has physically shown itself. That's not the real music anyway. Listen Goetheanistically, as if you were drawing a plant. I think you know what I mean. With the next attempt sing into the after effect. Find the good, the true and the beautiful in every attempt. Do this exercise. You may want to start with on **m**. one day and then add **n** the next. Important is repetition. Do this exercise at least three times during the day. Seven is even better. Now afterward, carry the experience with you and live into it. I know you are discouraged and fearful, but please try these exercises. It is important and I really believe it will help you immensely. I know from personal experience how powerful these exercises done in this way are. Write back to me. Love Teri

Darling Teri,
THANK YOU! THANK YOU! I am sitting here weeping, moved beyond measure, just rereading your letter. I will do this and think of you. I should have asked you ages ago. I am so stupid. I learn so slowly. Oh, how I wish I could be with you before you leave, but I think it's next week? I am so grateful, you can hardly imagine how deep it goes. Now I'm starting to sob again, so can't see the page. I am going to print it out, so I can begin this morning. I KNOW this is for future incarnations and I know it has to do with connecting more deeply with the Christ Whom I meet in you this morning. Now I'm signing off, so I can eat my cereal and get to work. Oh, how I wish you weren't leaving before Whitsun. We'll have to speak in tongues across the Atlantic! What you brought me this morning will go with me for longer than I think I know. I love you, Lee

Hi Lee,
I am now in Los Angeles. John has gone on. I am visiting my children until the 17th. Monday I'm flying to Portland to visit Marion for three days. You really won't believe this. I was given a book by a German friend last year, titled: **The Beggar King and The Secret of Happiness** by Joel ben Izzy. Have you heard about it? Well, again, you won't believe it. I took it with me, deciding that now is the time to relax and read a well-recommended book. Do you know what it is about? Joel ben Izzy is a professional storyteller. He was successful and had all that he could want. He wakes up one morning with gout in his big toe. He takes medication for it, but goes to get a check up a couple of months later. What does his doctor find, but that he has thyroid cancer. Before his surgery, the doctor explains to him that he may have some vocal trauma, but should be able to talk within two to four weeks. Guess what! His voice does not come back. The nerve in one of his vocal cords dies. The entire book is about his journey and discovering the reason why this happens to him. It does have a positive ending and there is a solution. But you must read this book. If you will send me your address I

will overnight the book to you. The book I received was in German. My friend gave it successively to three of her friends, so the thing has passed from hand to hand and has grown better for it. I gave it to John to take with him yesterday, because he liked it so much. I found another copy yesterday at Borders. When I got home and opened it up, I found that someone had returned it, after having probably read it. There is an inscription on the title page. Isn't it great? So now I will inscribe a greeting to you my friend so that you too can add your soul substance to it.

The other thing I want to say to you is this. You will recover from this. Not only will you recover but you will come through this transformed and ready to take on your work in a new way. Of this I am certain.

When my voice was injured, I cried and stomped and writhed. It came at the point in my life when I had to either shit or get off the pot, said in a vulgar way. I love vulgarity. It comes in so handy! My whole identity had been tied up in my voice. I often had the feeling that if I couldn't sing I was worth nothing. My father once told me that when I refused to be a performing monkey in front of company! Bless my poor father. When I began my lessons with Holger, he instructed me not to sing for six months. I had to completely accept my injury. I had to befriend it. I had to love my life and show compassion for my biography. I had to find meaning in my powerlessness. It was during this time that I thought I should become a priest. And that was correct. I have to become a priest in my life as it is. In my profession, in my dealings, in the small processes. That's what I learned. I really began to understand: "Not I, but Christ in me." My voice has come back. It is in some ways more beautiful than ever, But it has a slight limp and this is good. It keeps me authentic and checks my ambition. It is Michaelic in that it stands at the portals of the great door to the temple of the world and ask me: "Who are you?" Though I still sometimes grieve for my lost strength of youth, I am grateful for this and love this strict master very much. In my limp I am made whole.

You have been running around the globe giving workshops, certainly helping many people, bringing light into their lives. Then you come home to a place where you have little community and nourishment. Are you in the right place? Marion and I have talked about his. One reason we are returning to Germany is to connect up again with community. We need support, real live support, touching support, being in the presence of others who can also encourage us support, eating meals with others, working for the same goals support,… I'm not saying that this is what you should do. Really not. Just think about it. I'm sure you already do. Alright dear one. Give me your address and I'll overnight this perfect piece of healing. Love Teri.

The Beggar King and the Secret of Happiness arrives. One inscription reads: "To help my one-winged pal become two-winged again. Rick." And the next: "Dear Lee. Here's to going home by a different way. Love Teri."

I am not going to tell you anything about this book, only to say: "Go and buy it today." This is a book for all travellers on the road of life. Everyone needs a copy.

CHAPTER THREE.   SILENT SPRING..SUMMER.......?

"At first the silence is a silence only,
A huge lack rather than a huge something.
I listen for a voice in this dead vacuum,
Feel destitute, abandoned, full of dread..."
        The Silence. May Sarton.

Another month begins, ten weeks since I took my vow of silence, and five weeks since I couldn't break it if I chose. Unable to squeak or mutter, I pass the time writing the following little piece and rather daringly enclose it with first payment to the surgeon. (Oh yes, the bills have started coming in now!)

GOING OFF THE AIR.   *2 June 2006.*

When Bette Davis declared old age was not for sissies, she might have added: "nor is vocal cord surgery." Having one's vocal cords stripped is only for the young and strong. If, as I was, you are a smoker, you will also have been required to give up that delicious habit, and be feeling vulnerable and wretched,and lacking all capacities that made you function humanly even before going under the knife.

Before submitting to being "stripped" which, in the weeks following my surgery, I imagined resembled carving thick slices off an English Sunday roast, (maybe Americans can better visualize New York strips?) ask more questions than you've ever done in your life, get the answers in writing, and multiply recovery times by about four or five. These are probably predicated on extremely healthy nineteen year olds, not crumbling crones like myself. Then, who knows, you might be pleasantly surprised, as I always am when my Southwest flight lands early (I'm pretty sure that's because they add 20 minutes or so to the scheduled flight time, an excellent policy that I recommend to all stripper surgeons – make it 20 days at least, maybe 20 weeks to be on the safe side.)

You will not be able to ask questions after surgery. You will not be able to speak.

I'd suggest finding a surgeon within walking distance, or a short drive. Mine is a 240- mile round trip, so I can't show up in the office with placards: "Why did someone come in the night and attempt to wring my neck?" "Shouldn't I be able to squeak by now?" or, in a furious whisper, enquire: "Is it normal to feel as if someone else tried to pull my tongue out?" I am unable to show my surgeon the various expressions of misery, rage and mortal terror that I have been going through in the weeks following my "simple procedure".

When you are told you will not have a voice for a week or so, don't imagine a mild or even acute attack of laryngitis, a hoarse whisper. No, you enter a total dead zone, rather like driving into a canyon and the car radio cuts out. When you are told your voice will begin to return within 10 days to 2 weeks (as I was), multiply furiously. I anticipated a husky "Godfather"voice at my son's graduation, but had to sit silently, occasionally try whispering in very quiet corners, then bear the aftermath of a burning throat. That I later learned (emphasis on the "later") is a perfectly normal inflammation of the mucus membranes.

I was assured I could return to my work – public speaking, leading workshops etc – in three weeks. Some angelic guidance led me to postpone my teaching work in Honolulu scheduled exactly three weeks after surgery. I was still unable to emit a squeak or whimper. I'm happy to report that in the fourth week I discovered I could make a strange hooting sound rather like the Santa Fe express in a tunnel, but only on the in-breath. When I proudly demonstrated this to my neighbor, a hospice nurse, she cried: "Stop that immediately. It could be dangerous." Well, I wasn't told that either. I am now entering my fifth week of recovery. There are no signs of recovery, unless occasionally feeling I have a few strips of coconut matting caught in my throat signals progress? I don't remember discussing having to swallow doormats with anyone. Sometimes the neck wringing actually feels worse. I was told to expect things to get worse before they get better, and had assumed this to mean "worse than they were before surgery". While it is a fairly accepted truth that much of life tends to get worse before it gets better, there are also times when it gets worse before getting even worse. I do hope this isn't one of those times. While hoping to work again, as a public speaker there's not a lot I can do if I can't speak! I have begun to explore a late life career change, suitable for a mute: organic gardening? Massage? Horse Whispering? But it is late in life and every time I get a flicker of enthusiasm for some alternative, a member of my "public" writes saying: "we need your voice". Even if your work is non vocal, I think it's a legitimate request that yours also be returned to you.

If, as I do, you live alone, you need to set something up for every kind of emergency. How do you communicate if you fall and break a leg? How do you get a plumber when your shower springs a leak? You can carry notes with you to grocery stores. Be prepared for some interesting responses to your handicap. When I wrote my request for coffee at a local cafe,, the lady serving me dashed off to get her own paper and pencil to write back: "Room for cream?" Most men ask: "how can I arrange for my wife to undergo this surgery?" (My surgeon is male. Was there a conspiracy here?) When I whisper, several people begin whispering too. One young woman thanked me: "I feel as if you whispered a very special secret that only I can hear." A young man, who works in our local video store to supplement the meager income from his traveling band, suggested we went on the road together. I could whisper what I wanted to tell my audience, he, with his band, could loudly and flamboyantly deliver my message. I am tempted. I just wonder if I'd need to get all those tattoos?

Some people treat me as if I lacked all my faculties.

Be prepared then, for an utterly unique and frankly terrifying experience. Our voice is what makes us truly human and while there is certainly not enough silence in the world, and way too much bleating and blathering about nothing (turn on your TV for five minutes to be assured of that), it is still what *defines us, lifts us above all other creatures – at least potentially – and losing it for any length of time you may feel you have lost yourself. Before surgery, I asked my doctor what could go wrong, since our larynx was such a vital organ, and he replied – in a somewhat cavalier fashion, I thought; "what do you mean 'go wrong'? This is a very simple procedure." I think it can and does go wrong, all too easily. It's gone wrong when you don't recover as promised, when you need to cancel work, and are fearful of committing to other work even way in the future, just in case sound never returns. I've given some advice to patients, maybe I can end this with some for their practitioners. If it's really that simple, a quick snip snap of tissues, I'd recommend all vocal cord strippers and their staff to have the procedure themselves, so they know how some of us feel when we wake, try to speak, and sinkingly become aware that we are dumb, perhaps for ever.*

I may be inaudible, but the emails keep coming, now including messages of condolence and cheer from other members of my family.

***Sukie** –(who recently changed her name to **Salemla**) is my half sister and our brother Bill's twin. They arrived to upset my applecart after the war, my father's death and mother's remarriage. She is brilliant, beautiful, a fine spiritual healer:, the introvert, to my (formerly) big-mouthed extraversion, and therefore almost my opposite. Over the years we have built strong bridges to span our differences and the love that is forged now goes even deeper. She lives in Hawaii, is actually in process of building yurts - or "mandala dwellings" as these are called, with her daughter and granddaughter on lovely land close to Kamehameha's birthplace on the coast overlooking Maui.*

Sukie/Salemla June 1st Subject: How was the doctor's appointment?

Dearest Lee, How did it go? Was he helpful? How are you and your precious vocal cords? You are in my heart and thoughts and my prayers often. Much love, S. P.S. Don Antonio (her husband) re-sent his e-card to you. Did you get it?

Darling Sukie,
I go to the doctor this week – Wed June 7th (that's the 6-week mark) and I'll let you know what he says. I've had more help pouring its way, so I'm not feeling so depressed. Yesterday a deep soul friend and singer sent me an amazing email with instructions on how to "use" my voice, imagine sounds etc. I was sobbing reading it. I had a dream (one of my very rare remembered ones that captured the situation perfectly:

"I hear my neighbors talking in the driveway between our houses and go to meet them. When I get there, they have gone, the driveway is a very dark,

high-walled, concrete alley, swept completely clean, not even a weed growing out of a crack, or a garbage can. Then I notice the exit is also blocked off with a concrete wall. I can't get out. I stand there horrified (with an old cigarette stub in either hand!!!)

Don Antonio would appreciate the final image, I'm sure. No, his e-card never arrived. Bless him, and do thank him. It's the thought that counts. Saw pictures of the houses on the land from Laura. Wow, your hard work paying off at last. So much love, Lee

Dearest Lee,
When I ponder your dream and growing flowers in concrete, I think of the south end of this island – thousands of square miles of absolutely barren lava, baked in the relentless tropical sun, much of it rarely receiving rain. And then the miracle happens – little sprouts of green emerge from this apparent barrenness – occasional sprouts, clinging to seemingly inhospitable rock. Gradually these tiny, isolated, fragile shoots cluster together and attract more shoots. In time the south end of this island will become as verdant as Hawi. Slowly I have learnt how important it is to relinquish the logical mind and the apparent limitations of time and space in order to heal, and to take a page out of Steiner's book and act "as if". using the imagination to grow the garden in the "concrete' driveway. For it was only concrete on the night of the dream. It has no more permanence than that moment. Today it can be an English or Hawaiian garden, a marriage of spirit and body/earth birthed in love. For you to grow such a garden in your throat it would seem simply requires your love, your imagination and your willingness to bring your consciousness into your throat and allow/intend your images to be stronger than your physical experience. I write this as though it is simple. I know from many many days how challenging it can be to create an image of health in the presence of very contrary physical messages. I love you. S.

Darling Sukie,
Thank you for those lovely images. I have a wonderful Georgia O'Keefe card, sent by my friend Marietta, an art therapist, of a beautiful blooming crimson flower that I was imagining eventually unfolding, but a few darling little weeds (pardon the pun) will be good. Love, Lee

When I see Dr. W. at the six week mark, still in pain and unable to emit more than a whisper, he recommends I be seen next by a speech pathologist for a videostroboscopy. This procedure involves filming my vocal cords in action, and magnifying them so we can see what is going on. Vocal cords are so tiny, it is hard to do this through my nose. Dr. W. says scar tissue could be one problem. He also prescribes Prednisone for the continued inflammation. I don't tell him about the "lemon collars", arnica oil, aloe juice, *larynx levisticum*, rests, foot rubs, meditations, sturdy organic diet and other aids to healing I have been pursuing strenuously for the past six weeks. His tone verges on the contemptuous when I mention natural means of healing. I admit I am hardly a good advertisement for such cures!!

My friend Tina was staying and made the phone call to set this next appointment up. (Try living for a few days without speaking on the phone. It is quite an experience. particularly when it comes to someone telling you to make this or that appointment!) My choices over the past five weeks have been: a) email someone and ask him or her to make the call; b) drive to a friend's house so he or she can lift the phone and I can write or hiss the appropriate information, or: c) do nothing, suspend the life of dentistry, hair cuts, tree pruning, roof mending etc that are part of house and body holder activities while on the planet.) Until Tina arrived and took control, I hadn't realized how much I had needed this – someone just to say: "sit down, drink your coffee, I'm taking care of this and you." It is astonishing how tight we hold on to whatever is keeping us afloat, when we are solo on the ocean of life. I could feel my arms and shoulders relax the moment this beautiful and highly efficient friend came in through my front door. Oh how I will miss her when she moves to Texas next month. After she has left, I write the first of my group emails:

Silent Spring, Summer?...Fall? Group email: 8 June.
To all my friends.

I apologize for the group email, but there are so many of you who have been concerned about my voice and asked me to let you know what the surgeon said, so this is a newsflash from my session with him yesterday. We had a good conversation. He seems pretty concerned.   So maybe we can work together on this.

 The bad news is that he cannot truthfully say that my voice will ever return! He says the surgery has healed, but the cords are not performing as they should. He also can't tell with the naked eye (more tests need to be run) whether scar tissue could have formed or be forming along the edges of the cords. That would impede mobility. It could also be that the muscles had begun to atrophy before surgery. No way, he says, of knowing now. (I think that's quite enough anatomical detail.)

*So I'll see him again in a month, after I'm seen by another specialist who will film my cords in action, see where we go from there. Meanwhile I just have to face living and functioning in silence. (I can make a whispery sound, audible in quiet places, so you will all have to come closer to me to have a conversation.) I think in the next month or so I will have to decide if I will be able to work, so I will give ample notice.   I am so grateful for all your support and concern. Who knows? As Karen pointed out, this month's virtue is **Patience Becomes Trust**, so maybe that's what I'm called to develop! Love, Lee.*

Re: Silent Spring, Summer, Fall.....

Dear Mum, That is bad news. I'll get ready to sue the pants off him, so that at least you can whisper while living in a beachfront house in Australia. I just had a conversation with Marisa about her Dad, who had his larynx removed when he was in his early sixties (which is when he had Marisa) and spoke in a whisper for the rest of his life. She said everyone in the family just got used to it, and that she damn well knew the difference between his nice whisper and his "you're in trouble" one. She also knows some great throat doctors if you need a second opinion. Maybe it's time to work on some whisper nuances?

How are you feeling these days? It has to be depressing not to have any improvement. Have you started doing things you can do that don't involve full throated talking? Considering that almost all of your work is speech-oriented, this could be a significant shift. Want to come out to NY and watch movies on our couch? (*Silence of the Lambs? The Sound of Silence? Mute Witness? Look Who's Not Talking? The Horse Whisperer?*)

I saw Karin Schaefer two days ago, her shop is literally three blocks away. She said it was strange that I walked in that day, because she had just been thinking of you. I said it was probably because everyone was thinking about you for your throat and she must have just tapped into it. She sends her love. Studying is going fairly well. It is a bit boring reading about mortgages and real estate all day, but it will all be over soon enough. I hope you're doing OK? Let me know, when you get a chance. Lots of love, A.

From Dianna.. Dianna is a more recent friend, who has invited me to do workshops in the Reno area over the past few years. She has been an incredible, staunch supporter of all my work, overpaying me hugely: "Women are traditionally underpaid". When she first noticed I was losing my voice, she urged me to take care of this problem, saying: "I was first drawn to your voice, not just what you had to say." This compliment stays with me, though it is particularly poignant now that I may not recover it.

Dear Lee, Whoa. This *is* a lot. I hope there are friends close to hold you through this stage. Damn. Could this be the obvious and simple...that the healing spirits are demanding that you write? I wish I were close enough to drive over and at least offer a massage. After reading your email, I had to go outside to be in nature and water. Deep breath.

It must be that. Write away, dear friend. This certainly makes for a different sequel to **A Slice of Life**. And this one is *not* going to an Anthro press or any other *"can't make a dime for the author"* presses. Now I do hear stories on NPR about singers and others who lose their voices for various reasons and for distressingly long periods of time so I'm holding for it coming back at just the right time. There's a lot in this. I can't wait to read all about it Love and hugs, Dianna

Dear Dianna, Thanks, my friend! I *will* write, but not quite yet, as that is a pretty agonizing process for me, and enough agony for now. I was delighted when my anthro doctor said *"No mental activity"*! So first I am going to grubble in my garden, watch silly movies. I wish you were closer too, and not just for the massage. But I have truly good friends – just many are so far away. Much love, Lee

From Carol, a friend and colleague from Detroit now also in Arizona..

Carol to Lee
I am mourning for your voice!

Dear Carol, And so am I!!

*   *   *

 The following week I extend my roundtrip down the mountain to 300 miles, and meet with a speech pathologist in Mesa. This kindly man described the videostroboscopy he would perform on me. Basically, he would film my vocal cords in slow motion so we could see the state they were in. (He had other gadgets in his office to measure the intensity and quality of sound I could emit, but clearly that would be for a much later date, since I emit nothing measurable. I am, as appears in Dr. J's diagnosis: "aphonic", i.e. without sound)
The "action movie" involved plunging a mini camera on a metal rod as far down my throat as I would allow, and struggling to say "ee" while Dr. J. held my tongue (very tenderly) and attempted to capture a view of the cords when they briefly appeared from behind all kinds of other parts of my anatomy. We then both looked at the results, hugely magnified. Dr. J. looked fairly shocked, and remarked that it looked as though I had only had my surgery a few days earlier, not two months ago, as my cords were still completely raw. I hadn't known what a healthy, happy pair of cords should look like, but mine definitely fell short. Dr. J showed me a picture. I almost wept. They look like little labia, covered in beautiful thick, undulating white satin, embedded in rosy flesh. When they move they dance, shimmering and flickering and rolling towards each other like ocean waves. Mine were totally nude, no white satin garments, and as red as raw steak. One had an additional chunk of muscle missing and the other had clearly decided to play dead, and hide behind something else. Both looked as if they had been ceremonially skinned, sliced, then laid under the wheels of a tank. There was no way they had the strength to join. (And it is their meeting and dancing the dance of the seven veils that produces sound.) All in all, this family photo was not a pleasant sight, but a very clear explanation for my muteness.
However Dr. J. was cautiously optimistic. Both cords could move, so no nerves had been severed. Now it was a question of exercising them, at first gently because of the inflammation, then more rigorously, and the hope was that I could develop mighty muscles surrounding them so that they were

forced to meet head on. If I failed, there was another procedure available to me: injecting some kind of filler that would plump them or the surrounding muscles up again. Dr. J. said they used to use Teflon, but more often now used collagen. That certainly sounded preferable to the carcinogenic liner of cheap kitchenware. Quite frequently, collagen was extracted from some other part of one's body, so you could have the homegrown variety. That sounded good. I was more than prepared to surrender any amount needed from my hips, bottom or thighs. Giving up smoking has already had its effects, and I'm rapidly developing an acute case of the "Soggy Bottom Blues".

Dr. J. did murmur that my voice would probably never be as strong again and, if I did have to resort to the injections, there were a few potential hazards, one being that I could end up with a male voice! But he said we should work together for at least six months before considering any additional surgery. He stressed that I must not give up hope. I promised I would not. Grim as the forecast looked, I felt infinitely relieved to know the best and worst. And also that there were steps I could take to speed the healing process.

Group email. TO MY BELOVED FAMILY AND FRIENDS. Latest news.

Yesterday I had my vocal cords filmed with a speech pathologist. They aren't closing yet as they were completely skinned. Everything is still pretty raw. However, after we had worked a bit, Dr. J is hopeful that they can be strengthened and restored. If, in six months, I still cannot close them, there is a relatively simple procedure, of transplanting a little tissue from elsewhere (hips or thighs) and injecting this along the edges which were totally stripped of their outer membranes. (Knowing the generosity of my friends, I am still refusing any offer of transplants from any of your hips or thighs, I have quite adequate supplies myself!!!!!)

So, now, the work begins. Remedies, therapies, eurythmy, Dr. J's exercises, the beautiful singing exercises Teri gave me. I will write separately to those of you who were expecting me to "perform" in the next six months. Obviously I won't be able to work. Or use the phone. I can't!

Kind and flattering as everyone has been in saying: "Now is your time to write", I'm just letting you know I'm not planning on such an agonizing activity as writing yet.. No – I'm going to hike, commune with lizards and the wide wide sky, do my therapies, watch movies, laugh and weep (alas, soundlessly), be alone, be with friends.

*I'll end this by sharing a passage from Joel ben Izzy's book: **The Beggar King and the Secret of Happiness**. A professional storyteller, he has one vocal cord damaged when he has thyroid surgery, and is told he will never speak again. These are the words of the top specialist, when he breaks the news: "**What do the sages tell us? 'The voice is the gateway to the soul'. And before that gateway stand two guards - your vocal cords. To make sound they must come together - like two rabbis arguing about Talmud. But in your case, one rabbi is silent. Why? I wish I knew..... Perhaps he knows a secret.**" So, thank you all of you, for all your love and support. Now I'm going to listen to my silent rabbis! Love you, Lee*

From Adam
Subject: Darn It!!

Dear Mum,
Are they giving you something for the pain? Woowoo stuff is fine for lots of things, but it's not so good with the pain alleviation. This is no good if it's hurting you. Are you talking to that doctor? Next time you see him, tell him you have a litigious NY lawyer for a son who is ready and eager to bring aggressive litigation against him as soon as you say "go".
I wish I could take some time off and come hang out in Prescott with you, but I'm completely inundated right now. This bar exam review is definitely taking over my head. Meanwhile I hope you've got some good books and movies. I'll keep my eye out for more winners like *Water*. You are the one always talking about destiny and how things happen for a reason and how we need to pay attention to the signs. Something out there is definitely sending you a fairly loud (pardon the pun) signal about something. Who knows what the "something" is, but you're definitely being given some quiet time to figure it out! I love you lots, and hope you start feeling better soon, A.

Darling Adam,
Thanks for your lovely letter. As Suzanne said last week: "Who needs a husband when you have a son like this?" Now you really must sign off my worries. Don't forget to eat well – fish is good brain food. Love you, Mum.

From my D.D.R
Dear Lee,
When I got your letter today, I thought of my son Adam and the wireless public address system he's used for some years while teaching his class. He said a woman teacher with vocal cord nodules and a whisper voice at his school was thrilled to hear of his "public speaking" innovation. He suggests looking up "radios4you.com" in the internet. And do you have the larynx remedy from Uriel? It's for rebuilding a hoarse voice. If you don't have it, I'll send it to you. It has larynx in it, so I think it could be helpful.
I will be here in September when you come, and I'm looking forward to seeing you. The art in Italy doesn't begin till early October, so I will still be here. Let's plan on it. I've started painting the new Madonnas. The Madonnas of Pakistan, of Tsunami, of Iraq, of Darfur, of Hurricane Katrina. There are so many Madonnas I can't keep up with them. Bless them all. Thanks for your letter. Love, DDR
P.S. If you save all your emails, all you'll have to do when the voice is healed, is to edit them on the computer, interspersed with that humor of yours, and you'll have your next book of healing. You see how much you enjoyed *Joel ben Izzy*'s book. It will be effortless, and I will enjoy reading of your communion with lizards. That already sounds like the title. I had a pet lizard once and he was wonderful, and he could not make a sound. We used to go down in the backyard where the dry yellow horse tails baked in the sun, and

were topped by all sizes of drowsing house flies, some huge ones. I'd hold him close to the fly and watch him silently eat dinner. Two or three would make a meal. Since he was so silent, no other drowsing house flies would even wake up.

So if you are taking time off how about going to Italy with me. Since it is a healing painting trip, you can take it off as a medical expense. Three wonderful Italian meals a day, a private room and lovely people. I look out to see a hawk soaring in silence over Dolores Park and think of you. Love Rosemary.

My dear friend,

Thank you, thank you. I'd been thinking so strongly about you over the past two days and wishing I were closer so you could work your healing wonders on my neck. Still in a lot of pain. You call it cranial sacral work, I call it Rosemary's Healing Touch. I'll put the word out about Italy, but doubt I can come this year. Maybe next time. It would be the ultimate tragedy to be there and not to be able to speak Italian.

I can't believe you have such a special karmic connection with lizards. The first person I've met who does, so our own must run pretty deep. Or that you thought of the email book. I'd also had that idea. Thanks again. And much much love, Lee

Nancy. Now here comes one of my deepest "karmic connections". I was almost 50, and Nancy a decade ahead of me, when a group in Minneapolis invited the two of us to be the keynote speakers at a conference. We met and worked collaboratively as if we had been doing it for several lifetimes. "Well, we probably have," Nancy reflected. Nancy's specialties are birth and early childhood, then death and dying. Mine the years in between. So we make a great team. She has a vast array of interests and talents, an astonishing energy and commitment to others, and puts on – with Gordon, her husband, who gives the best hugs on the planet - the most marvelous celebrations of life events at White Feather Ranch. We did promise ourselves that we – like Granny D at 90 – would walk across America together. I'm glad I'll only need to reach 80, because Nancy, as you see below, is no slouch. I think I'll always be a little behind her in more than our ages!

Subject: The Great Leap Forward?????

Hooray! Sounds positive and hopeful! By the way Granny D had throat surgery, possibly a different kind, (also a smoker) and she is lecturing again – at nearly 97! I am off to La Jolla next week for my 75th to try a Para gliding jump off Torrey Pines. You could do that too! Love Nancy

To: Dr. J, Voice Therapist.

Thank you so much for our session and the hope that our work together may restore my voice. Yours, Lee

Lee, I received a copy of your surgery report right after you left last week, so I know a little more about the total procedure. The outer membrane was stripped almost the full length of the cords, rather than a small area. So that explains why you are not getting closure of the cords.   Due to the continued redness and extent of the surgery, we do have to proceed in a slow manner.. the coughing and "ee's" are pretty aggressive movements for the cords to be "slammed" together so only do these maybe once a day………..Please let me know how you are doing. You should *not* have pain associated with the exercises. Your cords are still so red that we don't want to create any more trauma. Yours, Darrell Jensen.

Dear Dr. J.
You asked me to keep you in touch with my process. "Progress" is not the word for it yet! I've been doing the exercises 3 times a day, but the coughing and "ee's" only once. Also humidifiers, and drinking way over prescribed amounts of water. You said the exercises shouldn't hurt. Problem is that I still have quite a lot of different pains....
1)   The "**Wake and Ache**", a low level continuous ache throughout neck and throat,
2) The "**Attack of the Big Bertha**". Feels as if someone took a good swing at my neck, jaw, teeth with a baseball bat or golf club. This is followed by the sensation that someone is trying to pull my tongue out by the roots. 3) The "**Burning**" in neck and throat, often after I have spoken a little, sometimes when I haven't. Where the exercises fit in all this I don't know! I have, however, cancelled all my work for the next six months, so I can go more slowly now if you would like. Yours, Lee

Lee,
Thanks for the update. It sounds like we can keep doing the same exercises for now. I was just hoping that they would not traumatize your vocal cords any more than they already are. Due to the extent of your surgery, we may want to consider the injections before the 6 month time period to get your voice back sooner. Yours, Dr. J.

Now I, and others, tackle the challenge. Exercise is limited initially. The pains are still acute.   It did seem to illustrate the theory that sometimes things do get worse before they get better. My first days after surgery had been blissfully benign. Doctors, therapists, friends, acquaintances began to pitch in. All these kind and talented people offered remedies of the natural (otherwise known as "woo –woo") variety. As a young friend of mine had once commented: "They may be woo-woo, but they work", which is more than can be said for the products of "Murk" and other pharmaceutical companies which may alleviate a minor symptom while afflicting you with a few terminal side-effects. (I'm almost happy to report that the Prednisone made no discernible difference whatsoever!)

I had compresses, mainly on my throat, but also calves and feet. One was the "lemon collar" Jannebeth had told me to wear for forty-two nights, a distinctly biblical ritual I managed to keep up for thirty-five nights – is that a world record? There were flower essences to dab here and there, homeopathic medicines for inflammation, cell and tissue repair, surgical trauma. Eurythmy exercises were sent from San Francisco.

I also began my own research. Not a great computer whiz, I nevertheless got "Googling" on the theme of vocal cords, surgery, injections and so forth. As this method usually brings up about 10-12 responses out of a potential 7 million each time, I was kept entranced. I saw pictures of vocal cords around the globe (all fairly similar – healthy ones being a glistening white, and diseased ones – well, we will not dwell on that.) I learned of just about everything that can go wrong, what can be done to put it right and, often alarmingly, what damage surgical and other procedures may wreak on the delicate organs down one's throat. I saw pictures that made me gag. I heard "before" and "after" voices. I learned what Teflon could do to tone, how collagen could migrate or actually vanish. I am rapidly becoming an expert! (Dr. Jensen even attended a similar surgery by another doctor who was able to do the job on a pair of very diseased vocal cords without leaving the patient mute. Wish I had been that lucky).

But happily, mail keeps coming, such as this from my British friend, **Linda.**

I've often wondered why Linda and I needed to wait 49 years before meeting, when she attended a workshop I and a Jungian analyst friend of mine were giving in Michigan. I had begun injecting a little anthroposophy to the purely Jungian perspective. One evening as I was walking to my car, Linda caught up with me and said: "You are on to something different, aren't you? And I want to know what that something is!" I invited her home, there and then. She became, and still is, the deepest friend I have on this continent – that extra dimension of speaking the same language just ices the cake. One of the greatest sorrows is that we no longer live in the same city: "No-one but yourself to blame," Linda is ready to tell me, as I was the one who fled west. That sorrow is now compounded by not being able to lift the phone and laugh till I cry. But no laughing now, for me, anyway, so probably just as well!

Dearest Lee, I was about to moan to you of my six week plus bout with chronic bronchitis, forced to go to a "real" doctor – Kate (her daughter) and Robert (husband and doctor) had gun to my forehead – and am scheduled for "THE WORKS' next week – feel more nervous than ever after hearing about your bloody awful experience. You don't say why the procedure was done? I am also suffering from miserably painful sciatica, but much to Robert's *horror* have chosen a chiropractor (several of the biography group go to him) who is, I believe, the only local who uses a low dose of laser beams (not yet approved for regular folk.) I wonder if the treatment might help you – will ask him on Tuesday. Footballers use it for sports injuries on the field, and racehorses with broken legs are saved from the bullet. (It is approved for vets.) Robert told me to tell you that Julie Andrews sued when this procedure changed her voice.

Do not do *anything* you do not want to do, and listen to *no-one's* advice, except perhaps mine, which is to read the collected poems of your old boss (John Betjeman, Britain's Poet Laureate) and **Knitting**, a novel by Ann Patchett – an Aussie married to a pastor. Anne Tyler's **Digging to America** is really good, and I'll ask Christine for "the list" as her memory is better than mine, and she keeps a journal, which I keep meaning to do, but it's rather too late now. When it comes out on DVD, **Water** is a must – the last in the Indian trilogy: **Earth, Fire** and finally **Water. Mrs Palfrey at the Claremont**? Don't miss Joan Plowright and her dishy young man!

Set no goals, just grieve – losing one's voice, no work, being alone, no cigarettes….(I'm thinking coffee/red wine)…that's a lot. My latest book is called **Death's Door** by Sandra Gilbert, subtitled **Modern Dying and The Way We Grieve** – she is a poet – Steiner is mentioned a couple of times. It's a *big* book – can't imagine it will sell well – thought I would support her "monumental" effort. What are you able to eat?

Ben has drawn you a sunflower, and Kate sends love (she will dig out some up to date photographs). Gabe will start at Oakland Steiner in September. If only you were still in Royal Oak. Hugs, kisses, tears and prayers. (I asked for prayers for you in Christian Community circle). Linda

My beloved soul sister!

First things first. Have you had The Works yet? If anything untoward, you'd better bl**dy well let me know, and we can escape to some island – taking Ben with us, of course. How I LOVE my sunflower, but I'll tell him direct too. Next, thank you thank you for your letter, and wonderful book. I'll only take your advice : "Don't take anyone's advice" and Adam's: "Come to NY anytime and lie around watching silent movies while I beef up on medical malpractice"!!!

Well, I had it done because I was losing my voice (remember in February) and I had a couple of months of the woo-woo stuff and voice rest, then this ENT bloke said: "You *might* turn around your condition that way in 5 years or so, I can have you back in traces in 3 weeks with this very simple procedure." I even imagined singing arias in 4!! Now it looks like nine months in all, then probably a second surgery where he (or preferably another) replaces the pound of flesh he took.

Yes, tell Robert I know about Julie Andrews. After three weeks I told the surgeon, and he said: "Yes, I know. That's why I don't like performing this procedure on singers." I said: "Well, you just performed it on a public speaker!" That got his attention. At the six-week mark I mentioned my son was an attorney. "*Now* you tell me," he said. I don't want to get adversarial yet. My main grouse is that I should have been forewarned, better prepared for such an eventuality.

Prescott turns out to be a pretty good place to be: village life good for such times. Everyone knows I'm mute and how I communicate. It's just rather weak on the medical front, so I have to drive these immense distances. I wear a whistle. Sometimes I think I'm crazy to be living alone: what happens in the night? Can't phone or call for help. Other times, I recall how my angel has always taken good care of me, probably hasn't given up yet.

Anyway, enough of that, and me. I am so sorry about your bronchitis and, even more, that sciatica. I do hope the horse laser stuff works. No, I hadn't heard of it. I've been having so many therapies: ozone treatments, pink lights, flashing red lights, blue too, none of which have had slightest effect on inflammation and nerve pain (nor, I might add, has Prednisone. **From Ozone to Prednisone** – now there's a title!) And so many changes of remedies I'm ready to open a resale shop. When one *woowoo* doc asked: "Shall I prescribe a remedy for grief?" I said: "The *only* remedy for grief is grieving, and it doesn't cost 45 bucks!"

Yes, it's huge. Yesterday I completed the handover of all my work – amazing how quickly that went, finding replacements – no problem, and being immediately addressed in the past tense: It was like attending one's own funeral – god, did I have to howl. But silently, which is *not* satisfying.

I wonder now if it would have made a difference knowing I was hearing my voice for the last time. (I am told it will probably never be as strong, or sound the same again.) Now I hear it in my head, like some ancient vanished ocean captured in a shell. And that is very painful too. How I love the sounds of language. (So many Americans think words are just functional. We Brits know better, don't we!) Thanks for Christian Community prayers. Thanks for all your book recommendations. My latest reads: **An Unreasonable Woman,** *Diane Wilson*; *Martha Beck's* **Leaving the Saints, Finding my Faith** and (fiction) *Miriam Toews* (Canadian) **A Complicated Kindness.**

I want to know how all your tests, aches and pains go. Now I think I'll go watch about 4 hours of TV pulp!!! I've worked hard today: meds, eurythmy, speech exercises, walk, swim, watering yard, reading your letter, (that cheered me up so much I haven't cried once!) and writing this. So time out now.

Oh, I forgot to mention that **True Botanica** do "Forte" oils: Just in case you are interested in slathering some on your sciatica. Love you, love you, love you... Lee

CHAPTER FOUR. AN INCONVENIENT TRUTH.

"There is an action, an allowing, a surrender within.... The ego experiences it as a kind of stoppage. It is a special quality of silence.... One begins to understand that it is only through that opening that one can love as one wishes to love. Then, truly, the world and life in this world, with all its pleasures and pains, with all its obligations and difficulties - just this world that you and I live in now - this world becomes my monastery."
Source Unknown.

I certainly don't compare my little ordeal with the fate of the polar bears and other tragic events catalyzed by global warming and outlined in Al Gore's movie, but this was the month it was released, so it seemed an appropriate title for this chapter. My own minor inconvenient truth being, of course, that I am still without sound, still in pain, still utterly floored by this turn of events and still surrounded by friends.

Entering my third month since surgery and knowing there is nothing more to do now than what I am doing, life begins to take on a daily rhythm. There's my usual awakening to coffee, the continued cravings for cigarettes, the rituals of meditation, eurythmy and voice exercises, a stint at the computer picking up emails, then a walk in my little local park, climbing the hill between juniper, live oak, manzanita as the sun filters through branches and before it strikes down with merciless heat. This has become the social highlight of my day. There are many dog walkers in these early hours. Each person, or couple, hails me with a merry: "Good Morning," and I need to cross the path and get up close and personal before either pulling out my note: "I'm sorry, I can't speak. I just had vocal cord surgery," or say this in a hoarse whisper. Then our conversations really begin. I am stunned to discover how common my situation appears to be. Almost everyone tells me of a parent, aunt, spouse, colleague, friend, who has undergone something similar, whose expectations of a full and immediate recovery were dashed. Some took a year to regain a voice, others never regained one as strong as previously. One woman told me her husband's surgeon performed three surgeries on his polyps, taking it in stages so he was never without a voice for more than six weeks. He needed his in his corporate job. Don't we all need our voices? In the next three months or so I count a dozen cases. This probably represents around 80% of my encounters in this small town!!

I meet others elsewhere with similar tales. In fact I don't think I had a single conversation over a 3-4 month period: checkout clerks in supermarkets, gas station attendants etc., who didn't know someone who had endured a similar ordeal. How could my surgeon have failed to run into this himself? Or *did* he know, and fail to tell *me?*! Once I take a chair to be reupholstered in a dim little store where the owner told me he used to be in a band that once opened in western Michigan for Johnny Cash. The lead singer had laryngitis and told him to take his place. When asking what he should do, the lead said: "Just belt it out, Man." Which he did, yodeling loudly, actually tore his vocal cords and never sang again! My darling elderly Estonian friend, Estelle Emmett, wrote sympathetically from New Mexico, telling me her friend, Bonnie Jean, a Native American singer, lost her singing voice for three years after a ferocious bout of laryngitis. It seems this organ is fragile beyond belief (I do so hope not beyond repair). These stories both comfort and appall me. Without the continuing support of my faraway people I might well have despaired. But see who comes again.......

From: My Dear Doctor Friend : Subject: Regaining Voice

I talked with Dr. B. today as you requested. He said that healing of vocal cords may take at least two months. He would like to examine you first before saying what should be done. He said that he could teach you to talk again. He no longer does surgery in the hospital, but has trained many good laryngeal surgeons over the years, and could refer you appropriately if need be. I had just read about the voice clinic at the university. Dr. B. said that he has heard of the voice turning masculine with the injections. At any rate I wouldn't think that you would want that doctor that did that surgery to do any more anything on you. So come on down, a consult with Dr. Barrios will give you the benefit of his 50 years of experience, something rare in this disposable world. You can stay with me. Love, DDF

Dear DDF,
First, thank you for speaking with Dr. B. This is all immensely reassuring to me. I can't come yet, as I am tied up here for now, and am working with a lovely voice therapist (he says 6 months before considering injections). Thank you too for the offer of a bed. Another time, perhaps. I'm so grateful. I'm doing Maria's eurythmy every day. Then I hope to get some chirophonetics in Sacramento. I just thank you again and again for all your support and that call to dear Dr. B. I'll drop him a thank you card too. Love Lee . (Attached is a piece I wrote that might make you chuckle?)

Dear Lee,
Thank you for returning my email so promptly. I liked your pungent **Going off the Air** message, I wonder if you would like to have me send it to Dr. B? He did say that 2 months was early in the healing. He assumed that more healing would be coming. It does seem that your doc underestimated the healing time. But then he probably hasn't been in medicine since the '50's either. Do you know Helen Keller story? I did hear from Maria who said that a lot of "Oo's" would be helpful. She added that she would like to see that you are doing it correctly. I probably won't be seeing you in October. That's a shame because I thought that Dr. B. could give you some tips, and besides I'd like to return the favor of putting you up as you did for me so long ago in Fair Oaks. Love, DDR

My turn to thank you so so much for all your care, concern, and really valuable help. I'd love you to send **Going off the Air** to Doc Barrios. I sent him a thank you postcard. I'm pretty good at Ooo's (and eurythmy in general, actually, but I'll get my buddy Ann Pratt to double-check me.)
I saw both the voice pathologist and my surgeon yesterday. My surgeon really went to town, stripping the whole outer membrane and dipping into muscle too. So, now I'm on a hefty regimen of muscle building. If I succeed, without the dreaded collagen injections, it will be a first for the voice guy to move me from totally aphonic to sound. He's rather excited at the prospect.
Of course I know about *Helen Keller* - amazing story. Do you know **The Diving Bell and the Butterfly** by Jean-Dominique Bauby? He was editor of **Elle**, had a stroke, was left completely paralyzed except for being able to blink and wrote his book by blinking (which meant "yes") at letters stuck round his walls, thus making every word letter by letter!!! Think you'd love **The Beggar King and the Secret of Happiness**, *Joel ben Izzy*. He lives in Bay area. Thanks again, and much love, Lee

To Adam.

Darling Adam, I'll be adding The Force (the invisible woo-woo bit) to the coffee over the next few days. Would be great if you would call me when it's over - 26 or 27th. Off to see Gore's movie tonight. Wonder if he'll have a stab at the presidency again. After all he won it once. No sounds yet. Definitely less pain though. Love you. Mum. (Oh, I saw a darling movie: *Conversations with Mom*, Argentinean, we need to see it together one day.)

Dear Mum,
Yes, lots of the force would be good. I'm starting to get in a good zone now, even though I'm not sleeping very well. I've kind of reached a point where any new information I put in pushes out a bit of information that I had before, so I'm probably getting to the point where it's as good as it's going to get!
Unfortunately, Gore is completely impossible as a prez candidate. America doesn't like "losers," even if they won. The more I think about it, the slogan "Barak O Eight, Why Wait?" sounds better and better. I hear the Gore film is excellent though.
Glad that the pain has subsided. Still no voice is pretty awful though. I'm off to a park to do some reading. It has been boiling hot lately, but today is perfect. Every once in a while, when I'm thinking how terrible it is to be studying under this much pressure, watching WWIII in the Middle East puts some perspective on the bar exam! OK, back to mortgages. I'll definitely call you when this exam is over: (26th). Love you, Adam

Darling Adam, SAVE THE FOLLOWING TILL 26th! Thanks for all news and reflections. This conflict is agonizing. Did you get to Beirut? I can't remember. Lebanon is/was one of the most beautiful places on earth, and I ache watching the refugees. Gore's movie is outstanding. Yes, it's WW3

basically since Bush went into Afghanistan. I agree Barak, not Hillary. Love you, Mum
(*Israel is busy decimating southern Lebanon in an attempt to wipe out Hezbollah, and succeeding in wiping out most of the civilian population instead.)

Dear Mum,
Just a quick message to say I DID read your email and thanks for the force. Unfortunately, my main comfort for the test now is thinking of all the fairly idiotic people I know who did manage to pass this thing. It's easily the most daunted I have ever felt: I can almost feel the last three years (classes, money, time) piling up on me just for this test. I can't wait for it to be over with. Will definitely check out the Gore film. Although I certainly don't need more things to be mad about in this world. Did you know that Bush forced NASA to remove any language about earth as our "home planet" in its mission statement? Because he wants manned missions to the moon and Mars. I keep thinking of the song **Moonshadow** by *Cat Stevens*, who prophesied your throat malady about forty years ago. You remember the lyrics? "And if I ever lose my mouth, or my teeth North and South, yes if I ever lose my mouth, I won't have to talk no more..." Now you just have to figure out what moonshadow is following you, and why! OK, back to evidence! Love you, A

Darling Adam,
The Force Cometh, and will continue to come for next couple of days. Two of my pool (as in swimming) ladies turn out to be lawyers, and are also in sympathy for you.
No, we have quite enough to rage about. Of course if Bush and his cronies go to Mars, that's fine with me. (I doubt he would be able to tell the difference between there and west Texas.) Interesting you should mention *Cat Stevens*. I just got a CD from Amazon, as I was missing him. (You know we hung out a few times in my rock concert days) I'm making a little DVD to share in my Biography Group, I was seeking some lyrics to accompany it - so, guess what, treated myself to **Sound of Silence** CD too! Let's forget atrocities. All that matters is whom and how we love. And gosh, how I love you!!! Mum

Signe is another friend from Emerson. What an astonishing time that was, opening us to so many people for our future. Her husband Chris founded The Center For Social Development in Forest Row. I worked there for 3 years, met Adam's father, and was thereby introduced to Adam! Her children, Stefan and Karin, babysat Adam when we all showed up together again in Detroit. We seem to be converging again after quite a long time.

Hello Lee, I am glad for the prompt with your email because I have been meaning to write you for ages. How are you now? Has there been movement with your voice? Is it back? Have you learned sign language?? (not meant as a tasteless joke, but I'm sure you have found whatever potential for humor this situation allows.) I just can't imagine how hard this all must have been and I hope it is moving in an improving direction. Have your inner dialogues been different in this time? Yes, the Gore movie is very important. We saw it the first weekend it opened in NY -- I think it was Memorial Day weekend. It is a real deed on his part. It's been interesting timing for Stefan's documentary on NYC traffic/gridlock questions -- in support of biking, rapid bus systems, etc. He interviewed people in London, Copenhagen, Paris, etc. about solutions to the problems of too many cars that are really working, even in huge cities. Everything is about being more awake, more aware, more responsible – so sadly against the mood of the times. And yet good voices are speaking out, and people are responding.

Linda's (Linda is Signe's sister, battling ovarian cancer,) situation continues on, but the pain is ever greater. It's hard for me to see how she can go on much longer. She is still so resistant to pain medication and only takes a tiny bit when it is really unbearable for her. It's hard to see her suffering so, and yet we still can have wonderful times together. I was there until Tuesday evening and we painted, wrote and even went out for lunch. Chris and I will go up there tomorrow evening for the weekend. I hope you are finding ways to enjoy summer. How is Adam faring in Brooklyn/NYC? I look forward to hearing from you again soon. Love, Signe

Dearest Signe,

It was wonderful hearing from you, and then I dreamed of us both together last night. I'm lucky if I remember 2 dreams a year, and recently I've begun dreaming of my friends, so maybe that's compensation for still being soundless. (Did I tell you I can have injections in about six months which might give me a man's voice?)

Linda must be one of the most courageous women I know. Can't imagine how it must be to live with that pain. 3 months of it myself (and only localized around throat and neck) has been quite enough for me. I've been an absolute bear. And now, thank God it is finally receding. Do give her my love. Adam is in throes of bar exams as I write this. So, although he's seen Karin and I think Chenta and Stefan briefly, he'll - he hopes - have more time when he begins work in October.

Some time, with or without a voice, I'll come and see you all too. He's looking for a pad in Brooklyn. I've also been thinking of you in connection with Isis and Lebanon. I'll never forget going to Byblos, seeing the Cedars of Lebanon long before I learned (probably from you) of Isis finding the dismembered remains of Osiris there. The larynx was missing, wasn't it? Oh, how I weep for that land, and people, for the earth these days. And I can't even make a sound when I do!!

Good for Stefan. Can't wait to see his first movie. I feel honored to know him and have had him as our babysitter!!! At times, it's almost overwhelming isn't it, this David and Goliath battle for the planet and humanity. Monsanto just won their case in California. But we mustn't be overwhelmed. Did I tell you about Ryan's Well? (1 800 475 2638) if interested in getting a video), Ryan age six began raising money for a well in Uganda and by age 14 had raised over $1 million and provided fresh drinking water to 300,000

Ugandans (same number Idi Amin had slaughtered) Wonderful little movie. Well, I'd better stop. Someone just told me that the length of time to order a book on Amazon uses 3 tons of coal for the electricity, so who knows how many tons I've used writing this! Much much love to you and family, Lee

*My brother **Bill** has been supporting me long-distance since the start of this thing. He lives with his wife Soraya, and their daughter Kara, in England and, more recently, France. (His two older children, Benjamin and Siena, have left the nest.) I wish I got to see more of them all. We seem to be confined to occasional email exchanges, phone calls, and a strong link through Adam, whom Bill invites to some of his more exotic travels. Climbing Kilimanjaro was the most recent expedition of theirs.*

Hi, Lee,
I guess you will keep me in touch with any progress on speaking. Have you tried SuDoKu yet, from the Times web pages? It is an entertaining "keep the mind alive" exercise for all and especially the over 50's.
Kara, Soraya and I are off to Greece for 10 days. Benj is hard at work at CIBC Bank and is now a full executive, having been a trainee until this month.
Siena is in (rainy) Belize, returning soon and starting legal training in Sept. She and Adam need to meet so that he can give her the low down. Love, Bill.

Dearest Bill,
First thanks so much for your continued concern. I was thinking that you and Adam are both such "tender and true" men. (The quote is from a favorite British movie: **Girl in A Café**). I feel I have protective knights in you both. No voice improvement yet, but the last time I had my cords filmed they - with exercises that I do 3 times a day – had moved a little closer. There will continue to be no sound until they can touch naturally at all times. It's hard not to be very angry with the doctor for not warning me.
You don't know your sister – at least this one! I've seen SuDoku. One glance is enough for me. I loathe those kinds of puzzles. I have a friend in Phoenix who loves them, so she showed me a few pages and I gagged mentally. Life is quite enough of a puzzle for me!
Indeed, Siena and Adam need to get together. Poor lad, he is into his last day (I think) of his Bar exams, then he flies (I think) to Cambodia to help set up another war crimes tribunal (I also think.) Given the world situation (don't miss Al Gore's movie, and we can't miss what's happening in Lebanon). I think the mission for us elders is to encourage the young never to give up hope. It's such a David/Goliath situation – hard not to despair utterly. Quite enough thoughts for now! Love, Lee

From Bill to Lee, I am collecting Siena at the airport today…back from Belize. I will suggest she talks to Adam. Yes, I agree about the world…it is tough for us 'elders' to accept relative impotence and hand over reins of control to the next generation as we have to ask ourselves what we have done to improve or change things and the answer is…very little.

No SuDoKu….so I will have to send books instead, chosen carefully as I know what a good chooser of books you are yourself. I have just done a week learning Spanish so I need to do some practicing; instead we are off to Greece for a week or so. Good luck, and much love, Bill.

Lee to Bill
You don't have to send me anything bar your long distance love. Have a great trip to Greece. I've been trying (and not trying) to learn Spanish for years! Love, Lee

Me to Adam: 26th July
Subject: HURRAH!
Must be over, I'm imagining you out celebrating. Oh, what a relief it must be to be through. Hope to commune with you before you leave. Don't even know where you're going? Love you, love you, Mum

Dear Mum, Yes, it is finally over. I had a few too many glasses of champagne last night and feel a little slow today, but overall life feels much better now. I don't know what I'll do if it turns out I have to take that again— maybe flee the country! (Thank you thank you for the card and cash! I opened it after the bar yesterday.) Here's my itinerary:
Bangkok and environs for three days, a little island off the coast of Thailand called Koh Tao for a five day scuba training session, one night on another island for the "full moon festival," and then off to Phnom Penh for a month, where I will be working for Open Society Justice Initiative on the criminal tribunal for the former Khmer Rouge. After that, I think I'll cross over into Myanmar (Burma) and do about a week there, followed by around ten days in Vietnam, and then back home to NY! I start work on October 10th and while I'm gone my friend Ashish will be getting an apartment for us both to live in. So that's the plan. I hope that when I get back we can have a real chat with your muscular vocal cords in full working order. Love you, A.

Darling Adam, Hurrah again and enjoy a glass of red wine on me (great antioxidant). Great to have your general movements. You've got me really nostalgic now for Bangkok. I wonder if the very grand Hotel Erewhon is still there where a rather delightful CIA agent picked me up with a Cafe Viennoise and papaya soused in limejuice, and the hotel gave me orchids thinking I was Shirley McLaine. You'll be careful in Myanmar won't you. Well, I think you have a good guardian angel. All sounds wonderful, BUT I may not forgive you if you fail to visit Angkor Watt. There's a huge stone Buddha tucked into grasses overlooking a lake that I'll never forget. Once, going around on the back of a little scooter, my guide pointed above us and there was a black panther lying along a branch just above our heads. Oh, and elephants darkening the windows of my cabin as they wandered past. I loved Phnom Penh too. Have a fantastic trip. Love you so much, Mum

Dear Mum,
I made it fine to Bangkok. Don't have much time online though, but just to say I'm safe and sound. Love you, A

Darling Adam,
Great news. Enjoy!!! I think you are going scuba diving where Michael Crichton was surrounded by sharks. Enjoy that too!! Love you, Mum

*I first met **Meg** in Sacramento, though I wonder where and when we really first met! Once, when we were sprawled across from each other on couches in my living room, she looked over, with a strange, intense expression and said: "Oh, I know where we were together. In Greece. I was older than you then. I may even have been your teacher." My whole body reacted. I knew she was right. I felt, in the way one does at such times, utterly and wholly "seen". I am so glad and grateful that our friendship continues to this day, years after we left Sacramento.*

From: Meg Re: An Inconvenient Truth

Hey Lee, I'm in New Hampshire and teaching away. Dennis Klocek and Michael D'Aleo (one of the more respected scientists in the movement) had serious discussions here last week about global warming. Neither of them are convinced by the actual scientific facts. They feel many of them are being manipulated. I was quite surprised, but they are fairly convinced that the jury is still out. Apparently some scientific reports of ice buildup in certain areas has been suppressed, and they feel the issue is being politicized because of a complex build-up around the sale of carbon emissions. They and others feel one needs to approach **"An Inconvenient Truth"** with good science. I'm not sure what to think. I'm off to Maine next week for the AWSNA meeting and then to Montana. Meg

Darling Meg,
Still no voice, but I'm working like crazy to develop new muscles that may close the gap. And in six months, if not successful, I have the collagen injections and may end up with a man's. Well, I frankly don't care what Dennis etc have to say. It is absolutely clear to me that we have been polluting and destroying the planet and if the jury just sits around wondering, the melted waters may just close over its head. Between that destruction and WW3 (oh, God, Lebanon!! I ache, I ache, I ache - don't you?) I weep, too, sometimes, for myself, as it's been as hard as anything to be soundless and weeping without a sound is not the same thing!! Love you, Lee

Lee, It's so hard for me to imagine you voiceless. It really got me when you wrote about soundless weeping. Concerning the environment, it's not that the jury is out on pollution, but what we should do about it. Apparently the hydrogen car is not the answer because of the issues of water vapor. What these guys are saying is pay attention to the science and make sure you know how and why the government is manipulating data. I am still working on this. In the meantime, I have managed to get my own eco footprint down from 35 to 14, which means I use only 3 times as much energy as I should for the health of the earth. (Oh, the shame of it). Just living in America is a problem in this area. You can check this out and take your footprint if you go to *redefiningprogress.org.*

It's great to hear from you, and I do hear you in my head with your voice of yore. I look forward to your new manly tones. Love, Meg

Then my therapeutic eurythmist, Maria, offers the following.

Dear Lee,
I wonder how you are doing.I just returned from the East Coast where I have been teaching in the therapeutic eurythmy training for a week.
I have been thinking about you, wondering how I could better help you with the eurythmy.
I think it would be better for you now to work with vowels and let the other program rest. I would think you know the movements for the vowels, A,E,I,O,U. A as in 'stars', E crossing arms, I stretching (EE). Always confusing with European/American ways of sounding them. If you could do them on a 5 – pointed star, forwards and backwards, starting at the head of the star and moving with A to the right foot, then E to the left arm etc, finishing with a circle around the star with one L.
This may be all too confusing for you? I can draw it for you if you send me your fax number again. You can continue with threefold walking, contraction, expansion and frame it with I,A,O.
When you do the U, you should put your feet very close as well as your hands, the palms of your hands pressed together, feeling that you draw all your forces inside your skin. Again, if you get another visit from your eurythmy friend, have her show you the 5-pointed star with the vowels.
The vowels should just be done archetypal and big. It would be very good if you could do them also with your feet in standing.
Tell me what you think. Greetings and love from Maria

My own son may be safe and sound, but on August 1st, I receive this tragic message from one of my dearest friends, Myra McPherson, mother of one of my favorite souls, Drew, whom I have loved since I met him around ten years ago. How do you howl silently? How do we respond helpfully? Writing this now, a year later, I barely remember what I did, only how I felt, and feel to this day. It was not a time for emails. It was a time for very practical responses: money, books, massage oils – and spiritual ones: prayers like I've barely ever prayed before. I know at some stage during the day, I lifted the telephone and dialed Joan's number. Since she couldn't hear a voice, she asked: "Is that Lee?" And after some strange hoarse hiss I made, she simply said: "Yes, I'm here, come on over." She and her daughter Faline could hold me for a long long time, while I sobbed (silently) and shook, and clung to their human warmth until I could find my own again. I think later I drove to the pink boulders where I had once taken Drew and which he had asked to climb. I had been terrified he might fall and hurt himself, but eventually reluctantly agreed, extorting a promise from him that he would only ascend a particular clump. I remember waiting, heart in mouth, as he disappeared among them and, what seemed hours later, seeing him emerge, standing triumphantly, arms spread wide against a blue blue sky – king of the universe. Later when I contacted Adam, he responded with his own heartbreak: "Whenever I remember Drew, he was always climbing a tree."

"Dear family and friends,
It is with deep deep sadness that I write this note, knowing that with the loving support of family and friends and the ever-present guidance from the spiritual world that our present family situation will be resolved.
On Sunday July 30 while I was in Nevada caring for my dying father (Dutch Stenovich,) who crossed the threshold on Monday July 31) I received a phone call from the park ranger saying that Drew had been in a serious accident at the river and I was to call and go immediately to Mercy San Juan Hospital. Being 7 hours away by car I notified Mic to go then found a ride to Sacramento. Michael Joyce my brother in law drove me given I was in no condition to drive myself. To encapsulate the nightmare, Drew was diving at the American river as he has done since he was able to take his bike down, crushed his C5, which has now been repaired through the miracles of modern orthopedic surgery and today we are heading to Santa Clara Valley medical center in San Jose California to commence intensive rehabilitation, at least 3 months. I will be living someplace close. We are taking it one day at a time And through the loving support of community we manage to eat a little and sleep a little. Someone will be setting up some type of web page on update on the mini Miracles of Drew McPherson. He is in good spirits, there is still a twinkle in his eyes and it's a long road to freedom. But I know that with the will this young man has and the loving support of everyone who knows and loves him, the challenge will be overcome. I would love to hear from you, but know I will be busy supporting Drew. My practice is closed for now and I am completely dedicated to standing next to this gallant young man as he climbs this summit. I ask for your prayers and hold us in the light of Christ. Todd has returned from New Orleans to be with his brother In love and gratitude Myra "

Thus July draws to a close. A month of deep tragedies, personal and international. In that context – Drew, Lebanon, the continued horrors of Iraq, and other atrocities - my little Inconvenient Truth, combined with the incredible gifts of this life of mine, must make me one of the most outstandingly lucky people on the planet today. And when I weep, still soundlessly, I am reminded of Stevie Smith's poem, capturing one of the deepest, necessary - if inconvenient - truths of all!

SO TO FATNESS COME.

Poor human race that must
Feed on pain, or choose another dish
And hunger worse.

There is also a cup of pain, for
You to drink all up, or,
Setting it aside for sweeter drink,
Thirst evermore.

I am thy friend, I wish
You to sup full of the dish
I give you and the drink,
And so to fatness come more than you think
In health of opened heart, and know peace.

Grief spake these words to me in a dream. I thought
He spoke no more than grace allowed,
And no less than truth.

CHAPTER FIVE. HOARSE WHISPERER.

"Prince Charles might talk to trees, but the Queen endorses the New Age practice of whispering to horses. The Household Cavalry recently hired an animal clairvoyant, Amelia Kincade to talk to their unruly nags."
The Independant, UK.

Before my monthly visit to Dr. J, I hear from one of my oldest and dearest friends, Sheila.

Sheila and I met in our counseling training at the Westminster Pastoral Foundation, London, in the early 70's. This was a time before counseling had even become a recognized, accredited profession, and our group was the last to be blown in from the four quarters, bearing rich and amazing biographies. Those of us who survived the first few weeks, and continued through the next 3 years were all "tenured professors" of life. Few had academic credentials, which were only required from the following group, and we claimed that things began to go downhill from then on!! Sheil's first job, age 17, had been deciphering German codes at Bletchley during World War 2. Later she became a film editor, needing a selective vision for what mattered in a story. If those aren't good preparations for counseling, I don't know what are? I believe about 10 of our initial 40 finally graduated. Sheila remains one of my closest friends. We write regularly so my little drama came in the midst of other news, other letters.
I think it would be hard for anyone reading her words to fail to understand how much our correspondence means to both of us. I often forget, until some deep exchange such as ours occurs, how much of my soul lies like a stagnant pond if there is no-one around to stir it, throw stones into it or, as I always feel when I open Sheila's letters, pour like some great waterfall into it, filling it with life again.

Sunday 6th August.

Dearest Lee,
Feast of the Transfiguration, no less! So, transformation is in the air and I hope some of it reaches you, in your dire predicament. I have been haunted by your story, having taken it in at some deep level where it begins to meet affinities (i.e. Jacqueline du Pre with her limp muscles, Beethoven with his deafness.) But these are extreme cases which proved irreversible, and yours is by no means beyond hope. Perhaps even now your Mormon friend will have rescued your voice? I'm listening as I type to a Prom on the radio, with a new piece, a setting (by Julian Anderson, not known to me) of a poem by Emily Dickinson: "Heaven is shy of Earth", woven in with sections of the Latin Mass – and somehow, bringing E.D. into consciousness adds something to the story of your mislaid voice. Is this because of her self chosen isolation, and the intensity of perception that came with it?

I was really moved by your letter, and by the Email on the same subject: perhaps that's why I had an unusually long and vivid dream the same night? (I hardly ever remember dreams at present, and feel hunger for them – a thanks for engendering one!) I'm enclosing a photocopy of the typed version. I shall share it with my analyst, Anne Maguire, at our next meeting in September. And, by the way, that will be our last meeting, for she is closing down her practice in Harley Street, and will spend her time instead writing. She is a consultant dermatologist as well as a Jungian analyst and writes books about the symbolism of body and illness. If I have time I will question her about the larynx, and pass on to you any offerings. She has been a splendid companion during my strange journey with D., before and after his death, and didn't bat an eyelid when it came to things like paranormal conversations! And now she has suffered bereavements of her own, and gracefully acknowledges that our sessions have sometimes been useful to her, as well.

Dream.

"I am visiting Lee in America for a few days. With her is a woman friend, strong, vital, short hair and of a similar build to Lee. I make an immediate and warm connection with her and she with me and as I recall it the conversation that follows is with her rather than with Lee. At one point in this conversation we hug briefly and at another she places her hand on my stomach – in the dream as in real life distended, but in the dream I can feel something hard there, even perhaps cancerous? A sense that Lee's friend may be alerting me to a risk I had not recognized.
We are out of doors, on open land, with rough grass. Lee's friend has suggested a swim in the sea, and I feel enthusiastic about this (though in real life sea bathing in now impossible for me). The day turns into evening, and we are still talking. We cannot now go to the sea, it is too late. I feel deep disappointment, but do not express this – instead I made a comment to the effect that plans cannot always be carried out. There is general agreement with this.
At some point, before or after, this episode, (but in daylight), we are in the same grassy setting and I suddenly become aware that an animal is stalking me. I can see it several yards away, lying low in the grass and beginning to approach me. Could this be a puma? Or another member of the cat family? Or is it instead a big dog, relatively harmless? I am very afraid and try to scream for help from other people (presumably including Lee and her friend) in the distance. I am not sure whether my cries are heard, but somehow the danger is averted.
Another snatch of activity: I am helping to pack fruit – possibly apples and pears, but in any case, round, individual items, not grapes or cherries – into a small white van equipped with trays slotting into the inner structure, close together for maximum capacity. The trays are nearly full – it is a bumper harvest.

Another snatch: At some point in the conversation with Lee and her friend, I am aware of the presence of Noreen L., with whom I have a now unremembered conversation.
(Noreen L. is an ex-client from very early days in my practice: we ended long ago, but remain friends though we seldom meet. She is in her sixties now, lives in Cambridge, and from childhood has been handicapped by severe deafness (and perhaps this is why she appears in the dream?) She has had to struggle with this disability, made worse by an operation that was not a success. She became an excellent senior social worker, and later added counseling skills which she continued to exercise after retirement.)

Some thoughts about the dream – and I welcome any that you yourself might have. "Lee" seems to be silent in this dream – it is "her friend" who talks, and who talks with all of Lee's immediacy and love of verbal communication. And of course I assume that some, or all of this dream is also about me, and what I project on to you. In fact I think dreams very often arise from the shared space between two people, especially when these two love and trust each other. I can't make sense of the hardness in my stomach, and do not feel a necessity to literalize the cancer idea, though indeed I do not rule it out. But could it be that I am finding it hard to stomach the news about Lee's voice? The swim in the sea, no doubt an allusion to the unconscious, and the need to draw on the deepest possible resources of the unconscious mind. In the dream I felt keenly, not mildly, disappointed. Tentatively, I wonder whether you have (or had, when you wrote your letter) not immersed the problem deeply enough, to the place where everything is alchemically reversed and where woundings become blessings? I recall the inner message I received over and over again during the major breakdown in my thirties: "Suffering is privilege". With these words came peace and relief and understanding. "Yes, of course!" But I could never hold the message for long enough. Please don't take this comment to be any kind of judgment. It is hugely difficult to reach this kind of reversal, and it often takes me weeks, even years to do so. But I think this is what Jung was talking about when he used to ask his patients the question: "Are you playing the game of life?" And then he would laugh. It seems to be about catching every ball that comes to you, whether you like it or not. And not just accepting it, but actually choosing it. And no, it isn't about becoming a martyr!

Believe me, I find it quite terrible to have lost the faculty that earns you a living, and that brings so much pleasure and satisfaction to you and to others. It is a kind of crucifixion – as are all major initiations, I think, undeserved and on the face of it, unforgivable. Do sue your surgeon, if your legal adviser (Adam, surely) thinks this fitting. But perhaps, also, he was obliged to make a mess of the operation because fate required this. This doesn't excuse him of course.

So, some thought about death and rebirth, probably the major metaphor in all our dreams, and all our lives. The idea in dreams is that whatever dies will be reborn (not always in the same dream), and when reborn will be subtly and distinctly different. Something will have been added, as seems also to be the case with people who have had near death experiences. They come back with gifts that were lacking beforehand, possibly healing gifts. This suggests that when your voice returns, it will be enriched, or it may have different things to say, or different modes of speech. What is required is that the death, however brief, has to be accepted as absolute. *It isn't recovery that is sought, but rediscovery.* (My italics!) The crucifying loss is a betrayal – the resurrection brings simplicity and a new innocence.

About silence, another thought. I've recently learned that the Pre-Socratic philosophers, including Parmenides and Empedocles, followed the Pythagorean tradition which had it that true philosophy could only be experienced and transmitted in a state they called "silence and stillness". And that the ability to reach this state was handed on by master to pupil in a ritual akin to the laying on of hands. This brought with it the gift, not only of philosophy, but also of poetry and prophecy, three linked capacities. Philosophy, it seems, was always expressed in the form of poetry (though only fragments now remain). Aristotle did away with all that nonsense. Books by Peter Kingsley (a professor of philosophy) proposes this idea, and you would find them interesting if you haven't come across his work. Enough! Ten o'clock in the evening, time for supper and then bed. This letter comes with much love, much wish for betterment for you, and a real longing for conversation. A dream is much better than nothing! I loved hearing about Adam's engagement with law. What a hope for the world! Much love Sheila.

Dearest Sheila,

Oh, thank you! Love and trust, indeed, brings us into the same space. I am awed, deeply moved, deeply grateful for all your "dreams and reflections." I'm sure all you made of the dream is wise and true. Couldn' t better your insights! Though I had a flash association on the "hard to stomach" bit, of a young woman returning wounded from Iraq and they placed part of her skull in her abdomen to keep it alive, while her brain healed. "Head below heart - for safekeeping"? Have you ever seen a cross-section of the larynx? Both male and female genitalia woven into this extraordinary design. The vocal cords themselves are tiny labia. And the way the whole thing works with the air. If you ever get a chance to see *Theodore Schwenk's* book, **Sensitive Chaos**, you can see how every form and movement in the created world culminates in this instrument. (It is also rather fascinating that I was first utterly silent, conversing with lizards and my horned toad, then able to make harsh croaks, this week can imitate seals, sea lions and, on a good day, a few frail dolphin songs, so moving up the chain!! It's also interesting to me that I can make vowel sounds – using a lot of arm muscle power – (the vowels are the inner life of soul) and I can also make consonants (these are from the outer world) but I can't bring the two together. I remember David telling me I had the challenge of "developing the muscle between inner and outer" – in what I spoke, in when I remained silent etc., as a counselor. Now I have to do this right into the physical. (Diverging from your dream here, sorry. We really

need 3 days and nights together, don't we, with both sound and silence. I am currently a Hoarse Whisperer, so not entirely without means.)
Next day.
Of course, as you say so wisely, there is always a gift, a resurrection. I'm aware of it moving towards me (actually always with me, but one mustn't hurry these things must one?) Here in the U.S, I find there's little ability to bear the necessary undoing, chaos, that precedes a new creation. It's a "problem-solving nation". And I suspect in many who urged me to write at once, it was a way not only of trying to end my suffering, but their own. Oh, as it has just darted up from your page, I love the philosophers' approach. Thank you for that. Have you, by the way, ever attended **Taize** services? Sacred song and silence, from the **Taize Community** in France?   Sure you know that beautiful George Eliot quote?
"If we had a keen vision and feeling for all ordinary human life, it would be like hearing the grass grow and the squirrel's heart beat and we would die from the roar that lies on the other side of silence." I can hear intimations. It's just too soon to shape the future, but it will mean more giving up, to make room for the new. After all, have to leave old pastures, all that over trodden, overgrazed grass, to find the new ones?
 I feel if I don't print this out and send it, I could get caught here forever. Our conversations have always meant so much to me. Thank you again for the dream. (A friend here just left a message on my phone to tell me she had dreamed of me speaking in a clear, pure, silvery voice!! It's lovely to think that that voice exists in other dimensions. Much much love, Lee

And after writing this, I remember a Rilke poem Sheila gave me years ago that resonated with Jung's comment about playing ball! If only......!

> *For as long as you catch what you yourself have thrown, all is*
> *Dexterity and allowable (venial) gain:*
> *Only when you become suddenly catcher of the ball*
> *Which (she who is) the eternal partner in the game*
> *Throws to you, to your middle, in a precisely*
> *Achieved swing, in one of those curves*
> *From God's great architecture of bridges:*
> *Only then is being able to catch a faculty, -*
> *Not yours, but a world's. And if then you were even*
> *To possess power and courage to return the throw,*
> *Nay, yet more miraculously, were to forget power and courage*
> *And had already thrown, ...as the year*
> *Throws the birds, the flocks of migrant birds,*
> *Which an older warmth hurls over oceans*
> *To a young warmth -, only then,*
> *In this risk, do you validly join in the game as a partner:*
> *Do you no longer make the throw easier for yourself, no longer*
> *More difficult for yourself. From out your hands proceeds*
> *The meteor and speeds forth into its spaces...*

I now enter my fourth month since surgery. Every morning I wake to pain and the question: "Will it be the same as yesterday?" I try to make sound, lying in bed, but none comes, bar the harsh whisper most of us can make when deprived of vowels. I hear my voice inside my head, like some ancient vanished ocean captured in a shell. Will it ever sound out again? I have a video of a TV talk I once gave, but can't bring myself to play it. Next, I think of those young soldiers wounded in Iraq, and how much much worse it is for them. Then I wonder how it is for Drew. Waking, does it dawn on him sharply or slowly that he cannot use his lower limbs? Does he dream of dancing? Apart from my concrete driveway, I have been almost dream free. I get up and remove the lemon collar. This "solution", like so many others, is becoming something of a problem now. The lemon leaves my skin pretty raw. So now I have to put creams and oils on it. I do all the others things I am supposed to do, which takes almost two hours: coffee, meditation, eurythmy, rest, voice exercises (or more accurately, my bench pressing, bicep pounding actions, since my voice remains discreetly uninvolved), picking up my emails, all before breakfast and morning walk. This is still the great – only! - social outing of my day. Well, not the only social exchange, for, like those ladies from bygone days, I have my daily correspondence.

Group- email. Sent: Wednesday, August 09
Subject: Hoarse Whisperer

Dear Friends,
 My predicament may be such old news by now, you don't want to hear any more about it. But, a brief update, having just had my third Action Movie (vocal cord filming) to let you know both my voice therapist and I are cautiously optimistic that I may be audible within the next 3-4 months (we had given it 6 months before feeling a need for another procedure.) The cords are no longer completely raw (and the pain is diminishing), and when I do certain exercises to "smash" them together they can now touch! My voice may never be as strong, probably slightly hoarser (due to scar tissue) so I doubt I'll sing soprano at La Scala. But I'm very happy to see these improvements. I'm sure all your loving support has helped. Now you can turn your thoughts and prayers to other folk who are really suffering in these times!! Much love, Lee

*   *   *

 *I mentioned **Marion**, the music therapist who moved to Portland, and who has been sending loving cheer for the past months We have been coordinating my visit later this month. Just being with her is enough to heal anyone, never mind what she might pluck or twang in my presence.*

Dear Lee.
I do love hearing your progress and frustration so I can share in it! love,
Marion

Dear Marion,
Maybe I should bring my family photos then? Three filming sessions of my vocal cords??? Almost with you, girl!! That will be wonderful. Love Lee

From: Nancy: Subject: Re: Hoarse Whisperer

HOORAY! You always had that low sexy voice as a trade mark, we will assume it is even more so when this is over. Much love, Nancy

Dearest Nancy
Thanks girl. Yes, nothing bell-like this lifetime, or probably any to follow! Love you, Lee

From: Steph

Dear Lee,
Sounds like relatively good news. Thanks for relaying it! So next May (2007) will most likely be on for you, and I'm very happy to know that. In the meantime, you are at least surviving financially? I'm taking a week off in Oct. to attend a class reunion in Porterville CA. I'm really going in order to see the core of the people I used to hang out with - but after having connected with the three other women, I'm not sure if the plan is such a good idea. For sure, it will be interesting. In short: The wildest of them is a recovering alcoholic; one blew up in body weight (from steroids for asthma) and almost died but is still alive after 3 husbands and eight grand children....Another couple who married at 16/18 later had them growing marjuana to alleviate pain of his diabetes and her fibromyalgia, which led to numerous busts and finally, arrest with $500,000 bail. They were the first test case for California's medical marijuana law, and eventually everything was overturned. Okay...you get the picture! One might say it's a rather good thing that I got out of there! Much love to you, Steph

Dearest Steph
I don't know, girl - shouldn't you spend a week with me instead? Golly, would I love that! Sleep on it, please!! Though ghastly events make the best stories, don't they? You truly surpassed me there with those tales. How about this from last week, after I'd been weeping soundlessly because one young friend jumped in a river, has spinal cord injury, another brain tumors, Israelis bombed Baalbek (God d*mn them!) - then I bumped into the guy who "hijacked" my house so it doesn't fall down the hill. He married recently, lovely girl from S.Africa, we all hung out together a few times. So I congratulated him. He said T. (his wife of 2 days) took his truck, totaled it against a cabdriver's cab and went to live with the cabbie! We were in stitches, doubled up in downtown Prescott and, as Garry said: "Nothing bad happens to a writer!" All grist to our mill, eh! Take care, love you (hugs to Sam too) Lee

From: Signe
This is goodish news -- encouraging! I spoke to someone last week whose husband had similar surgery and also lost his voice -- hard because he was a professor -- but it did come back within months. It's still kind of husky, but he still sounds like himself and has had no further problem. You never did sing soprano did you??!
We are having so much fun with Cyris! Who needs work? Such a miracle to watch human development at work -- he is talking up a storm now, sentences, paragraphs, real conversation. And every day he tries some new thing physically. And his sense of humor is a joy! Keep getting better, Love Signe

Dearest Signe,
No, never could sing a note, that's why I was hopeful!! Enjoy Adirondacks, and Cyris - thank God he has humor, will need it mightily. Can't wait to see him when I visit Adam in NY. (He's currently in Cambodia.) Love Lee

Dear Mum,
Good to hear the news on your throat. I am just about to get on a plane to Phnom Penh, after about ten days wandering around islands in the gulf of Thailand. I'll write a longer email soon. Love you, A

Darling Adam,
Even better news to hear you weren't eaten by sharks. Longing to hear more. (Oh, you might enjoy this: My voice therapist introduced me to a young singer about to have her polyps removed. She was clearly a little nervous after I had hissed at her, but I assured her that if she had found a good, sensitive surgeon, she would surely be fine. She told me she had, one of Phoenix Top Ten, Dr. W***! I gave her my card, told her to wave it under his nose before he picked up his scissors, so he would be sure to treat her with consummate delicacy.) Love you, Mum

*My friend, **Marianne**, and her family count as "adopted" family for Adam and myself, meeting in Sacramento and bonding through losing both our homes to floodwater. This really cemented our friendship. (Nothing like having all one's physical possessions swept away, to strengthen the human connection!) As a single parent, I cherish the families who offer a true home from home. Marianne, Dave and their children have certainly done that over the past decade or so. Now we meet in San Francisco whenever we can, Marianne and I sometimes managing to extricate Dave for lunch at a little Vietnamese restaurant before we go walk on the beach and catch up our lives.*

Hi Lee,
So great to hear your news...you are daily in my prayers and thoughts and I know you will recover...in any case your voice will!!!! Yes, there is so much suffering in the world again and this blasted war in Lebanon has me wondering how I can withhold my taxes in protest of supplying Israel with

weapons....I'm at my wits end! I'm off on Aug 22 for 5 days with the Dutch family and 3 days with Bron...a fast trip but I am so looking forward to seeing my family again after 6 years!!

I hope you are keeping as cool as possible and send you lots of love and hugs, also from Cynthia Aldinger who is at RSC for her Lifeways training course in 110 degree heat! I drove over to have lunch with her a few days ago and was greatly relieved not to live there any more...how did we ever stand it there? I am sure you've heard about Drew McPherson who did himself very serious injury while diving into the American River. Take care, Lee, keep in touch, hugs, Marianne

Dearest Marianne,

Thanks so much. Yes, I heard about Drew – unimaginably terrible. Of course, as we all are, I'm praying and imagining angel's wings and who knows what else every night. We **Women in Black** do extra vigils now, with these new Middle Eastern atrocities. Some can't eat or sleep (more advanced souls than me,) so we just go stand together instead. Lebanon may be my favorite country, too. I was last there a week before the Six Days War! Think, as the Brits did in India finally thanks to Gandhi, Israel has lost its moral credibility (I don't mean many Israelis, I've seen them trying to stop this thing too. I mean the Govt. Our current lot never had any to lose!) What a choice point we live in now, eh. Everything is one now, from the smallest trifle. I inadvertently bumped someone's fender in a parking lot yesterday on my way to the voice guy. No one in sight, only slightest paint scrape, could have left etc., then told myself "No" and was writing notes etc to the owner, hoping not to be late for my appointment.

I don't know if I'll come to SF after my bio retreat in Sacramento. Being voiceless is really frustrating and I'm sure I won't have it back by then. When one's feeling "*peelywally*" (a lovely Scots expression") one needs one's own bed and special blanket. I'm like a 2yr old. I'll keep you in touch. Maybe you would come to Sacramento for a day? I miss you all, just have to focus on healing right now. Love, and to Dave and the family, Lee

Dearest Lee,

Of course I would love to see you but I understand feeling *peelywally*...just let me know what day in Sacramento would work for you and I'll make a go of it...going to Sacramento with a purpose is much different than just going to Sacramento for the scenery! I have 2 days a week of teaching plus our new Lifeways family life class - up to my ears in darling moms, dads and their children...we are making flower presses, dyeing silks and making lanterns as well as felting small rugs, slippers and berets....all this summer long. This is the most fun I have had in years!!! Love and hugs! Marianne

Darling Marianne,

Maybe I should come and stay with you for a couple of days and do felting. I LOVE felting. I'll let you know my plans. All I really want to do in future is feed birds, rock babies, learn to make silent movies, and write rude letters in vague attempts to stop this world going to hell in a hand basket. Oh, and BE WITH MY FRIENDS!!! Do give my love to Bronnie, and lots to you of course. Lee

*   *   *

It is one thing writing letters, another actually seeing, being with a friend. Yes, our hearts do actually jump for joy. Mine leaped like a salmon seeing Jannebeth at Portland airport, after the ludicrous journey through Homeland Security.

If it wasn't enough to be with her, her beautiful home was right in the heart of streets lined with every English tree I haven't seen and have sorely missed since living on this continent. I had had no idea I would find massive beeches, London plane trees, oaks, sycamores, and when I snatched time from our wonderful kitchen table conversations (or Jannebeth gently extricated herself so she could prepare for the conference) I walked and walked, combining awe and delight as I caressed bark, leaves, even snuggled in among massive root systems, and also did my speech exercises. One distinct advantage of being soundless is that I can do these in broad daylight, in public places, without anyone knowing or my disturbing the peace. That's until they see my lips moving, but hey, who cares.

Then Jannebeth and I really caught up. It's been nearly a decade since we spoke. I had forgotten we are possibly the only two people on this continent who know or knew many of the same people: Dutch doctors in particular, several of whom have now died. Recalling them, our memories of our times with them, was astonishing. Again, another example of how these regions of our souls lie stagnant until another revivifies them.

As if this wasn't enough, there is Marion too. And the conference itself. I am for the first time in quite a large gathering. I enjoy my own silence, which carves more inner space to listen to others. We draw leaves, and blossoms. We go in the Arboretum and paint scenes. We make music. Or, more accurately, the others sing, I listen again. Marion places me between two circles of people sounding tones towards each other. I can feel the vibrations in my throat, and sense these healing me. I remember Marlo Morgan (Mutant Message) describing watching the aboriginal healers singing broken bones back into place. I'm surprised after every session not to have a full voice again. But still I feel healed in some mysterious and even more significant way.

And still more mail awaiting me on my return!

From: Dianna
Dear Lee,
Your predicament is very much of concern to me so thank you for the update. It is a relief to hear of some improvement. I am wondering how you have dealt with the frustration and fear this sort of thing is bound to have wrapped

around it. You always make your e-mails sound so positive. Now are you still planning to present at the Homeschoolers Conf? Seems that is coming up quickly. Had a visit from an old college friend. He's an energy economist and first person I heard use the term "global warming" which was 34 years ago. The information I had to coax him to share was not too encouraging. We've all got to get ourselves in order so that we are able to assist each other. By the way - remember Rachel Corey - the young woman who stood up to the Israeli bulldozer? **The Nation** magazine had reported a story - her story had been produced as a play in London and scheduled for showing in NYC. The theater got cold feet and dropped it at the last minute out of concern of offending NY Jews. I heard that Seattle (just as I thought) will be taking the show. I'll send further info as I find it. Continued good thoughts your way - don't ask people to turn them away just yet! We want you fully healed. Lots of love and big hugs - Dianna

Dear Dianna,
So good to get all your news. Thanks so much. I must say, lovely as Portland is, place and people, I was rather relieved to get back to a little sunshine to warm my old bones. It is only August!!! And 4 out of the 5 days were cloudy and dank! No, I won't be at Rahima's. I've basically cancelled all work for this year, which may mean I'm looking at a very different future that does not depend on the verbal. Thrilled to hear about Rachel Corey play. Have to hope there'll be a movie, then I can get to see it. Much love, Lee

*The simple reason I have not yet included anything from my beloved soul sister **MaryJo** is that I lost her previous emails! Don't think for a minute she hasn't been by my side (at least spiritually) probably since the world began! She's a smoker for one thing! There is quite possibly no deeper karmic bond than that, and I have met many of my companions for this lifetime in the few and ever fewer spots allocated to us addicts. We are definitely an endangered species. (But, hey, I got to meet Nina Simone's percussionist at Detroit Metro airport when he asked me for a light. My smoking encounters could be the subject of my next book!!) Anyhow, more than nicotine binds MaryJo and I. We met in Detroit. We cannot go for long without spending time together. She is a remedial teacher, she is a gorgeous personality, we have worked and played together over the past twenty years or so. I hope we have many years still ahead of us.*

Hello dear
AArgh. It is middle of August and I have tons of writing, prep work and AHE business to finish by month end. I need the beach again. Cardinal rule: get to the good spots any way you can. On Tuesday, the painter came to do the deck - of course in the wrong color, not like the sample - but I was too apathetic at that time to make him go back. I figure one or two years and it will weather to a nice moldering grey (right now it is bordering on orange) While he was here the furnace folks came to install the new boiler. While

they were here the water heater started shooting flames. Thank God it ended there - of course we had to get a new hot water heater too. Today my printer won't work and I was going to print out the grants for mailing. Oh well I don't think there is anything more frustrating than trying to make house repairs - unlike people, I expect a certain return for effort. It all seems to domino.... Well more later. Love to you, MaryJo

Hey girl,
I'm just back from Portland - great city, great people and it was grey and chilly four days out of five and I couldn't wait to get back to my lovely sunshiny spot!! So I won't be moving!! I'm just deciding to tell my very own biography research group that I don't think I'll be coming in October. All part of letting go, dying to yet another part of myself. What I enjoy most is my morning walk with Cas (new found friend) and her dog Molly, who loves me to pieces. And reading. And feeding the birds. That's it!!! Anyhow, that's my news. Love you, Lee

*I met **Drew (Andrew) J.** fairly recently. He attended an Angel Workshop I gave in California, made such a fine comment at the end that I went afterwards to thank him, and that was enough to get the ball rolling between us and, later, his whole family. He is a therapist, working with Aids patients among other people, and when I go (or went) to San Francisco, we discovered we lived on the same street, and had lovely walking, talking and coffee drinking conversations. It has been wonderful to extend knowing him by meeting his wife Gabrielle, and remarkable children, Emanuel and Miriam (now 3, and with a hearing challenge).*

Dear Lee,
So sorry to hear about your operation. Gabrielle talked with Meg on Saturday at the school's workday. We cannot imagine how you manage without your voice. You, who have so much to say and enjoy people so much. It must be very frightening and frustrating. Our hearts go out to you. Knowing nothing of your physical condition, we pray your speech is restored before long. Emanuel is about to begin first grade. We are all very excited! We also had a wonderful *spaghetti carbonara* luncheon with Lalla and Paolo after their return from Italy. If you are in the mood to write, we'd love to hear how you are making sense of this new turn of events. Thinking of you. Gabrielle and Drew

Dear Drew,
Yes, it's been bad, and I won't be coming to SF for a while. Here are some of my group emails, to catch you into loops again. Just think – next time I come and we go for coffee, YOU can do all the talking for a change!! I am a Hoarse Whisperer, so not all is lost, and even more may return with therapy in 6 months or so – enough to function at least, but no singing soprano at La Scala and maybe no more workshops etc, just chats with buddies which has to

be good enough for me. I'm still hoping to come your way next year. Give my best love to Gabrielle, and Emanuel and Miriam. Tell Emanuel I hope he has a great start in First Grade. I bet he will!! Did you ever read *The Diving Bell and the Butterfly*? **Jean-Dominique Bauby** wrote it with his eyelid (blinking a "yes" for each letter after a massive stroke.) I'm still in really little league!! Much love to you all, and thanks again so much for writing. Lee

Jackie is a friend and colleague from our Detroit, Ann Arbor days. She was the Director of WTDA Summer Sequence Program (Waldorf Teacher Training) in which I taught for several years. This cemented a friendship that began when we both went through cancer. She spent a week with me once here in Arizona, ostensibly recruiting for the program, but having an incredible time traveling around, sharing stories. One treasured memory is of us needing to change out of jeans into full length dresses, covered heads and ankles etc to visit the Greek Monastery in Florence (Arizona, not Italy) across from the State Penitentiary. As we were struggling out of our clothes, we realized the monks could probably see everything, if any were peering over the walls. We got a bad (good) attack of the giggles, which seriously impaired our attempts at modesty!

Hello Lee: I was in Ann Arbor to visit relatives and we went to the Treasure Mart where I ran into Linda (sorry can't remember her last name). She told me that you have no voice. She said you had sent the surgeon's report to her husband but she didn't give me any details. First of all, let me tell you how sorry I feel that you, of all people, have lost your voice. What a loss for you and for everybody who has learned from you in a workshop or classroom. I'm sure you have and will discover ways to live and rejoice even as you whisper. I also wanted to tell you that my son-in-law is a voice researcher. He has a Ph.D. and is one of the foremost person's on this continent concerning voice rehabilitation. He has worked at the University hospitals in Iowa City and Madison but he is now working for the Denver Center for Performing Arts. He is vocal coach for the performers but continues to do research on the larynx, surgical options, rehab; he now works primarily with singers, actors and others who use their voices professionally. Would you like me to ask him to review your surgical report to offer an opinion on rehabilitation possibilities? I would be happy to do that...The DCPA has a voice clinic right within the complex. I look forward to hearing from you and, in the meantime, my thoughts are with you. Yours, Jackie

Dear Jackie,
Wow! How wonderful to hear from you. I've missed you, us, our times together, so much. And now this amazing news about your son in law. I'm working with a voice therapist in Mesa. I think my surgeon (I had vocal cords stripped) was a little over enthusiastic with his scissors. One has quite a slash out of it, and the other tried to play dead after surgery. It's perked up considerably. I get them filmed monthly, which is rather fascinating, seeing

them in action. It has been pretty brutal. I will keep you in touch. We've given it six months, then, if needed, collagen injections are proposed, which could land me with a man's voice. Next lifetime is soon enough for me. I am definitely not going that route without 2nd/3rd opinions.

Of course, I'd love to meet your son in law. I have great records (including my "action movie pictures") because Adam wanted me to sue the surgeon for performing this without my "informed" consent, as no one ever suggested this might happen, and it happens more often that I like to think. Meanwhile, I've had to give up all work for 9 months - maybe I'm gestating a new, late life, non vocal career change? Anyhow, I do thank you deeply. Who knows what the future will hold? By the way, if we never get to meet, your son-in-law might like to have a copy of Joel ben Izzy's **The Beggar King and the Secret of Happiness**. It's wonderful! It got me through the worst beginnings of all this. He's a professional storyteller, who lost the use of one vocal cord, but it's a tale for all journeys, interspersed with stories from around the world. A singer friend of mine sent it. A copy in his office might comfort and inspire other patients, as it does me. Anyway, thanks again. I'd love YOUR news too, my friend. Much love, Lee

CHAPTER SIX. SNAKE CHARMER

*"In my name, they shall cast out devils; they shall speak with new tongues,
they shall take up serpents...."* St Mark 16: 17-18

Before I leave the realm of utter silence, which actually occurs this month, I
should mention two other conversations I have been having over the past
months. Neither use words.

One began one day on my walk in Acker Park, when I noticed some lovely
Andy Goldsworthy- type piles of stones. A couple of these "sculptures" were
low, perhaps unfinished, so I added a stone to each myself. Next day some
stranger had added others. And so we began. Every day each of us would
add a stone. About once a week the whole pile would be knocked over. We
simply began again. To this day – a year later – I continue to create these
sculptures, just as others continue to kick them over.

The second activity was my silent communion with lizards and my horned/
horny? toad. Every day I spent time in my back yard, just sitting, looking at
the earth. Lizards would come and stare at me.   Soon my little toad appeared.
I am sure he is the one – grown somewhat – who hung out with me last year.
But this time our connection is even stronger. I crouch close to gaze into his
glittering, hooded eye. I swear we are speaking to each other. I seem far
closer to plants too, now that I share their silent state.

How I envy the birds their voices, and how I long to call out, even a solitary
note.   Yet I feel my silence has drawn them closer. They seem less afraid.
One little sparrow alights on my hand. Twice, very small birds fall in my
driveway and lie stunned. I carry the Ruby Crowned Kinglet in the palm of
my hand into my house and nurse him until he regains his wings again. The
hummingbird is even more fragile. I slide a thick sheet of paper under him,
lift him into the ivy and feed him sugar water till he, too, is ready to fly.

Group email: Sent: Wednesday, September 13, 2006
Subject: Snake Charmer

*Latest bulletin. Happy to report I can now produce sound. Do not confuse
sound with "tone", the former having more to do with animal than human
kingdom, i.e. ravens, arctic foxes etc. My therapist is thrilled. We got a
reading on his sound box for first time, though I go off the charts in the wrong
direction. (Like a lot of my life?) Cords are looking pretty good now. They've
moved from rare through medium rare, now just a few "Pink Bits" which, like
the British Empire, I am hoping will be lost by next month. And they can
flutter a little. They can close when I use a lot of bicep power, and are almost
closed when I just try to speak. All in all, pretty hopeful now. We are only at
the halfway mark too. In 3 months I hope to have something serviceable at
least. Singing arias is I think for next lifetime. I exercise them for 2 hrs a day
and when/if I falter I am inspired by thoughts of darling Drew, whom many of
you know, but for those who don't, he's a young and very special friend,
meeting the challenge of a spinal cord injury. I just say to myself: "I'll bet*

that Drew is workin' away right now, come on Lee, you can do it." Thanks Drew!!!

Of course these months have offered an opportunity to question if I will be working in a vocal field in future. (I'll still want plenty of fireside chats with friends.) I simply haven't answered that yet, for myself. But I should tell you that the day Steve Irwin (Crocodile Hunter) was killed, I found a 2ft snake in my bedroom (which I then lost so it may still be there) and then went for a walk and a 6ft snake crossed my path, so I wondered if it was a sign that I was supposed to wrestle reptiles from now on? I'll keep you informed. Love, and thanks again to you all for all your support. Lee

From: Marion

You crack me up! So proud you can produce sound. I know it isn't tone! You keep sounding girl!!! That was quite a story about that snake. Keep reading those signs... Love from still sunny Portland (I bet you had more rain than we did in Aug/Sept!). Love, Marion

Dear Marion
And I bet it was that wonderful music I stood in the midst of that helped heal them. I still hear it. Well, off for my morning walk and snake hunt! love Lee

From: Adam

Dear Mum,
That's great news! Hopefully you'll be fully up and running by the time you visit NY.
I'm in Hoi An, about halfway down the coast of Vietnam. It's a small town that specializes in tailoring, and I'm spending a couple of days here getting suits made so I don't have to pay NY prices. They are quite incredible here, and it's nice to be out of the cities for a while. I took an overnight train down the coast to get here and stayed in a cabin with three very drunk Australian arms dealers.
Next I'm going a little further down the coast to a beach town called NghaTrang, and then on to Saigon. I'm taking it fairly easy, reading quite a lot, and just wandering around. I've met some very nice fellow travelers, but am looking forward to a little time alone out here. Then on the 23rd I'm meeting Kim in Bangkok, and on the 24th I'll be in Myanmar (Burma) for about ten days.
Keep pumping iron on those vocal cords. Oh, and did you get the photos? If not I'll send a stern email to Kodak. Love you, A

Darling Adam,
Yes, I even had two teeth pulled last week, so I can chew again in two months. I'll be ready to visit in 2007. Probably able to sing **Moon Shadow** by then! Loved getting all your news. Honestly, if you hate the law, you can be the next Bruce Chatwin. You are such a good writer. These little vignettes

of arms dealers and cheap suits are so good, (isn't it amazing what folk do overnight? You bring it all back to me so vividly.) I guess you are very well guarded, not allowed off beaten track in Myanmar, but that in itself looked pretty wonderful. Yes, I did get the pics, thanks. Is the baby yours? The cutie, playing with your shoes? What do you think of my future as a snake charmer? Go well, have a grand time, love to Kim too - do tell him about Drew. Love you hugely, Mum

Martine is (can you guess?) a beautiful Frenchwoman, masseure, in whose home I stayed last summer when MaryJo and I attended the Bay Area Training Arts Week in Santa Cruz. A few months later, she helped coordinate a workshop I gave in Monterey, so I had another, all too brief, visit with her in the fall.

Dear Lee,
I am so happy for you that your voice is coming back. You have really planned for yourself quite a challenging biography when you came to this life! You are such an inspiration for all the people who are lucky enough to cross your path. I feel fortunate that I am one of them. We met briefly, but you really touched a cord in me. Your depth, common sense, great sense of humor, and taste for life are just wonderful. With love, Martine

Hey, my friend,
Just don't think of us in the past tense (a lot of people refer to me that way now and I feel as if I'd died) because I'm hoping we'll spend time again together - please!! Go well, till then. I do hope your son is doing better? I so often think of you and our conversations. Much love, Lee

*I met **Estelle** and her husband **Ben**, at a conference in Arizona, then they invited me to give a little workshop in Albuquerque. I stayed with this beautiful couple, now in their 80's, in their little cottage in the woods. It was like entering a fairy tale! Over that evening, I told Estelle – who is Estonian – she should write her biography, and she kindly sent me what she had written up to age 28 when she met Ben, in Paris, I think where he had gone to paint. She really needs to write about the next 60 years !*

Dearest Lee, I was shocked to read that you don't have a real voice yet – all my good thoughts are with you. That must indeed be terrible. My Indian friend, Bonnie-Jo, here had layryngitis, she is a singer – it took her (without an operation) *3years* to be able to sing again. No, I don't quite see you in the midst of crocodiles, with or without voice! And I sure hope you will get it back again. Actually, I am now walking more with my cane than with the walker, exercises help. Our son Andrew suggested "Eat right for your type", (diet and blood types), I want to try it for my arthritis. There are some goodies on the list that I love and are "no-no's"!! I will certainly give Sally your love. Here is ours multiplied, Estelle and Ben.

My monthly group email obviously excludes much of what happens. One visit I seldom allude to is to my surgeon. I am always struck by the immense difference between that and my session with my speech pathologist. The latter has a modest office in Mesa, always open so that even if I arrive early (which I often do) I can sink into a comfortable couch in a cool, shaded interior. There's also a bathroom key, which comes in handy when you are driving around 120 miles to get there and drinking just under the lethal limit of water to keep your vocal cords moist. Dr. J. is invariably ready for me, even a few minutes early, greets me personally, welcomes me warmly, treats me tenderly, and sends me forth feeling hopeful and encouraged. Even the procedure of thrusting a metal "boom" to the rear of my throat so we can film the cords is really quite acceptable.

I stop off for my appointment with the surgeon on my way home, after a minor detour to Trader Joe's. The first appointment after lunch works well for me. I always prefer a first as there is less chance of things running late, and I hope to hit the freeway back to Suzanne's before the afternoon rush-hour begins. Dr. W's office closes for lunch. That is rather unusual. As someone committed to punctuality, I tend to arrive early. It is also hard to calculate a 30 mile or so journey to the nanosecond. This means I generally have to spend 10-15 minutes propping up a wall in 115 degree weather, so that the moment the door is opened I can dash in, and probably use the rest room again. Then my punctuality is seldom if ever matched by Dr. W's. The front desk folk are very nice, one even once supplied Kleenex so I could mop my sweaty face (I have wondered however what it would cost to ask one person to eat sandwiches there each day, so patients could get in during lunch hour?) The couch is a tad less uncomfortable than the chairs, so, unless there are several of us waiting to storm in, I am usually lucky there. After another 15 minutes or so, while my sweat dries in the blessed air-conditioning, I am summoned into one of the back rooms, and told Dr. W will be with me in a jiffy. A "jiffy" is usually a fairly decent unit of time.

He eventually arrives, with my file. While always perfectly pleasant, he needs to subject me to what I call "specialist syndrome". Thus I sit in my high chair like some recalcitrant toddler while he shuffles through my notes. I've never known whether this is intended to convey: "I have so many patients I can't remember who you are, or what I did to you," or is a mode of establishing supremacy, or maybe simply a way of putting off the evil hour when he needs to address me personally. I suspect many surgeons prefer carving folk up to actually relating to them.

Over the months Dr. W. has expressed concern. He claims he is at a loss to know why this has happened – a first for him. He suggests I wait to sue him until I know the extent of the damage, my losses. He wishes he could let me have a stipend to cover my financial deficits. All this is good to hear. His assistant at one meeting, when I say it would have made an immense difference if I could have been forewarned that this might occur, laughingly replies: "Well, ignorance *is* bliss, isn't it". Her ignorance? My bliss? I am

too stunned to respond. Later, however, I give her the benefit of the doubt.
Some people find it really hard to face the pain of others.
As I continue my own research, learning from so many others how common
my predicament is, I begin the inward struggle to accept both my condition
and my lack of preparedness for it. I also begin exploring my legal options,
getting referrals for top notch medical malpractice attorneys. It is clear there
is always some case to bring, even though Arizona, typically, doesn't
recognize "battery" a suit I could have brought in other states. Several
attorneys send messages to me, via my various friends, that I should give
them a call. Since this is just what I can't do, I don't yet. At least there's a
couple of years before the Statute of Limitations expires.

I have always been amazed at this litigious society. And I am reluctant to join
it. It does seem legitimate to claim some compensation for financial losses
and considerable pain, without due warning. On the other hand, the negative
energy that all adversarial situations create, is a big issue for me as a self
professed "peacenik". So I dance back and forth on this. It would not be
enough to decide not to sue and still remain riddled with rage and bitterness
(which I must confess erupt like boils all too frequently). Something will
have to be done at some point, but the days pass without my being able to
decide what that something should be. I'm in "process", I guess, so long as
we don't confuse that with "progress"! And to be absolutely truthful, I admit
that I might never have had these letters from these friends had this disaster
not occurred.   This month they come pouring in from around the globe.

*As I mention later, **Patricia** was a fellow student at Emerson College, coming
with her friend, **Dawn**, from Australia. I will say more about both of them
anon. But Pat and I – thanks to another Australian artist, **Jennifer**,, who
lives in the Bay Area – had reconnected last year, when Pat came to
California. We had a wonderful lunch at Fisherman's Wharf, and resolved
not to lose touch again.*

Oh Lee!   What an absolutely disastrous event you have had dished out to
you! I am so sorry to hear the news of your non-voice - you who have
retained your English quality of language, relatively uncontaminated by
Americanisms, being deprived of the instrument of your livelihood by a
careless surgeon. (You have the gift of speech you express so well in your
writing. Maybe this can be your partner sphere in future work) . It is amazing
that it was the nonreceipt of the attachment on your first email (**Love is more
powerful than hate**) that connected us again. Thank you so much for
sending GOING OFF THE AIR with its truisms and humor, as well as your
feelings about what happened. I'd certainly like to receive the news updates
with info. about your progress.   Incidentally, were you able to confront the
doctor with a written report of what was happening to you? I have given
Dawn a copy of the emails and she will contact you as soon as she is able to
access a computer. I don't know if you know RS's meditation:

Spirit of God fill thou .....(Lee)
Fill her in her soul.
To her soul give strength,
Strength also to her heart,
Her heart that seeks for thee
Seeks thee with earnest longing
Longing to be whole and well
Whole and well and full of courage
Courage - the gift from the hand of God.
Spirit of God fill thou ...(Lee)

This is my wish for you. I will remember you each night. Much love, Patricia

Dear Pat,
thanks so much for your words on mine!! It takes a non-American to even understand me and language, and what it means to me. I'll keep you informed. Just got home after another trip to surgeon and voice therapist, so a lot to catch up. It's progressing. I can register a sound now (not tone.) Had a bit of a run in with the surgeon who of course claims he did a perfect job. I'll have to ponder whether I spend the rest of my days suing him, while he prances around carving other people up, or leave it to karma, tighten my belt so I can still party on $129 a month social security. Alas, these last 9 months of earnings would have hiked that up a bit, and my last chance as I turn 65 at Christmas. Well, most people have to live on less than $1 a day!! I'd better dash. Thanks again, and for letting Dawn know. Much love Lee

And **Pat** is shortly followed by **Dawn.**

As with so many others, we met at Emerson College (a training center for Rudolf Steiner's work, anthroposophy). My Foundation Year at Emerson was one of maybe the three greatest life changing experiences. My son's birth and emigrating to America are probably the other two! Dawn went on to do the Speech training,and I had the privilege of working with her which deepened our connection even further. Our paths then diverged. We were always on different continents. Now, at least in this mode, we can connect again.

Dearest Lee, I am so amazed at all you reported in your history of what has taken place with your larynx that it is difficult to focus on other things like saying hi and telling you about my life and why I have been below the horizon for so long and also to tell you that the very week your email came to Patricia I had said to her that I must get your address from her in order to write to you and see whether you were still thinking of coming to visit next year as we had talked about. We were talking about the places we would like to take you to, not to mention all the catching up I had in mind.
I guess the answer to that last one is tied up with what happens to your recovery. However, we were very heartened that you mentioned still the

possibility of coming. Since that first communication we have received the second that tells of your first audible sound. (Can there be an inaudible one?) To you first.

What a journey!! On top of all the others!! The first thought that flashed across my mind when I read your story was that it sounded like some very individualized form of certain stages in the old initiations where someone undertakes a vow of silence. Now I don't know very much about it but I have a strong feeling for the idea that one makes a decision to consciously hold back the free expression of certain forces so that capacities develop at another level which can then be released with far more potency and consciousness. I would love to explore this with you further if you come. Somehow your experience all feels very connected to the task of the larynx in the future.

Anyway, by going off on this level I don't want in any way to overlook the level of earthly experience which has completely disrupted your life as you have known it till now and must have been indeed terrifying at times. Your description of that is as usual, very honest and powerful and I am sure important to be written down. Dear friend, my heart goes out to embrace you .

As for whether I can be of any assistance with speech exercises. I don't know. The therapeutic (in a clinical sense) level of the speech work has never till now been my task to develop. However all I can say is that if when you come you are willing to engage in a process of research together as to what might be possible then I should be privileged and honoured to 'have a go'. That is a funny expression for a sacred journey!

My life also has gone into a complete makeover. Chosen on a somewhat more conscious level only because the necessity for fundamental inner transformations became so pressing that I felt I could not work again until something had changed. My initial way of dealing with it was to freeze. Being inside a frozen mountain for quite a few months was at least helpful in stepping out of my life as I had known it till then. Gradually the mountain has thawed and now I have moved into the liquid state. I have been a chrysalis for a few months. Everything of who I have thought myself to be and the work I have thought I was doing all these years has dissolved and become a mush. I do not know who or what will emerge from this but am beginning to be interested. It is nearly a year since I 'worked' in the sense of my profession. But it has been the hardest 'work' of my life.

Part of all this journey has been searching for a place to live. I have bought a small house which I hope one day you will stay in for a time. It has been amazing how this earthly necessity to engage with the business of selling and buying has served my inner work. The other aspect of my life has been 'grand mothering'. I mean that destiny has brought me to live in a wonderful family where I have a deep connection with both children. The younger one has just turned 4 and is adorable and I have been able to do quite a lot of child care for the mother when she works. This has been very healing for me and awakened a facet of myself that has never before been able to unfold.

Well, dear Lee, perhaps this enough for now to make a beginning. Here I am again and very happy to be in touch and sending you lots of love, Dawn

Dearest Dawn,
I will probably send several emails to reply to yours. Well, this is the second, so let's make it threefold at least.
You are ahead of me - well, you always have been!! I'm planning to try to sell my house in the spring, so I won't come to Australia until you are in yours (WHERE? I'm clueless, is it Adelaide or thereabouts?) and I am out of mine. Then, who knows how long I might be tempted to stay!!
Yes, it's probably for next lifetime. At 63 I thought we were supposed to be off the hook of planned karma. I've wondered if it was for the surgeon to learn something. I'm making his life as miserable as I can! May even file a suit as Adam thinks we should get our Australia trip covered. I don't know how many times I asked him: "What can go wrong?" And he said: "Absolutely nothing can". He'll be a little more cautious with his surgical scissors on the next victim!
Anyhow, of course I'm learning all kinds of fascinating and fruitful things, but these wonderful opportunities are only wonderful when they are OVER AND DONE WITH!!! Quite the worst part I think has not been being able to HOWL, to WEEP, even to LAUGH WITH SOUND.
 I was stunned to hear that you gave up your profession, went in the frozen mountain. This is what I am doing now. No one really understands, do they, unless they've done it. I think it takes unbelievable courage. Which you've always had. It was so interesting when I had to cancel my work, find replacements, folk started addressing me in past tense as if I had died. God it hurt! Still does and can. The other thing was everyone telling me what I could do instead - write novels etc., which I began to feel was their way of protecting themselves from pain. There aren't too many who dare die to it all! It was also hard, because many folk here use their voices functionally, have no sense of the sounding power of a voice, or language, which is my true love, how we can move and heal (and indeed destroy) with our words and tones. So people just said 'get one of those gizmos that amplify it'. All the time I can hear my voice inside my head like ocean captured in a shell. Has it vanished for ever? I still don't know. I have myself on tape, but haven't had the guts to listen yet.
Anyhow, I know telling you this, you will know, and that's what is so stupendous. And I think I know what you must have been going through, and even I begin to feel a little thawing now, and a sense that something may come of it all. It will be nine months before we consider a second procedure, so I now have 3 months to go. Is it a true or false pregnancy??
I am so happy you have grandchildren. The Word was your child, but it is lovely to think of those little ones. I'm going to sign off here because I've got to get some household things done now, but I am so FULL OF JOY that we know each other, love each other, have found each other again, and will actually get to see each other within a year or so. Oh, I should tell you I got reunited wonderfully with Esther. Its amazing that so many of us are re meeting after 33yrs, I have Patricia to thank for getting us together again. That's all for now, but not for ever. Love Lee

This seems to be a time for reconnecting with some very distant figures. First the Australian contingent, now Judith.

*I think, apart from my siblings, I've known **Judith** longer than anyone else in this little record of friendship. We are both British and when I emigrated I saw much less of her, alas. We shared a flat in London during the 60's. We shared a lot more besides! Once (and I write of this in **A Slice of Life**) she came to stay with me in Detroit for six months when I was healing my cancer. Realizing I have her email, I begin to include her in my group letters, and thus we connect again.*

Lee, this is awful, I had no idea you had been suffering so! I will take your word for it that you are getting better, but really, the thought of you not being able to speak for months is too terrible to think of. And in pain too. You sound incredibly brave. And there was I whingeing about my minor and perfectly manageable ailments. I'm so, so, sorry. However, e-mail is the perfect means of communication in these circumstances. Are you ok for getting about etc., or have you needed other people's help with everyday things? What about driving? Is Adam nearby, and can he help you at all? As you say, thank goodness for the NHS. What would you do if you didn't have any money? Are you totally non-resident now, or could you come back and avail yourself of our free services if you needed to? You could always come and stay with me, I have marvellous GPs here. Please please do stay in touch and let me know how you get along. If not, I shall pester you until you do! Meanwhile, on quite another tack, you have been very much on my mind as we have been celebrating **Mr. Betjeman's Centenary**. Nice bits of archive film with Jonathan Stedalls's voice and presence, though he seems much aged nowadays. Surely he's no older than me? Still hoping to visit before too long, perhaps next year, or the one after. I'd love to meet Adam all grown up. Jon is currently staying with me due to home problems, temporary we hope. However, as you know, he is very domesticated, and has just finished the washing up, as well as having cooked a delicious fish stew for our dinner. Which makes me think: what about eating? Oh it does sound awful. DO hope you get better soon now, lots of love, Judith

Dear Judith,
First thanks so much for all your sympathy. I really needed that today as I suddenly felt very sorry for myself - actually bl**dy angry with the surgeon who simply said this week "well, you were just one of the unlucky ones." Indeed, by choosing him! One of the greatest trials has been my inability to yell, curse, swear, howl. The worst is definitely over now, pain receding, I'm just left today with fury! So your letter was very welcome. Your ailments don't sound minimal at all. Angina hurts. So does arthritis. This is the "arthritis state" by the way, so much copper and so dry, folk come from all over to get relief. Come on over.
No, I wouldn't return to UK, have crossed some kind of line. I'd move to Australia if I were younger. (Adam is 3000 miles away, I don't see him as

often as I'd like, alas.) I got about OK, though Adam insisted I wear a whistle round my neck, mainly to repel mountain lions as I doubt I'd be raped here in Prescott, (which is like an English village with cowboys and a few cacti, so very cozy and helpful). I haven't used the phone for 5 months - that's quite an achievement. I will keep you in touch, I promise.

My best friend on this continent, still in Detroit, Linda, a fellow Brit, sent me the lovely illustrated version of JB's poems and I wept - silently - because I couldn't quote them with fervor and feeling and sound!!! How interesting that Jonathan looks so much older than us. I remember a friend of my brother's (with whom I had a delicious overnight after Bill and Sukie's 21st birthday party, asking me how much older I was than they. When I said 28, he said: "*goodness you have worn well*". I wonder what he'd say today?) One of the curses of this surgery was having to give up smokes, which I still crave every minute of every day, and have started putting on weight, the "soggy bottom" variety, alas. And dark French truffles seem to slip down more easily than anything else. Vocal cords don't affect eating capacities, alas. Oh, how I'd love to see dearest Jon again., and wish I could have shared a bowl of fish stew. Thanks again for your support. So much love, Lee

*I met **Michelle** when she was a student at Rudolf Steiner College and I taught there. Later I would visit her in Louisville, and give workshops at the various schools with which she has been connected. Her latest enterprise has been in public school. Her class comprises 14 families from Somalia, and when she put the word out I sent a contribution. She is an utterly remarkable human being and enormously gifted teacher.*

From: Michele : Subject: goodness

You are too good. I cried when I got your card. Sending you photos. Please send me your home address. Come and rock babies any time. It will heal anything needing healing and fill you with a light unimaginable.

I have never worked with children who are completely free of any television, etc. no cars, no nothing. They are so very very different. I can feel something in them I have never felt anywhere else. And here they are now in our country to teach us. I believe it is possible that they have made the ultimate karmic sacrifice to come. Love you so much. M.

> *"Children of the world, you have the right*
> *To sing and dance, run and play, let your dreams take flight,*
> *As the innocent die, you rulers carry the shame,*
> *And if we stand idly by, we share the blame."*

Dearest Michelle,

Well - I JOLLY WELL WILL then! Just want enough of a voice to be able to growl or squeak a little lullaby, though they would probably heal my voice right there and then. (I sent your letter and pics to just about everyone on my mailing list, I know a few are thinking of you, who knows if anyone will DO anything!) Truus Geraets, who is in mid 70's now and began Waldorf Ed. in the townships of S. Africa, was deeply moved, said you must be an extraordinary soul. I told her you were. She has no money to send. But she is an utterly genuine supporter. She brought eurythmy to the Detroit prisons years ago, married a lifer, all before heading to Africa. You may need to meet each other sometime. Can't wait for the photos. Love you, loving them, Lee

*To **Teri**, after she wrote me something which I have lost! John, her husband, had a stomach tumor, and she let me know the general picture was optimistic for him, benign (if something that is cluttering up your tummy can be called benign!)*

Hey, my dearest dearest friend. It was Sooooooo good to hear from you, thought I'd lost you for ever. Glad too that John is strengthening, just sounds as if you might be weakening, so please take good care of your hips and thighs and whatever.
Well, tell me anytime about snakes. Yes, it was in the bedroom! I know in the Demeter Mysteries, the women had an annual ritual, first turned the men out of the house, then went to the cornfields, spent the first night yelling about what a terrible year they had had, and how awful the guys had been, then took their knickers off and menstruated all over the fields, then went under the earth (dug a hole I guess) and took energy from Snake (which incidentally was a female power, none of this penis envy stuff). Then they had a huge feast, went home and were fortified for the year ahead. Is this the sort of thing you meant? Lee

Adam, bless him, continues to keep in touch.

Hi Mum and Dad,
Just a quick note to let you know I'm doing fine. I'm about 3/4 of the way down the coast of Vietnam, staying in a small beach town. My bungalow opens straight onto the sand and it's perfect weather. I also got my advanced open water scuba degree in a town called Nha Trang a couple of days ago. We saw lots of moray eels, did a night dive and saw squid, and did a 30 meter dive where I saw some scorpion fish and a big barracuda (no, they aren't dangerous).
In case you haven't been watching the news, there has been a coup in Thailand. I'm flying into Bangkok in three days and have thoroughly checked: there is no problem at all. It's not dangerous, they aren't closing airports, and tourism is unaffected. So nothing to worry about. OK, the beach is calling. Lots of love, A

Darling Adam,
Great hearing from you. I am most impressed by your underwater skills. I HAD heard about the Thai coup, just didn't know you were returning to Thailand. I won't worry (worry never helped anyway). I was confined to a sleazy hotel in Damascus for two days while the Syrians psyched up for the 6

days war with Israel, so I'm hardly one to tell you to be careful. Have a great continuing trip. Love you, Mum

Now here comes someone I feel so honored to have met, and she deserves a long introduction. There are some people in our lives we meet so briefly, yet who make such a deep impact, we wonder why our physical connection has to be so infrequent. Well, I suppose I should just be grateful I got the chance to meet Yvonne at all. Here is a fragment of her story.

*About five or six years ago, I was invited by my friend **Julia** to give workshops in Alto, New Mexico. Julia was busy writing her book **Remembering Wholeness,** and had flatteringly devoted a chapter to me and my work. She picked me up at El Paso airport with her friend, **Yvonne,** and after a spiffy lunch in Las Cruces, headed in what we thought was the direction home. It wasn't, and thus we were able to have a very extended conversation between the three of us in the course of which Julia asked Yvonne to tell me her story. This beautiful blonde woman with big brown eyes, began. She had been deaf until she was 35 and they invented some gizmo that enabled her to hear. She'd been brought up by the kind of Christians that spend at least 3 hrs in church on Sundays, testifying and whatnot. Since she couldn't hear a word, she happily read the Bible, and developed her own approach to Christianity, which included reincarnation (as it is loud and clear in the gospels) and avoided quite a bit of the tub thumping simplicities of her parents' faith. She loved wild flowers, and collected them frequently, but whenever her mother suggested putting them in water, Yvonne was happier letting them dry out and crushing them for the smells and oils. When she was twelve she had a powerful experience of a "Being", as she described it, and after that wanted to be with Him, and leave the earth. (As she was speaking, I was reminded of **George Ritchie** and his book, **Return From Tomorrow**) . The only way Yvonne could comfort herself for Him apparently refusing to allow her to leave the earth, was to dig her hands well into it and be close to plants. She came to realize this Being lived here now within the earth itself. As she was telling me, I was looking at her, and I said: "Yvonne, the Being you met is what I call the Etheric Christ."
"So you've met Him too?"
"No. But when I look into your eyes I know you have."
Years later her husband grew sick, and no one knew why, or could help him. Yvonne thought:: "The skin is the largest organ in the body. If I feed that, maybe he will recover." She gathered plants and began to make soaps and oils and unguents. And – what do you know? Her husband healed. This is what she now does. Everything she makes heals something or someone. Her last question on this drive was: "Can I tell you something else? It's a bit strange." I told her: "Just try me!" And she shared that she got the strong impression little fairies were around her when she brought the plants in to make these substances so, in a whisper (so the neighbors wouldn't hear her) she invites these elementals to help her as she stirs her cauldrons of herbs and oils. Well, I expect you all want to order some right away. Her "company"*

(that's Yvonne and the fairies, is called Madalyn Rose, in Ruidoso.) I had asked her to send Myra, mother of Drew, and her family some of her wonderful healing remedies.

Dear Lee,
The package to your precious friends went out the day I came home. I sent them 2 bags – one Vitality and one Serenity - one for when they need a little lift, one for when they need to relax.
Years ago I read a book by a woman who died, went to "heaven" and then came back to share what she learned while in the presence of Christ. Besides what most of us already know – we are here to love one another – she said our superficial understanding of karma causes us to miss out on some of the most profound lessons in compassion, courage and gratitude, offered by some of the most powerful and loving beings incarnate. When you told me about your beautiful friend, Drew, and his parents who endure this with him, I knew in the depths of my soul they are among the angels who came to touch our hearts in ways ordinary life cannot. How can we say "thank you" except to love them, to move beyond the pettiness in life and love each other with everything we are. What else matters more? I am so glad your polyps are benign *and gone!* But I want your voice back. The world needs your voice. Please exercise, exercise, if not for yourself, then for us…. Lee, I know we are always in communion with each other, but I love your letters. More please. All my love, Yvonne

Lastly, Linda sends me the illustrated poems of Sir John Betjeman and I think it's fitting to end this chapter with my response to her!

Dearest Linda,

Well, that was a lovely package – thank you thank you. When the tree cutting guy has come and gone, I must go searching for a good snake picture for Ben. Bet he wouldn't get "wigged out" if a snake came in his bedroom? (You are just as likely to have one entering from Wing Lake as here!!! We're not talking cobras or rattlers. However a rather nice German fellow and his son, with their air duct cleaning service, Gesundheit, vacuumed thoroughly yesterday, and no reptiles came flying out. Don't know whether that is a good or bad thing that he/she has defied German thoroughness?) Speaking of which, I have a newfound friend, Cas, we walk together with her dog every morning and she is a great resource as she grew up in the valley. So – when I was looking for a medical malpractice attorney in case I sue my surgeon, she said: "No problem. My friend, B., will take a look. I would have married him 30 years ago if I hadn't thought I'd probably strangle him." When I told her a friend of mine was having a 6hr brain tumor surgery, she said: "Dr. H. is the best neurosurgeon in Phoenix. We were lovers 40 years ago. German precision is great for brain surgery, just not so hot for sex, so I went off with his partner." Alas, she didn't romance a good laryngeal surgeon (in case I need the injection procedure,) but Jackie Beecher got in touch after she ran into you, and told me about her son in law, one of best in nation for voice retraining, did I want her to contact him? I said I seem to be going along OK for now, but if Sean Connery booked into his clinic (or a few others come to think of it, as he works with actors and singers) to let me know and I'd be on next plane. I'd better milk this thing for all it's worth, eh?

Since you never told me about the Works, I'm assuming you have nothing terminal? This wretched sciatica sounds wretched! What more can I say? Well, a little....

The only person who has alleviated pain for me has been Terri Kosmicki with her quantum energetics (she comes to stay with MaryJo periodically.) If the horse laser guy doesn't succeed, you might – or indeed might not – want to try her. I find all these *woo –woo* people an interesting bunch. Main problem is few know their limits and believe their "modality" can heal all ills. One recently worked so intensely on muscles damaged in that car accident I had, that I had to go twice to my no nonsense chiropractor so he could put back all the bones she had dislocated in her over- energetic energy work! The other possible solution is one my dear mother found. She had utterly awful acute earache for 2 years. It was dreadful, and terrifying. The only thing that worked was yoga – 15 minutes a day – sort of Dr. Bob stretch stuff. And if she missed a single day, the pain came back. That's another thought. God, this aging is hell, isn't it!

I say, you are getting adventurous with your cooking. A Thai Rosh Hashanah no less? My big thoughts right now are about selling my house, getting somewhere smaller and simpler and wondering how to prepare for a future, with strokes and broken hips etc!!! Well, I'm going to leave this for a bit. Tree guy hasn't (of course) shown up and Prescott College emailed me to say I had won a t-shirt in a raffle I didn't know was happening and I need to pick it up. I'd prefer a cap. (See what a rich and fruitful life I lead here – a real contribution to humanity!!!) Give Ben a big hug from me. Love you, Lee

CHAPTER SEVEN. THE BULLFROG THAT SWALLOWED A MOUSE.

Practising Love.

Walk the one path many a time
Not for knowing but for greeting
the tree at the corner,
for becoming familiar
with the grassy valley
and also the clearing
that again and again
lets in the sky.
Walk the path many a time
until it is yours.
You are practising love.
(author unknown)

October begins wonderfully with news from Adam . I wish my own could have been so cheering. I seem to be making no progress whatsoever. However, the golden daisies still flourish in a golden light, and each tree turns in exquisite shades of gold, umber, burnt sienna and red. So I walk the "one path" every morning and try to forget my own woes, which is relatively easy so long as I keep my mouth shut!!

Oct 2, 2006 3:06 AM
Subject: Back from Burma

Dear Mum,
I am safely back from Myanmar, after an amazing week of traveling around with Kim. Burma/Myanmar is the most untouched place I have ever been--no banks, no ATMs, no fast food restaurants, no credit cards, no cars made after 1975, the roads haven't been repaired since the British left in 1948, and almost no white people at all. Also, the government censors the internet, so I had no email access!
Kim and I managed to get around despite a series of idiotic mistakes: we ran out of money (as there are no ATMs, so I had to go onto the black market, pay a $60 fee to someone who was undoubtedly unscrupulous, and get some); we didn't realize that it was off season, so none of our anticipated transportation was running; we constantly left important things behind, or out in public (Kim, for example, dropped his boarding pass somewhere in the airport); and we accidentally showed up a day early at the airport in Yangon. But the locals were so kind, honest, and generous, that we were OK. They spoke impeccable English, never took advantage of our idiocy, and were constantly on the lookout for us. One woman who owned a cloth store told Kim to come back and pay her later, because she trusted him. That would never happen anywhere else in the world, and definitely not in SE Asia.

We saw a plain with over 3000 pagodas, a festival where 43 boats pulled a floating temple across a lake, a man repair the gear box of our bus at midnight with a screwdriver and a brick, a 1.2 kilometer bridge made out of teak, one million gold Buddhas, and some of the most incredible countryside I've ever seen. I'm definitely going back for some trekking (as you can imagine, Kim wasn't into the idea of walking around in the mountains, it might ruin his $300 shoes!).Now I'm back in Bangkok, babysitting a one year old for a friend of mine here. She reminds me of Sophia: blonde, fiery, big, and very independent. I'm taking her to a playground today and will have to stop her from bulldozing the other kids! I'll be back in NY on October 6th, but my phone has been cancelled, so it might take a while to contact you. I'm also not sure if your voice is back yet, so maybe we'll stick to email for now. Lots of love, A

Darling Adam,
How glorious hearing from you. Your trip sounds astonishing! Enjoy your last days out there, and I hope the return isn't too depressing. I'll wait - obviously - till you get a phone to hear your voice. Mine can still hardly bear that name. This month seems to have brought no progress. Other than that, I'm fine and the weather is wonderful, and all the hills are covered with golden daisies, so I'm off for my walk with Cas (a new found friend) and her dog, Molly, who loves me to bits, which sets me up for the day. Hope you had a good day at your park with that little warrior girl. Love you, Mum

Dear Mum,
Just a quick note to say I'm back in NY, safe and sound. My apartment is beautiful, even though I installed the curtain rods at different heights! I'm in kind of a jetlag fog right now, so lemme get a few pragmatics out of the way: (1) Here's my new phone number; (2) Dad's OK (in case you saw the chemical explosion on the news, about two miles from his house;(3) I'll have photos as soon as Kim gets off his butt and emails them to me. Now I have to go wait for my new mattress to be delivered: the usual four hour window during which they might deign to arrive. Lots of love, A

Darling Adam,
So glad you are back safely and apartment good. Different curtain rod heights very artistic, probably reflects the years I invested in your Waldorf education! Glad Dad is OK. I hadn't known how close that ghastly spill was. I'm off to Phoenix in a couple of hours for my "action movie" session. No progress this month that I can see or hear, but maybe the therapist will. Love, Mum

Group email: Subject: The Bullfrog that Swallowed a Mouse
Date: Oct 11th 2006

Well, my friends, and family, I have become totally transatlantic! As some may know, we Brits hope to go to our graves without ever mentioning physical pain (that's "discomfort", by the way) or referring to a single

dysfunctional body part, whereas here, as my mother once remarked: "Ask an American how they are feeling, and, alas, they TELL you!!" Here am I giving my monthly update, and you never even asked!!! I promise there will be none in 2007.

Saw my voice therapist yesterday, and he both saw and recorded my cords. He is "tickled pink" he told me, at the progress I/they have made. This honestly surprised me as I still sound like my letter title most of the time, also with long periods when the bullfrog hibernates. But he has technology that can pick up the sounds and vibrations only audible - I imagine -to dolphins and whales. Anyhow, he is now optimistic that I may not need further surgeries. He has taken me off the bench pressing. The cords can now close, are just still very tender and raw, and have not developed their pure white, thick, blanketing covering. However my "mucosal wave" is developing tsunami proportions, and the auditory numbers are approaching the human - at least some of the time. (He insisted on 3 attempts before he finally recorded me as the first two went off his charts.) And that's about how it seems from my position. I simply never know if I'm going to produce sound and if so, what sound. To my delight, vowels and consonants can now hold hands, though not exactly dance together. For the past 5 months they have reminded me of my awful boarding school (single sex) dances, where we girls stood on one side of the hall and the boys 100 yards away on the other and you didn't know which you dreaded most - spending all evening standing alone, or having to foxtrot with some terrified pimply youth.

The pain (sorry, "discomfort") is only periodic now, and I think I've linked it to whenever I am in situations with more than one or two people talking. As some of you pundits know, the larynx imitates all movements of other larynxes, so mine gets a little fried in company. I will continue my life of occasional movies with friends, otherwise totally reclusive. The phone will certainly be the last thing I return to. I have set up a pretty full program of activities for myself that do not depend on the vocal. And I'll be continuing all my therapies in the hope they continue to be therapeutic. I will also send a November installment!! Love to all of you. Lee

From: Myra McPherson

Great to hear from you Lee. Sounds like the cosmic and earthy Lee are beginning to dance together a bit. Hurrah!!!! I love you deeply and will write soon about Drew's adventures. My, is it difficult sometimes to keep my head above the water, actually at times I just weep the day away. Love to you. Myra

My darling Myra,

I know you must sometimes weep the day away. I carry photos (of you too) and every time I look at them, my heart just cracks apart. I had my dear friend Yvonne send you a little care package, and I just forwarded a couple of pages from a letter she wrote to me, speaking of you all, as I thought at least a reminder of who you really are might, for a few moments lift you up. What an etheric heart you must be fashioning. I also just plain miss you all so much. Please let me know if there's anything more I can do. Love Lee

Marietta is Jake's (and Hallie and Gideon's) Mom, and a whole lot more besides, and she only appears now because she has been sending me fabulous handwritten cards with Georgia O'Keefe crimson blooms that lift my spirits and I honestly think I could bear anything with her and her family beside me! As an art therapist, I remember her presenting at our teacher training program in Ann Arbor. No-one could leave at the end, even though it was lunchtime. We all just wanted to go home and paint with her. Jean, her husband, and I have seen more of each other, happily, when I have been working in San Francisco and he has headed west for his own work. I don't think I can be completely happy until I have somehow finagled our lives so we are within a few miles of each other!

Marietta. Oct 11.

Dear Lee, It was so good to hear from you. Your voice may sound like a frog but your words come across crystal clear! We *all* are sending good thoughts and I hope Hallie is doing her part by e-mailing. She was desperate for your address this summer – had lots she wanted to talk over with you…. We saw Jake over Labor Day…he looks really good, about the best I've ever seen him. Was with Julie, his current "significant other" I guess you could say. Gideon keeps getting promotions…he makes way more than me $$$. Jean is doing lots of traveling, mostly to Sacramento. Too much, I think. I am just finishing up my requirements for my masters. I am wondering if we will ever make it to Portland. No houses are selling in Michigan. Take good care of yourself, now, Lee. Much love, Marietta.

This letter is shortly followed by a phone call from her son Jake, who lived with me for a year when he was a student at Prescott College. Oh did *that* cheer me up!!! And now darling Dawn again!! Lifting me up from Down Under!!

Dearest Lee, How wonderful to receive your update on the state of your larynx. At some future stage of evolution this incident will be part of the history of the ' new larynx'. It will be quoted in the textbooks and in the akashic record as a seminal moment in the metamorphosis of our human species towards the new androgyny and the capacity for creation through the word. Although I say this to make you laugh I do believe there is some truth in it which I suppose there must be in all humour. But really I am full of admiration for all you are doing and seeing and understanding. I so look forward to having you over here in the next couple of years with or without your voice as I remember it. I will be going to England for two and a half months to teach at Emerson and the Speech School for 8 weeks. Any chance you'd be there? Now it looks that I shall be moving in to my new house after I get back from England, then getting ready for your visit! I feel I am beginning to emerge from my chrysalis and the sign of that is that I am looking forward to teaching in the new year which up until quite recently I could not have said. I feel that the focus on my spiritual work has really begun to change some things. About time!!! lots of love, Dawn.

Dearest Dawn,
Isn't it lovely to know that "when we laugh, the angels come a little closer"! One challenge here is that many Americans are - as one Californian put it, rather "irony deficient". I am not going anywhere until/unless I get an error on part of INS (now renamed Homeland Security) in my Green card info, which I only discovered when I attempted to sign up for Medicare, and my splendid $129 a month Social Security. They may just decide to deport me and solve the problem that way. So maybe I will see you in UK. Or emigrate to Australia? I just found some speech exercises in my piano stool - Kim Schneider Vyne's. So I think I'll add these in to my pharmacopeia. Love you, Lee

From: Signe. Re: The Bullfrog that Swallowed a Mouse

Oh, Lee, You make me laugh! I am so glad things are moving in a good direction and I feel sure the frog will find your own unique transformation. Hey! How about a Prince? Are there any left?
Yesterday I was in Brooklyn to babysit with Cyris, and I stopped briefly to see Karin at the store, and she told me that Adam now lives almost directly across the street. Isn't the world always so funny and small?? I guess he had stopped in the day before. So she looks forward to seeing him in the future. I look forward to seeing him before too long, and you too! Any trips on the way? Chris and I are almost ready to begin looking for a small apartment in Brooklyn. Big changes are in the wind. Chris is already half time now at the College and I will give up my full-time work in December. Well, thanks for keeping me posted. I do think of you often and send waves of sound. I hope you'll be coming this way before too long, Love Signe.

Dearest Signe,
Of course I'll be coming your way – when I can have a conversation and we can all get together with those fantastic children of ours. Adam only got back from Myanmar 3 days ago – already in to see his old babysitter (Karin)! I'm beginning to enjoy my monastic existence and think it may be a good opportunity to retire and play on my $129 a month social security which I may not get because I lost my birth certificate and am having a problem with INS, so may also be deported. All that matters now is being with those I love. You would be awed as a lover of the Word and the future human being (becoming) to see what the vocal cords look like. Signe, in a world of red, they are – or should be – this extraordinary, pure white, satiny little orifice. Amazing!!! Love to you both, Lee

Dear Lee,
Can things get worse if we keep laughing?? $129 ------!! And I thought ours
was measly. We actually met with a TIAA advisor yesterday to see how our
pension can be useful to us – pocket money basically. But oh, yes, we do
have fantastic kids!! I love the image of satiny white vocal cords in their red
world. See you soon, I hope. Love Signe

*Can't believe I haven't introduced Lalla yet, or her family. We met when I
went to spend two months in San Francisco and we found we had an Italian
family in common, that I had met 40 years ago when I was at school in
Florence and spent several summer holidays at Bolgheri Castle -
immortalized in a Carducci poem. An immediate, firm destiny connection!!!
Lalla now invites me to do work at the school whenever I go to San
Francisco.*

From: Lalla: Re: The Bullfrog that Swallowed a Mouse

Yippyyy! So good to hear news of your cords responding to the calls of
doctors and angels!!!! Please keep on sending the news. If Americans like to
tell about their pains, well, Italians cannot live without telling and they feel
really weird if you don't tell about yours, like it is some cosmic injustice that
we aren't all suffering in some way (and I mean suffering!!!). Maybe it all
comes from Dante's Inferno being so strongly in the folk soul's unconscious,
or some esoteric reason of that sort.
I remember when my philosophy teacher sent me home with the question
"Are you happy?" and I dared pose it to my father. His response was " Since
when are human beings on earth to be happy?!!!" Then he went on
with complaints on the state of the world since people had started asking these
kinds of questions.
 On another note, I am about to complete the CHILDHOOD MEMORIES
class and I look forward to sharing some thoughts with you. The participants
seem to be getting a lot out of it and I feel confirmed that we need to continue
offering these opportunities. For sure the hardest thing is to keep people to
time when they share. It seemed that you did that so graciously! Lots of love
and blessings, Lalla, with Paolo and the gang.

Dear Lalla,
 Perhaps that's why I love Italy and Italians so much! I always felt I was
living in a tragic opera: *"Caduta Massi"* *(Falling Rocks), "evitate rumore
inutile" (Avoid Useless Noise).*   So glad your class went well. I'm sure
Karen was wonderful too. Miss you, love you, Lee.   •

*Maree was a Prescott College student who lived with me for half a year. Her
boyfriend, Greg, joined us soon after she moved in, preferring my home to an
8-week class in Death Valley - sensible lad?. We all became very close –
surrogate children? – who knows. (Greg's mother, a Detroiter, died when*

Greg was 17, so I think I'm entitled!) I just know I grew to love them both dearly, and am so grateful for the continued connection.

Hello Lee! It's Maree.

I just received your postcard. So nice to receive a message from you. I am sorry that you have had such traumatic recovery from this surgery. Seems you have been afforded a vacation from work and perhaps other obligations. I hope that you are being well taken care of and receiving lots of love. Do you still get to swim? Where is Adam living these days? What is he up to? Do you see the Berkowitz family often?
Yes, I agree, Arnold Mindell's stuff is so incredible. We had some very intense moments together very quickly in our group process sessions. Now it's the task of translating or integrating all that came up and was processed and spilled into everyday life. The workshop was truly amazing. I've just signed up for the 3rd portion of the program in January, in hopes that they will be able to afford to go through with it. Due to the economy, they may not..I'm coming up on 30 this winter, wow, time truly does just move right along. It felt so good to spend a couple weeks on the west coast again. It just seems the general climate (environment/people/attitude, etc) is more suited to my soul person. I just have all these ties with family, a fear of leaving, yet a fear of staying. I feel I am sort of at the tipping point with many things. Feeling really ready to move on to the next phase. Getting back to movement and finding really inspiring channels for it. I think about getting back to teaching, possibly even getting a Masters in some type of dance/movement/somatics (more like the stuff I was doing out west-theater of the oppressed, process work, authentic movement type things) so I could teach at University level. But teaching is coming back into my mind a little.

Isaac and I have been living together here in Cleveland for about 1 1/2 years. He is a really amazing individual. Saw Greg while out west. We had a good time together. Will (Billy) is doing ok. I really wish for him all the time that he would find a good social support network other than family. He really wants the traditional life--marriage, decent job, family. He's just had rotten luck. But, he's enjoying serving and is going to school for an associates in business, I'm really proud of him! I just always wish there was more I could do to help him. My parents are doing ok. I think they are both very tired. Part of the reason I feel the need to stay close. It was so great the way you crept into me during that exercise (see postcard I sent). It was as if you were there with us. I was remembering the time that we were standing on your front lawn talking and a car was coming down Senator Hwy, and we heard a woman scream. Before I could even have a thought or reaction you were already running up the hill asking the woman if she needed help. That has always stayed with me. Look forward to hearing from you, much love, Maree

Dearest Maree,

How lovely to hear from you with all your news. As you see, I have bowed to the computer age. I haven't used the phone in nearly 7 months, or smoked in 6 months!, so I don't really deal with anything anyway. Think Billy would understand! Give him a big hug from me. Hope he's still writing poetry? I've still got the one he wrote for me.

And you, my dear friend, so good to hear even your dilemmas - really belonging out west, yet feeling this true and necessary pull of family. It's the tension, often conflict, between Sun and Moon Karma (Sun, the deep impulses we bring to earth that can run in many forms through many lifetimes and take us and humanity into the future) and Moon (generally the relationships we pick up along the way and we owe them, need to fulfill promises etc.) Both will have to be completed, fulfilled eventually, sometimes one is put on hold (folk who sacrifice family for public work is a good example of Sun making way for Moon) or those who tend close personal relationships as a primary "work" and one often thinks "what a waste of talent" etc. (Moon takes precedence over Sun) It's never an either/or, just which/when? Next 3 years will be crucial, fascinating - the years the Christ worked on earth, having entered Jesus at the Baptism. You may discover your deep destiny, and will have to find the courage, capacity for sacrifice, to realize it. (Oh, I didn't acknowledge Isaac, that relationship yet, can't cover all the bases in this letter, which is already long and will be longer. Another time, maybe!!)

I'm sorry the Mendel training may not be able to continue. So few things of value can these days. Just Halliburton and the arms makers, and oiligarchy. My little blip on world radar barely shows!! Yes, it's been rough at times, particularly when I handed over all my gigs to others. I don't think I'll work again in the vocal field. Who knows how long the healing will/may take.

Adam is his usual brilliant self. He finally graduated both Berkeley Law School and Fletcher (Tufts) and is working for a horrible NY Law firm. When he's paid off student loans hopes to do projects for UN - Sudan, Cambodia, Congo? I'm still here. The big drag about not working, is that folk used to pay my flights, it would cover costs for a glorious dalliance in SF etc. Miss that hugely. Good to hear of Greg too. Every time I worked in Reno I would let him know, but our paths never crossed and that's another place I probably won't go to again. Better dash now - yes, I do swim and it's time for my morning constitutional!! Much much love, Lee (Oh, I just got your amazing postcard – thank you so so much!!)

(*Maree's postcard*: " *I just returned from my Arnie Mindell training in San Francisco, We did an exercise where we had to think of someone who embodied what we were studying called Deep Democracy (embrace and value for all things and people in life) I found myself embodying you. I got to share a little about you. Just wanted to thank you again for making such a strong impression on my life, as a phenomenally strong and compassionate woman...*")

And Maree's response to my Bullfrog email, and **Going Off the Air** piece.

Wow Lee,
So, you are to pursue massaging snakes with tattoos while traveling with a
rock band, eh? I can not even begin to imagine what your experience has
been. Have you at least overcome the pain from the surgery? Do they have
you participating in any kind of therapy? I do have to say that your writing
continues to be very powerful in a very palatable way--you get straight to the
point in a round about sort of way, I treasure your humor and that it involves
some darkness. I am so sorry to hear that you had to cancel so many of your
great teaching gigs, I know they meant a lot to you for more than one reason.
I think all the people writing to you are correct that your voice, both written
and spoken are so valuable, and if it's not available vocally right now, the
written is certainly as powerful. In public must be very difficult, the
Starbucks story you told was amazing, was she trying to be polite or a punk?
This says to me that we just need to be generally more sensitive with each
other. More perceptive. And the smoking--you know, I started smoking
when I was 13, quit on and off all the way up until I was 28 (I was in a break
period at Prescott) so I understand that and feel for you there. Billy will
definitely give you props. He hasn't been writing poetry lately, but has been
busy with school. I was trying to do interviews with him to write about him,
but he sort of lost interest in that. He wants to open a coffee shop. Sounds
like Adam is doing great.

I like what you said about which/when, the sun and moon. Anna Jo's mum
was saying that age 29 is when your connection at the top of your head closes
from the universal energy in some way and that it leaves you more to make
decisions on your own, which is exactly how I have felt this past year---
"Where are my guides? Hello, is anyone out there?" I used to get gut feelings
or intuitions, now I feel lost in having to make a very conscious decision
without feeling like there is a right or wrong answer, so how do I know what
to do???" Becoming a bit more calm now, but decisions are tough. Anyhow, I
have to run. You are in my thoughts. So great to be in touch! Lots of love,
Maree p.s. Do you care if I forward your attachment writing to Greg

Dearest Maree,
How wonderful again to get your words!! 29 is, of course, your Saturn
return, when Saturn returns to where it was at your birth. Saturn was the Lord
of Destiny (until the Christ took over) but it still carries the deeper meaning of
your existence, why you came and for what, and really confronts us with
those questions. Its metal is lead. It can be a very dark and demanding year.
I remember four people came to me for counseling around the same time and
I suggested they started a Saturn Return group (sort of AA. Misery loves
company. I've never been that good with the depressives!!) So, all in all, you
are right on target. New forces will start to flow in, in the early 30's, but it is
still a pretty critical time. And every new life phase is heralded by loss, and

letting go.Wish you could come and visit some time, but maybe when I can talk more again. (Though it's a great opportunity for those who thought, rightly, I talked too much!)

Billy should definitely open a coffee shop and they could have poetry readings and who knows what else. But it better be good coffee, tell him! Organic, fair trade, and STRONG! None of this American dishwater. (Starbucks sneaked a fast one, and have reduced the strength of theirs surreptitiously by about 25%. I know these things. In an earlier life, I was a food (and drink) researcher. We used to analyze meat pies for their actual meat content, and what was "meat extender" a kind of ghastly glue. Enough of that in life itself! Well, better let you go.   Much love, Lee

Ann and I met briefly in New Hampshire, a quarter of a century ago! She has been involved in Waldorf Education her whole life. She moved to Arizona a year after I did, and would come and stay with me. The second time she came she shared a dream. We were in some monastic space. I, as a man, dressed in a white robe, was older, or superior to her, and although she tried to capture my attention, I ignored her and continued embellishing some sacred text. It became a humorous currency between us, for she stayed frequently in my home, when she was advising a little local charter school, and we also ran a 2yr Foundation Studies program together. As I doled out dinner, I would ask : "Satisfied yet? Is our karma balanced now?" Well, whether or not my previous neglect of her has been redressed, we are certainly eternal spirit kin.

Hello my dear,

I feel connected to you via your emails about your "condition", but I don't really know how Lee is bearing up. So...won't you write and share some of the "inner" news? Please?

We perk along slow, slowly, slower and slowest. I have little work, but some. So, there is time also to peruse -" those books for later, when I retire" on that special shelf. I have taken up two loves - the elemental beings and the meaning of the trinity. Funny to have such a difference, but they feed my sanguine nature and hopefully sustain my spiritual life. I attend the class on a regular basis now and since it is just down the road instead of down the big hill, I can attend almost every month.

I have become the "care giver" here, which is alright now that I am accepting my destiny more, and working on trying to be a "community member" As you probably remember, I cannot do that!! At least not without working super hard to achieve interest and equanimity. Next life perhaps. Or......did I do it already? Wouldn't that be a treat?

We like our home (apartment) with everything done for us, just at the edge of town. We don't drive as much - gas being the price it is - but we don't need to. It is great (as you said several times) to be in a town where we can shop easily, take in events as we want to, and yet hear crickets at night. Although that event has stopped now. Now there is a tang to the air - that makes walks invigorating. Hearing from Katherine and having the pictures I feel we (you and I) have produced our first trainee grandchild! Aren't we grand?

The world is totally falling apart, but as we know, it is part of the "grand-plan" as he says. It is nice to know that we will not have to be here much longer, but will our work strengthen all those souls who will? That is my biggest worry at the moment.

Do let me know the news of "your listening area"? I'd like to keep up a little. A group of 14 of us are now working on the grand plan for a therapeuticum/assisted living/hospice/ something. I not sure I will ever see it completed, but you never know. Enthusiasm is high . There is a meeting on the 29th so I'll report again after that. I'm so pleased that you are mending well. Keep it up and please send a word. My love to you - Ann

Dearest Ann,

It was so lovely hearing from you. At first, I thought : "Oh. God, here comes another active, spiritual person to remind me of what a blob I am, and I can only tell her there is no "inner Lee" these days. True, but here goes, anyway. I am completely withdrawn from the community, pull back more and more each day, and it is going to take me at least 3 more lifetimes before I really want to be part of some jolly human family. I really dread life after death - no getting away from others!!! So, in a nutshell: I don't *think* anymore. I don't *do* anything any more, apart from a morning walk in Acker Park, all my therapies and the usual business of keeping a house together (all the doors shifted and I can't lock myself in or out any more). Quite a lot of *feeling*, mainly for the world's anguish. Have utterly no sense for any future. Only am pretty certain now that I have given up my whole past. I doubt I will work in the vocal field again. The past months have been a letting go, passing on my work, sometimes thinking it was just temporary, now beginning to realize it may be permanent. Of course there is always joy connected with hearing of someone else doing it. There is also pain. I, with two others, pioneered biography work in the English speaking world, 31 years ago. And I've been flying solo ever since, making it up as I went along. In all the forms it has taken, it has really been a quite individual work, and the thought of bringing it to an end isn't easy. (Must, though, by 33 years, I decided). But as a wise friend said many years ago: "So long as you are occupying the ground, no one else can stand on it." I am clueless as to what, if anything, might follow. Must just go into the dark. I would love to have enough of a voice to be able to croon huskily to babies. And I'd like to have the vocal strength to hail a NY cabbie at JFK and go visit my son.

Obviously I'm pretty out of touch. I do know M.Oaks had an awful sewage overflow, and many classes have had to relocate till it is sorted out. Sharon is exhausted. Please congratulate Alice for achieving *sprachtgesunheitfarenheit abbschluss whatever* - my German is not absolutely fluent, but you know what I mean.

I will do some writing, but neither of my computers are bending to my will these days. So I am being challenged on all fronts. However, lest you think I am falling apart completely, I already fell, and am fairly happy sitting at the bottom of the heffalump trap. I'm glad you can walk to the shops - vital, as long as we can still walk!

I wish I could say I was doing grand spiritual work, but I'm not. Just connect with you all thrice daily, read a bit, ponder a bit, pray quite a lot - for the earth, for the world, for all those hurting folk. Oh, last of all, I had been thinking of you yesterday when I found a little Tupperware with your name on the lid. I'm not sending it back! But I love you, Lee

15th October from Sheila

Dearest Lee,

Your wonderful August letter, full of rich thoughts and interesting stories. I especially enjoy the glimpses of Adam you sometimes give me – the way he seems to make bridges so easily, with other people and between different aspects of his own life, brings hope for the rest of us. I suppose if you are christened "Adam" you can't help being an initiator, the first one to take the plunge. And he does appear to enjoy the role! You have every reason to be proud of him, and proud of the parenting you have given him.

And what about you? I have a feeling that your "hoarse whispering" stage may be over, and that the silvery 'bel canto' may have emerged (although I liked your voice the way it was, and I wouldn't really want it to be improved.) What matters is that your voice should be your friend and ally, faithfully responding to the energy vibrating between heart and soul and mind – and that is what I greatly wish for you. I like your thoughts about Isis, and about the structure of the larynx, and about the nature of vowels and consonants, and I'm glad to know that seals and dolphins are playing a part in your recovery. Perhaps that's why I felt in the dream so concerned about swimming in the sea?

For fun, I'm enclosing a photocopy from The Independent, a couple of years ago, from their 'silly' page, which usually has items that are true but in their eyes absurd. And another quotation I found at the **Kandinsky** exhibition a few months ago. And finally a passage from Helen Luke's last book: '**Such Stuff As Dreams Are Made On".** That book is half an autobiography, and half a selection from the journals she wrote late in life, calling them her **Diary of Vowels*.** You would enjoy this book.

This is a hugely challenging season for me, and will be so at least until January or February: they call it 'Major Works" which means a new roof, new radiators, new double glazed windows and other undesired improvements. I'm surrounded now by scaffolding draped with green gauze, so can't tell what the weather is like without going downstairs to the street. On a sunny day the green is rather romantic – otherwise, it is simply an impediment. I have one new radiator that leaks, defying the efforts of a team of charming young plumbers who spend hours here with spanners and wrenches. And another radiator that remains defiantly cold. I dread the window operation, which may not start until December (so Christmas celebrations will be a bit draughty). Work sessions continue, threading themselves in and out of the surrounding chaos – so far, without disturbing clients. I'm trying to hang on to the certainty that all this is necessary and has meaning for me, presumably because of 'major works' on the inner plane – but sometimes I feel like chucking in my hand! Then, I come to and look for a lifeline, perhaps Schubert, or an exhibition (we have Rodin at the moment, and Modigliani, and I want to go to Holbein at the Tate) or a friend who can make me laugh. And it helps to be given quotations, like the marvelous George Eliot one in your letter. Thanks for this! Oh yes, and last week I escaped to a matinee at the Old Vic – Eugene O'Neill's **Moon for the Misbegotten,** brilliantly played by Kevin Spacey and Eva Best. If you don't know the play, it is his last – about poverty and deprivation, and love, loss and redemption. Big hug, lots of love, Sheila.

A DIARY OF VOWELS
In August 1976 I had a dream in which I was told by a voice that it was time for me to become a diarist of vowels. This puzzled me until I realized that the vowels of language are the sounds that are not interrupted by consonants. They are the pure sounds of the breath – "the central sound of a syllable," as the American Heritage Dictionary defines vowel. The word is derived from the Latin "vox" – the voice itself. The consonants are the sounds that accompany, "sound with", the vowels. Therefore I knew that my diary should contain the "central sounds" of life – the meanings, the unblocked sounds from the unconscious as they came to me day by day.
Such Stuff As Dreams Are Made on: Helen Luke

Dearest Sheila,
What a feast of quotations. Thank you, thank you. I sent the **Kandinsky** on to four friends, 2 painters, 2 musicians. I love the **Helen Luke**. Can you imagine what life would be like without these quotes? Like being a vegan, I fancy, just living off tofu.
It's been a hard couple of weeks with **John Betjeman's** centennial and I really had to scour the town to find anyone who had ever heard of him! Finally ran into a British Anglican vicar. He knew! My religious attendance is now pretty much confined to my silent vigil with **Women in Black,** and my monthly **Taize** service. I just get increasingly monastic. Think I may be running out of words too.
The thought of you having to endure all those repairs – never mind pay for them – is pretty bleak. At least in this climate, if things are horrid at home, we can go to a sunshiny hilltop and forget for a while. I just began **John le Carre's** latest. Was chuckling in bed last night: *"The England that awaits (him) is a rain swept cemetery for the living dead powered by a 40 watt bulb."* (A little cruel, but he has a point...). Had one of my very rarely remembered dreams last week, in which a woman I hadn't seen in a long time, but knew well (not in physical life) came and said: "Oh, my God, I had no idea your voice was this bad." I flew at her: "You should have heard – or not heard – it before. It's way way better than it was." That's pretty much the tension for me now, both being true, yet I oscillate between the "oh, my God," and the

"well, it could be worse, it has been worse!" Well, my hands are cold this morning and I'd better push on with a few errands. Just so wonderful every time I hear from you. Much much love, Lee

And to end this month, lovely words from Jane.

Dear Lee,
I am so glad that you continue to make progress! I don't know if I would have as much patience as you have been having to develop!
When I was a child, there was a Carmelite monastery near my house. There were pink walls around it and beautiful gardens within. Sometimes my mother would take me there to the chapel at dawn and the nuns would sing in Latin from behind the grate. So beautiful. I used to think I wanted to be a contemplative nun when I grew up.
Well, I know you are not singing behind the grate over there, but I think your experience has cured me of wishing to be a contemplative!
I have just started reading Dennis Klocek's book, *The Seer's Handbook*. Here's a quote you might like: " *The capacity to perceive within the silence of the spirit is the root of inner development and the hallmark of exact seership... All insights come from the silence and all images received in meditation are to be dissolved back in the silent, creative darkness from which all light of understanding flows.* " And a poem that I have also been finding inspirational, love Jane.

from "The Secret Iron of the Heart" by ARVIA MACKAYE EGE

> *There is a golden merriment*
> *No evil can destroy*
> *Or ever touch,*
> *No shadow scar,*
> *Because its quality is such*
> *As no impurity can mar.*
> *There is a joy,*
> *Of such unburdening degree,*
> *No enmity can ever grow*
> *Within its glow ---*
> *So free*
> *That it can dwell*
> *And spend its fervency,*
> *Its loving, high festivity,*
> *As well*
> *In heaven as in hell.*
> *There is a beauty,*
> *That turns all labor*
> *And all duty*
> *Into love,*
> *And brings to earth the flavor*

Of the starry meadow-land
Above.
And there is then a trust,
No matter what we must,
That flows
Into the soul
From each undeviable star,
That knows
Itself at one
With the vast, sparkling whole,
Its innermost confiding goal,
That is the cure
For every human ill ---
And will
Throughout eternity,
In pure,
infallible security
Endure.

CHAPTER EIGHT. THE VOICE OF THE PEOPLE.

"How do we know where we are going?
How do we know where we are headed
till we in fact or hope or hunch
arrive?... Navigating by chart and chance
and passion we will know the shape
of the mountains of freedom, we will know."
From: Perpetual Migration. **Marge Piercy.**

Since this is one of the most depressing months as far as my own recovery, or lack of it, is concerned, I need to celebrate all the people, old and new, who came to my rescue. And, of course the mid term elections.

From Bill - my brother
Hi Lee
How are you and how is the voice?
I was thinking of you yesterday when Soraya and I drove past the old Hammersmith Hospital where Adam was born. It is now a head quarters for Sony Ericsson. (*plus ca change.....*). What a star Adam is....hooray. I was also remembering that you had a stillborn child..........and somehow this horrible event for you, which must have been so difficult never really got recognition and proper respect ....I do not know where I was at the time or why I was not helping you, I just remember that I was not, and have always felt that you were let down. You have dealt with the troubles that life has thrown at you so well....and you are doing the same with this one. I do hope that the light is visible now..........good luck. Love Bill

Dearest Bill,
Thank you so much for your lovely words. You know what I remember, outstandingly, was the incredible, fiercely loyal support you gave me over the whole Paddy business. You were only 15 at the time, and at Winchester, so hardly ever around, so I don't even know how you knew what was going on. I was utterly awed by that. I can't even remember where you were when I lost my daughter, so how could you have done more?
Adam certainly is a star (well we may learn this month that he didn't pass his bar exams, but that is the least of it). His chief claim to stardom is his tender heart and he shares that with you: seems to come down through the male members of our family. I'm not half so loving - in fact pretty grumpy and fierce most of the time! Anyway, even if I'm not singing, last week was magnificent, the voice of the people speaking loud and clear in our midterms!! Hurrah. Just hope something can be salvaged from the last 6 grim years. So much love to you all. Oh, I do wish Benj and Siena would come my way sometime. Is Siena in law school now, or what?? Of course you too, Soraya and Kara. (Tell Soraya I'm delighted with the purple sponge bag.) Love Lee

Yes....hooray also for the good voters of the USA; the threat of another McCarthy era has dissipated. Good luck with the voice quack. I do not recall much about all the Paddy issues and was indeed only 15/16 at school. However thanks for the thanks......Good luck to Adam in his exam results. Siena started at Law School a week ago. Love Bill.

Sophia *is a young (young to me!) Dutch woman I only met in the past couple of years in the Bay Area. She was running a round the clock child care service in Marin, and beginning the Waldorf Teacher Training program. I've been missing everyone I know and love in Northern California, which may account for my note to Sophia*

Dear Sophia,
 Was thinking very strongly about you yesterday, so thought I'd write and ask how you are doing? Love Lee

Lee,
Wow, that's amazing. You and your formdrawing spirits! I gave my first formdrawing lesson yesterday, while doing my three week practicum, which is rather hectic. It went quite well. I'll graduate next summer and have no idea where I'll go. I follow your news, and keep you off and on in my prayers. I'm so glad you are on the mend.
Will miss seeing you puffing those fags though. I keep on trying to find out what the true nature of addiction is, so I go off and on. As long as I can't have a pack in the house without smoking them (I do fine when they're not around), I know I'll be waiting my time on them in kamaloka. Definitely connected to the will forces and the astral.
Hope to hear that low, husky voice of yours again one day. Got to run to school. Summerfield in Sebastopol, can't be late for Main lesson. Thanks for thinking of me, I bet it helped my formdrawing lesson in this class of 32 second graders! Much love, stay in touch Sophia

Dearest Sophia,
How utterly wonderful to hear from you. A lovely Rumi quote: *"There's a voice that doesn't use words. Listen!"* (I must have tuned in to that speaking silence!) I have missed California and all of you so much. Oh, I'm not saying I'll never smoke again.   I'll probably get arrested one of these days for pursuing men with fat cigars, or fat men with thin ones, (I ain't fussy) for my secondhand thrill! And still a big question whether I will ever get a voice back, and certainly whether it will sound anything like my old one. So you are teaching at Summerfield? Thought that was in Santa Rosa? I know you are fantastically busy, but just stay put in California till I can get to visit with you. So much love, Lee

Margaret *found me many years ago, when she was living in New Orleans (as she does now, bar not having a house to live in) and later moved in with me in Detroit for a year or so. Later still, she arranged workshops for me in "The*

Big Easy", so I was able to visit that lovely city, work and play with many of her friends. She has continued as one of my nearest and dearest (not ever physically close enough) friends.

Dear Lee,
I did think at one point I should call and leave a sympathy message for you when I was virtually voiceless for about a week with the flu last month, although I would have had to have my father make that call on my behalf...So how are you? I was so heartened to hear in your last message that there is real progress. As someone who 14 months later finally has walls in her house again, I can truly appreciate any degree of progress!
Thank God the Dems won back Congress - now let's see if they can offer some real alternatives! Sending you much love and looking forward to hearing from you, ever closer to being able to actually hear you! XXOO, M.

Dearest Margaret,
Well, it's pretty slow. Maybe when your house is completed I'll have a functional voice. Though glad to hear about the house, I've wished that the first rebuilding of your city could have been to let silt out of the Mississippi to begin to recreate the barrier islands. After hearing the author of **Bayou Farewell**, I'm convinced there's no other true protection, and it would only cost what we/"They" are spending in Iraq every week!! Thank God, We the People have been able to make a statement at least!!! Love, Lee

Group email 16ᵗʰ November: Voice of the People.

Dear Family and Friends,
Well, I hope you agree that far more important than hearing my voice again was the result of the mid term elections?! A chink appearing in those dark and ever darker clouds that began rolling over in 2000. For those of you outside this country, it was quite remarkable. Even in this "red" state, folk had a light in their eye and a lighter step on Nov 8th. Except one poor lil ole lady who clutched my shoulders and said she'd never be able to sleep again as she was sure terrorists were heading for her bedroom as we spoke, and now, with our saviors, Bush and Rumsfeld cut off at the pass, had a clear run. I tried to reassure her that she was much more likely to die from a lightning strike or a fellow American gunman (close to 12,000 are shot here annually). Well, enough of political commentary!
This is the LAST time I will treat you all to a dissertation on the health of my vocal cords. Thanksgiving and Christmas are almost upon us, it is time to think of other things. So, assume no news is good news after this. (Of course, for those who ask it will be given!)
Andre Gide said: **"We must go too far before we know how far we have to go,"** *and alas, I rather overdid the exercising this month, and have a few hemorrhages in my cords (have to use that word - medically correct, and in my notes now -because I think I've spelt it right, and our vocabulary is*

diminishing daily), and also the beginning of vocal cord nodules (different from polyps) where the scar tissue is. It is not to be worried about, (at least yet) I just need to calm everything down, including my voice exercises. I've been so scared of them not closing, the muscles weakening again, that I forced them in the other direction, rather like asking a 3yr old to train for the Iron Man Marathon. My therapist is still optimistic, but has prescribed fewer and gentler exercises and only "confidential conversations." These are the one on one, up close and personal, chats I can have in a very quiet space, or out walking with a friend because, happily, the air up here is so thin and dry that you can hear someone fart 5 miles away, so I don't have to project my voice at all. I mustn't use phone, sorry, it takes a lot of force.

So now I'm backed into a corner and have to write. Writing, for me, is like having perpetual acute toothache. I will try to intersperse it with such uplifting activities as walking, housecleaning, even house fixing - I'd always, as I was doing last week, rather mix cement than words. I hope to arrange my life in such a way that I can spend time with those I love - you all, for starters!!! I will try to sell my house in the spring, which will give me more mobility and more cash to travel. Hey, my $129 a month Social security starts in two weeks. Watch out, I could be heading your way before you know it. Have wonderful holidays, all of you. Much love, Lee

From Nancy
Lee! So good to hear from you and Yes, somewhere that deep good will and common sense in Americans is coming up to the surface after having been fooled for so long. You can fool some of the people some of the time but not all all the time as they say.

So glad you are making improvement though the hyper activity sounds over the top. What an incredible discipline! I know you didn't want to sign up for it but it is truly a mountain to climb. More power to you Lee. And you are a good writer.... will this one become a book? We are fine and so busy. Gordon just passed his flight physical and we shall be continuing to enjoy the skies! Expecting the large gangs for Thanksgiving.... will be good to see you when it is all possible. Our wonderful news is that Colin and Wendy are expecting a baby and we are thrilled. Will be such a great event for them and they will be wonderful parents... Much Love, Nancy

Hey, my dearest friend.
I was thrilled too when told a few months ago about Colin and Wendy. Hard to be too serious about one's "vowel movements" once you have a child! Who knows if I'll write anything. I do correspond with my Anthro Prison Outreach fellows - that's always lovely - and, to a limited degree, I am incarcerated, so feel a little closer to them. Well, go well, hugs and to Gordon. Love, Lee

From Lalla, Dearest Lee: It's so good to hear that you are ploughing ahead, or maybe were "ploughing ahead" so much that now you are more securely "plodding along" instead. No matter the speed, it all sounds very good! I have been reading Theosophy, the part where he says how many different kinds of spiritual beings there are, and I can see lots of little and big angel types sitting around your house delighting in your accomplishments! They probably don't give as much importance as we do to how loud you are able to speak, bless them. It would be wonderful to see you in the spring, truly would be a gift.

Our family is well and Paolo and I are very much enjoying seeing the first fruits of Waldorf Education in our teen age children. Pietro had his interview at the high school today and brought a self-portrait in the form of a collage composed inside his guitar case: many pictures from his life, the Beatles in pictures and song lyrics, many cover pictures of his favorite books, quotes from Tolkien, a hip-hop song called *Where is the Love*, and in the guitar pick case, together with his precious guitar pick, a picture of the first Judo master and a little wooden statuette of Saint Francis. Sibi was elected to the student council and would like to convince her peers that we don't need to be a prep school. She shared with Paolo that this is hard because she can't explain to them what is behind Waldorf education (which we never thought she herself had any awareness of)! Little Tommaso is delightful, now in the stage of telling me, as we get out of the car at the grocery store, "Mamma, now I am going to ask you, *May I run?*, and you have to say, *No, it is too dangerous in the parking lot!*" His way of taking control, I guess, being surrounded by so many big people! Love and blessings, Lalla

Hey, Lalla,
This must be quick because my computer is playing up. Lovely hearing from you, with all your esoteric and other news. And about those lovely kids of yours. Each and all sound marvelous. Well, I hope to get to SF for a couple of nights. Otherwise the fall, when Meg will be back, though of course there's someone now sleeping in *my* bed!!! Love to you all, Lee

Thanks Lee! We have a sofa, but long lines for the bathroom...Love, Lalla
:
*Jennifer is an Australian, living in the Bay Area, a friend of **Pat** and **Dawn**, and I had a chance to meet her again when Pat visited San Francisco last fall. She is a quite wonderful painter, and I will leave her website here, so folk can look at some of her paintings.*

Dear Lee,
Patricia has kindly shown and forwarded me your recent emails. I have been variously shocked, inspired, humored of course, deeply moved, and heartened by your accounts. What an initiation you are going through! I know that sounds banal, but I think it is true. It seems like a trial by fire, but I am not sufficiently knowledgeable to really know. However, I see that you have been stripped bare (even literally) and been given a new birth into another way of being. It appears to me that whenever we undergo a profound transformation, there is a generous dose of suffering to go along with it. The

way in which you are approaching your latest destiny challenge is nothing short of Michaelic and I wish you much courage and strength as you continue on this most difficult and rewarding path. Please don't feel that your words are unnecessary or inadequate. You are indeed still teaching and the lessons are essential and wonderful. I, for one, would like to be added to your emailing list and to hear the details as you see fit to publish them. Despite the "toothache", you may have another book gestating.

My personal response is to offer you some painting sessions when you are next in the Bay area if that is something that appeals to you. I can do it without much talking at all. That has become my practice with one of my clients. It may not be your cup of tea and that is fine. I know you are not financially flush, so would only ask a small donation towards gas. Unfortunately I find myself looking back on Waldorf work as lucrative!! Meanwhile, it is a long time since I saw you and we dined with Patricia. I participated in the annual North Coast Studio Discovery Tour in September, went to Australia for a month, returned and moved to north Berkeley. A few weeks later Emily, my landlady, who for 12 weeks had been commuting weekly to Reno from the coast (about 7 hours) for alternative treatments for her aggressive breast cancer, was hit head on and ended up on life support for 3 weeks, then entered the zone called rehab - you know the one - for many months. Apart from the shock, grief, and organizing a ritual at her house with her goddess friends and others, I ended up doing property maintenance whenever I was up there, instead of painting. Emily came home after 6 months and is still recovering in a very determined, disciplined, and good spirited fashion. Another member of your sisterhood!

My painting continues nevertheless. Step by step I have been finding my voice in the realm of art. Recently I have branched out into acrylics on canvas, working larger than the watercolors. I have my first solo show coming up December 1 at the Sea Ranch Lodge on the coast. It is not a fancy gallery, but it is a gorgeous room oceanside, with a large fireplace and lots of rich visitors traveling through. I hope they are in the mood for some expensive Christmas presents or just a splash of color amid the dreary winter grays.

I rushed off to be with my very sick father in Adelaide for five weeks after the latest September studio tour. That was where Patricia first showed me your emails. Well that is probably more than you ever wanted know, so I'll close for now, except to say that my partner, Osha, is a wonderful spiritual human being and I feel blessed to be with her. Being a step mother to two boys - 10 and almost 13 - was completely unexpected and has its hairy moments, but I have a lot up my sleeve to rely on, so that helps. Love, Jennifer

p.s. so glad you could protect the old woman from the terrorists

COLORS FOR THE SOUL
original paintings, prints and cards
lessons for individuals and groups
http://www.jenniferbundey.com

Dear Jennifer, I was just quietly rereading your email. I wanted to add how awed I am by your own journey, how grateful I was to hear more, feel more connected. In fact your letter may have been the "final straw" to my imagining that I wanted somehow to get back to California, even find a funky apartment in Berkeley! Financially it would be challenging, but as my mother used to say "shrouds have no pockets"!!! Just thought I'd let you know that your letter might well have acted as a final spur to even considering this. And then I'd love to paint with you. Hope you have had a great Thanksgiving, also with those boys. Hope to meet them someday! I have quite a thing for those young lads. My own is now 28, just got his NY Bar exams, is on his way, thanks in great part to Waldorf education!! Much love, Lee

From: Judith: Re: The Voice of the People!

Hello Lee, I have been meaning to write to congratulate you and all Americans on the result of the mid-term elections. We are generally all so awful about America and the Americans most of the time, but now I have to hand it to them - a complete change around politically, and not a shot fired or a drop of blood spilt in the process. THAT's democracy. I really only found out what democracy means (and it has to include universal education and access to information too) when I lived in an African country that didn't have it. I'll never forget visiting the small British Council Library in Asmara to find it packed with Eritreans fervently reading elderly copies of the Times, Telegraph and Guardian! They had the English, but not the newspapers, only the Government-sponsored one, which was complete trash. So thank god for America in this case, and we are all looking forward to what will happen next. At least they (with partners in the wider world, hitherto largely ignored) may now be able to stop this terrible slide into hatred and murder. Perhaps. It is terrible to think of you with no voice, but you sound as usual indomitable, and what is this about selling your house and going traveling? Any chance of coming this way? I'm STILL waiting for my angiogram (could get it private tomorrow, or of course if I were an emergency also), and until then I can't get travel insurance! Stay in touch, much love, Judith

Dearest Judith,
Lovely to hear from you - yes, let's keep this up, I hate phones and have had a rude message left by a friend about 6 months ago that says: "Lee won't be talking on phone for 3-4 months, find another way.." I may keep it on for the rest of my life. Though I do miss chats with my beloved son. Yes, it was a good statement, and maybe Bush can do less damage, and maybe we can get a little more back into the global fold. I just can hardly bear the pain and suffering this nation is causing. The Bobby Kennedy movie will be out next week, timely reminder that there was a finer impulse in America. Well, while we are all trying to sort this out, China will clearly take over. Apparently the Mayan calendar gives the world till 2012. Five more years, we'd better enjoy them. So I'm going to get dressed and go and walk in my little local park

which is very lovely, full of birds and dog walkers. Please keep in touch, it's so good hearing from you. Much much love, Lee

Aloha Marietta,
 Have been thinking of you a lot, and hoping you are settling in all right in Vermont. I think I remember you telling me that Jean could join you for Thanksgiving? I do hope you have someone with you, I know it won't be the whole glorious family. Hallie and I are in the loop again, I'm so happy. I spent yesterday morning, Sunday, in my pajamas, dreaming of us all moving to the Bay area, maybe an improbable dream, but it comes with love, Lee

Hi there----You were probably thinking of me because I needed psychic strength from all areas of the country to get through my first week at this new hospital. What a bleak unit....I feel so sorry for the patients to have to endure the way things are set up there. I have lots of ideas...and have said so...but no one has sat down to listen to anything. I'm going to wait a few more days and then make an appt. with my supervisor...and out it will come. I realize I have to choose my battles and prioritize potential change (not to alienate people) but it is hard to wait on some of the things. Anyway, I'm plenty busy. And yes, Jean is coming on Wed. for 4 days....I can't wait! Too short, but lucky that he can come at all. Thank you, Lee, for your thoughts of me...and for your moral support of Hallie. I am very grateful! Marietta

Well, I'll picture and pray for you mightily. You are the most amazing healer. I'll never forget us all sitting there in Ann Arbor with our mouths open, drinking it/you all in, and asking to go home with you. It's utterly daft that the world won't say "please come, do whatever you want, we'll pay you whatever you want..."   I think I got a swiftly passing stomach flu yesterday (seem fine today) and I fainted 3 times! It was interesting and strange to find myself staring quietly and happily up from the floor with no memory of getting there, but the idea to move to Berkeley came even more strongly. Now you tell them what for at that hospital, and keep warm, and have a lovely time with Jean. And I'll send you as much force as I can, because I love you and can't bear thinking of someone so wonderful not being happy! Lee

Lee, You are so good for the old morale! Thank you for your confidence in me and belief that I can make a difference out here in the cold, remote world. No wonder Adam turned out so terrific! Now, I want you to report to someone about your flu. What IF you had passed out for much longer....who would know or call on a regular basis? Who knows, Sean Connery might be volunteering that day & could make a house call to revive you. I know he could raise ME from the dead!!   All the best, Marietta

From: Esther. Hello my lovely! How super to hear that your voice is returning! And that it is not a high-pitched squeak!... Our dear Helga has lung cancer...I know she has had a pretty good "go", but I still find it hard, especially since she is not up to seeing anyone. Steven is quite shattered...they have such a close relationship. Huge hugs and love , Esther

Dearest Estherbelle,
I am so sorry about Helga, any place I can send a card to?   Blast! I'd like to connect with both of them. Do give Stephen my love and sorrow. Keep lots for yourself too. Lee

From: Adam Day
Subject: My B-day Present

Wow, that DVD was amazing. Thank you so much! I didn't know you still had all those pictures and I really liked seeing them all with the music playing etc....I'm in the middle of a really long day at work and have to get back to it, but wanted to say what a wonderful present that was. I could see how much time and effort went into it. Love you lots, A

Darling Adam,
Glad you like it, I enjoyed creating it. Hope you got, or get, to seeing it on a really big screen with Space Odyssey playing really loud! Love you (well I seem to have said that rather copiously in the DVD) Mum

Dearest Pat,
 I wanted to let you know how intensely grateful I am for your linking me first to Dawn and now to Jennifer, from whom I had a long and wonderful email. (In fact, as I wrote her back, I told her her letter may well turn out to be the final impetus to my considering moving back to California, and forward to the Bay area!) Still plan to visit Down Under, but not much point until we can have a conversation, even if I keep my big mouth shut a lot of the time! Maybe I am awaiting a meeting with a kangaroo. Do you know your myth, that when God had created the world and animal kingdom, he needed to bestow speech. All the animals refused the gift, and at last the kangaroo suggested they (he) gave it to humans, because speech was so troublesome, and we were just idiotic enough to deserve it! (I think it is a bit grander and more poetic that than, but that's the gist of it.)
I do hope you are doing well. Jennifer is very impressed by you - as am I - and your strength. I already feel very crumbly. Anyhow, I just wanted to say hello, and I often think of you. These threads of friendship are all that matter to me now, and I'm just going to pull myself along them somehow, so I can be with those I love. Amazing this 33yr cycle, I seem to be reconnecting with all my Emerson buddies now. Love Lee

Dear Lee,
I am delighted to have received your email. I didn't know the Kangaroo myth - but there are so many aboriginal legends that it doesn't surprise me that Roo has a special one. I used to have Ainslie Roberts' (a painter) books of illustrations and legends when I was a teacher, but handed them to some child

or other. I must see if they are still in print, for I am sure that you would find them interesting.

It is a miracle that we have reconnected - as you say at the end of the 33 year cycle from Emerson days. Jennifer seems to be an important link between us now.

I am hoping that I may have enough strength, endurance and courage to make another pilgrimage to the beautiful Californian north coast, redwoods, Lake Tahoe, and Bay Area in 2007. It is my octogenarian year, but I would dearly love to be able to come when Jennifer is showing her work. Of course I would want to see you too, and who knows, you might have A VOICE TO SING WITH (title of Joan Baez book). Though I seem to remember you were not a participant in the Italian Art Tour Palestrina Choir at Emerson! Perhaps we'll settle for a VOICE TO SPEAK WITH!

Life goes on here. The joy of my life is Pete my Dachshund, with whom I spend my Dog Days. He is very much a mummy's boy - quite indulged, but sweet. His unconditional acceptance of my every mood, my joys and sorrows makes up for his misdemeanors.

I endeavour to keep my mind active by doing the crossword each day, and keeping up with my share portfolio on the computer. (It's one way of financing my retirement, and of maintaining an interest in the world of business.) I get The New York Times political news via the web each day, together with the Review of Books and Films. I follow with glee the downfall of George W., but wonder how ever the US will extract itself from the diabolical disaster it has created in Iraq. Will the Arabs and the Infidel ever find a peaceful way of living together? How many more centuries will it take for the world to live in peace? In the words of John Lennon:

> *People will say I'm a dreamer,*
> *But I'm not the only one.*
> *And I hope some day you'll join us*
> *And the World will be as One.*

I try to support the Planet, its creatures, its needy and suffering people, and my friends who are contributing to the world through their artistic gifts. - The Threefold Social Order, I guess, though I don't belong to the Anthro. Society these days. I'd better stop rambling! I hope you continue to make steady progress and look forward to keeping in touch. Much love, Patricia.

Dear Pat,
Well, I do love these reconnections, and I hope you return to SF in 2007. I read the kangaroo myth in Thomas Keneally's **Woman of the Inner Sea.** I recommend it. No, I never made it to the Palestrina Choir, that's why I was so hopeful I'd be singing after this thing. My connection with Joan Baez is confined to our Rock Concert days, where we supplied lighting and special effects and she gave a benefit concert after Hell's Angels destroyed the Isle of Wight concert and we had to pull out the balloons and performing pigs!!

I don't know how this utter agonizing mess of whole Middle East can ever be healed. Jimmy Carter said he thought going into Iraq was the single worst foreign policy decision in US history! Worse than Vietnam. Colin Powell spoke yesterday saying how hugely he regretted his role. But that doesn't help the families of the dead and wounded, does it, and the utter agony created in that region and for the returning soldiers and if I have to hear another statistic (fewer killed this week than last or whatever) I may run through streets screaming. Folk have become so deadened. There was some silly talk show yesterday on "why are children violent here".. It is pretty straightforward isn't it? Because the adults are! Well, if it comes your way, see Bobby - the Bobby Kennedy movie. And take Kleenex. He quoted Aeschylus on the night King was assassinated (I've always thought Democrats worked more out of their Greek incarnation, Republicans being the decadent Romans).

> *'Even in our sleep,*
> *Pain, which can not forget,*
> *falls drop by drop upon the human heart,*
> *until, in our own despair,*
> *against our will,*
> *we come to wisdom,*
> *through the aweful grace of God."*

Well, on that note, I'll leave you to you stocks and shares. Much love, Lee

From: Signe

Hi Lee,
I hope you had a good Thanksgiving. We had 28 people, including 5 boys under 6! The strangest thing happened late Thanksgiving night after things had gotten quiet. Stefan was doing the last round of dishes and he was washing an old bone-handled carving knife from my family. He noticed some writing and a drawing carved into the blade, and called out that it was made in Finland (where Judy's father's family came from).Then he said with a more excited voice: Heh Chenta, this was made by Johannes Lauri. So Chenta called Judy in Maui, only to hear that her grandfather's grandfather was named Johannes! It was the middle of the night and you can imagine how we were all feeling -- Stefan just kept laughing, and we were all amazed. We always knew that Stefan and Chenta were connected, but this? I really do love biography ... Even of a knife!!
I've been thinking of you lately because Stefan was just visiting Shirley MacLaine, at her ranch near Santa Fe. He has been working on a script for her, through a friend of hers who is the father of a friend of his. It has had several drafts and now was the time for them to actually meet. So over the weekend we (Stefan, Chenta, Chris and I) watched a couple of her movies-- **The Apartment** (she really did look like you!!) and **In Her Shoes** (for a more current view). He was with her on Monday and Tuesday, home late last night and feeling quite encouraged by the meetings. My days at Sunbridge are numbering down. What are your plans for Christmas? Love, Signe

Dear Signe,

How utterly extraordinary, that story. Indeed these stories are amazing, and they should be told, somehow. Maybe Stefan can make a film. Did I tell you I was given a huge bouquet of orchids when I went to the Hotel Erewhon in Bangkok (1960) to have a nostalgic Cafe Viennoise and papaya and lime on my return from Hongkong, as they mistook me for Shirley McLaine? So, she lives in Santa Fe?

Well - Christmas - my beloved son is flying for 3 days, returning on red eye Christmas night, to work on 26th, just to be with his ole Mom, what more can I ask? Think I'll wait till early summer to come visit him, also in the hope that you will be there then. And the evenings are longer and lighter and I can tootle around while he works and maybe have a voice approaching the human range. Have a great Christmas. How lovely to think I will be able to catch up with you all now Adam is entrenched. Love, Lee

Laura is my beloved niece, and mother of 4yr old Sophia, also busy erecting her yurt next door to her mother's. I can hardly wait to be with them again, next May, having missed last year's visit.

Dear Lee,

Your voice healing seems to be like our house building - two steps forward, one step back. Hopefully soon, both processes will be complete. Your advent calendar arrived today by itself. Thank you so much. Sophia was very excited. Much, much love and hugs to you. Laura

Darling Laura, Yes, I see how we are both rebuilding in same fashion. Let me know if another package doesn't arrive. (It's a world puzzle - just the sort of thing to get stuck in the cracks of a half finished house in an earthquake!!!) Tell Sophia I miss her so much, can't wait to see her again, and she can do ALL (or most of) the talking now!!! Love, Lee

Joan lives in Prescott so we don't have to email each other that much. She's really the reason I moved here! I lived in her home for the first three months. She is a remedial tutor of children, which needs, as she does, a whole chapter. Just imagine a beautiful bird-like woman, serving her children tea in tiny china cups, candles alight, maybe singing a song to them. Well, I'll let her conclude this next chapter, hoping we have many more chapters together in our lives.

Darling,

Just back from Phoenix (a very fine time, with the work going well) and read your letter! So sorry about the recent set-back. I suppose the delicacy of the situation demands a much gentler approach. It is sounding so hopeful, and a small set back is just that. Isn't it curious that this recovery is so tenuous, from what seemed like a routine procedure! Well, darling, I will be there, all the way! I assume that this impacts your ability to speak at the January

Conference, since it would require a good deal of speaking. It is about 7 weeks away. Beautiful weather, beautiful air, and winter is coming! Love and many hugs to you Joan

Hey darling,
Sadly, sadly, it's probably better if you can manage without me/my voice. God, these are hard choices. Just don't put me in the flyer. I really wanted to support Betsy, so if you can do without me maybe you should. Love you, Lee

Honey! We don't want to do it without you! Maybe we put your name in and see how you are by then? It's really your call, as only **you** know how to pace yourself, and how you are coming along. If it will strain you to a point of relapse, then..... But only you know that. I know Betsy would feel the same, that we want you there, but only if you feel it is what you should be doing! I've never been one to "preach" to my friends or anyone, about what they should or shouldn't be doing! This is such a deep, far-reaching experience for you, and you are truly the one to set the course. Don't you think we put your name in, and then see? Or does your doctor feel that that kind of strain would be detrimental. You just let me know, and I will gladly proceed as usual. Or, honor what you need. I wish I could be of more help, as I know it is agonizing. Loving you! Joan

First, my darling, You are the best help anyone could have!! Oh, yes, put my name, it will cheer me up no end. Maybe I can put duck tape over my mouth!   So, count me on/in. I used to be in the circus, maybe time for mime? Hugs, love you, Lee

CHAPTER NINE. ADVENT.

In this suspense of ours before the fall
Before the end, before the true beginning,
No word, no feeling can be pure or whole.
Bear the loss first, then the infant winning.
Annunciation. **May Sarton.**

Now we enter Advent, always a dark and challenging time. The state of the world certainly gives us nothing to feel optimistic about, and my voice relapse echoes this all too pathetically. One thing to be inching forward, another to go backwards rapidly. But this month was utterly redeemed by first a visit from M., and later from my son.

I had slightly dreaded having a houseguest, even one I love as much as M. I imagined strains, in speaking, in adapting to company. How could I have been so silly? From the moment she descends from the airport shuttle, my heart lifts, and doesn't fall back into place again until she departs. I had completely forgotten what it is to sit and share to all levels, to laugh and laugh (even if the sounds I make are revolting) to have someone who looks out with similar eyes on both the beauties and absurdities of the place I live in. M. is actually very impressed: "For such a small town, Prescott has remarkable resources," she tells me, pointing out many of them, and bringing me out of the negative space I often occupy here. Our walks are glorious, and it is wonderful to have a friend to share these with, and who could call out if a mountain lion descends. I had really missed Granite Mountain, and the day we went we even saw a great flock of Western bluebirds. She bought me a bird book so I could begin to identify those that flock to my feeders and, later the following year, even rest in my hand.

Our highlight was an outing through Skull Valley to lunch at the Buzzard Roost Café. It took a while to get off. I must have paused the car in the driveway at least four times. The last time, M. asked: "What have we forgotten this time?"

"My teeth," I told her, before dashing in to rescue my partial plate from its glass. This aging business is quite an ordeal.

"Did we really sign up for this?" M. asks again as we exit finally. Like much of life, it is probably better not to know *this* future in advance!

The Buzzard Roost Café has gone through many changes since I've lived here. First time I came it was with Trudi, a splendidly large Austrian friend in her 70's with an admirably uplifted frontage. We are sitting outside, sipping Sarsparilla, surrounded by fake graves, a single boot marking the resting place of One-Legged John, our conversation occasionally interrupted by a plastic rattlesnake shooting out from the stones and hissing loudly, or a similarly lurid frog croaking to announce the arrival of another diner, when we look across at each other and wonder how we, sophisticated Europeans, used to dining in Vienna, or London, or even Paris, have come to be here in the wild west. It is quite a moment for both of us. Now the café has really expanded. Our cooks, a Welshwoman and her cowboy spouse or sweetheart, serve quite excellent food of its kind . (I can speak with authority, I used to be a food writer, in an earlier life). M. is enraptured, and needs to follow her strip steak and grilled vegetables with several scoops of local ice-cream. It is hard to say goodbye to her. But she has greater travels to take, as her "sabbatical" will be spent visiting and helping initiatives around the world.

So, after farewell, to this my Sister of Sisters, I receive the reminder – as if I needed one – from Barbara. Here is a brief excerpt.

To my dear friends, who are really "sisters" ...
Sisters are the mainstays of our lives. After more than 58 years of living in this world, here is what I've learned: THIS SAYS IT ALL: Time passes. Life happens. Distance separates. Children grow up. Jobs come and go. Love waxes and wanes. Men don't do what they're supposed to do. Hearts break. Parents die. Colleagues forget favors. Careers end. BUT......... Sisters are there, no matter how much time and how many miles are between you.
Barbara

Dearest Barbara How lovely, my sister. Thanks, and thanks for being one of mine. Love you, Lee

Then we move towards Christmas, graced by a three day visit from Adam, flying back through Christmas night to be at his desk the following day. I feel fortified for the months ahead. What a present! Then, on my birthday two days later, Kim and Tina show up for a pajama party. How lucky can a girl get? I'm ready for 2007 now!!

From: Adam Day : Sent: Dec 27, 2006 Subject: 65!

Dear Mum,
Happy Birthday! It was great to see you and I'm sorry I'm not around to drive you to your massage. Hope you have a wonderful day. Roman and Kenny send their love. They have been in NYC for the last few days. It's been really good to see them--it will be also really good when they go and let me normalise my life again. **The Book of Evidence** is brilliant. I'll be on to the Civil War Pulitzer winner tomorrow and will give you an update. I think I might have to read all of Banville's books sometime soon. I have to get back to work, but I hope your birthday went well and I'm excited for your Spring trip to NY. Love you, A.

Darling Adam,
You gave more than I could have expected by coming as you did. Hope first day back at work wasn't too horrendous. Can't imagine how you are managing with the bathroom, needing to shave and get to work. My love to Kenny and Roman too, and speed them well (away!!) Glad we agree about Banville! Yes, I read another - **Shroud.** He takes some beating. I just

finished Malouf's **An Imaginary Life** - the Aussie/Ovid one. That was pretty remarkable. Assume you didn't get fired, or haven't been yet? .I had a smashing 65th. And when I went on my own for my "Riparian (Hyacinth Bucket) Entertainment " along the trail between the pink boulders a few days ago, I saw: three pure white freshwater pelicans, two swans, a grey heron, a kestrel, and two juicy male kayakers through Ma's old opera glasses. Doesn't get much better than that! Hope you get a little rest, a long shower, a good night's sleep soon. Love you, Mum

From: Sophia: Dec 28, 2006 1:31 PM
Subject: Alison

Dear Lee,
With much sadness I have to let you know that our dear Alison, the giant, the powerhouse, who seemed to be able to win any battle, crossed-over this morning at 9:45. Even on December 1st she was still up, bright and expecting to heal. But since then it went very fast, with fluid in her lungs, and around her heart. And besides having the fluids removed to improve breathing, she refused regular medical treatment. She died at home, surrounded by many, many loving friends. She leaves behind her partner and their 3 year old son. Please keep her in your prayers for the next three days. Much love, and of course the wishes of the season, AND of course a great improvement in your health in the new year. I have a feeling they won't let you go so soon, whether you want or not! Sophia

Dear Sophia,
Oh, I am so sad and shaken, and was thinking of her, and talking about her over Christmas with my son. Yes, what an incredibly courageous soul. Another Holy Night crossing - so many seem to choose these days. Could you send me the name of her partner, whom I never met, so I can write her? I'm so glad and honored to have met her. You go well now. I'll let you know when I'm headed your way. Don't leave. Love, Lee.

Dear Lee,
I'm hoping for the 1st grade job at Summerfield in Sebastopol, but if that doesn't happen, it seems I may be able to get the job at Marin Waldorf. Here is Alissa's email, their son's name is Zaiden: I just looked through some emails, even on the 18th of December they still had all kinds of plans. But on the 20th Alison was told she only had 24 to 48 hours to live. Amazing how she lived so fully right up to the end. Sophia

Dear Sophia
Thanks - though I'd hoped to spend time with her and Zaiden when I got to Berkeley, I guess I just have to be so so grateful to have met her - thanks to you - and now we can visit each other any time any place. Much love, thanks again, Lee

From: MaryJo

Hi dear one, All OK here in FL   Easy day yesterday, out of it from allergies but today got to the local park on the bay. The bay water is brackish and not good for swimming but they have a nice little pool and a Bocce court so I got to swim and watch little Italian men and women play.   Tomorrow I see an old friend whom I used to be in a drama group with and hopefully get to do some work on my workshop. On Saturday (14th or 13th) I will have a Extra Lesson in the Living Room with local grads from the program. This is in keeping with my desire to not go hither and yon all the time. Well the dinner bell is ringing. Can't wait to see you . Hugs, Mary Jo

Hey darling,
Watch the crocs and come home safely. I had a lovely birthday, massage and pajama party, but yesterday learned that that lovely Alison (black woman I thought was a guy in Santa Cruz) died yesterday morning. Cancer raced through her. Don't know if I told you I had spent a glorious day with her and her son, Zaiden, on the beach in San Francisco. She was one of the gutsiest souls I ever met. So she, and Suzanne Bishop down this Christmas (or "up" I should say?) Guess I'm just so glad to have met these folk, but I always ache, don't you, when someone you love crosses. Raises whole question of where I truly want to spend my fast declining years. Did I tell you I've been having *mild fantasies* (why do italics appear I wonder?) of renting a 1 room apt in heart of Berkeley after (if there is an after) I sell my house, and tottling around those lovely streets among all the ancient hippies like myself? I think that's where I have been happiest on this continent. Prescott is being steadily ruined by overdevelopment of the most hideous kind.
I have a new and lovely hike for us, don't have to watch feet, all along through the pink turds, and blue water, and there have been sightings of white freshwater pelicans. I saw a flock of western bluebirds!!   Hope you are still smoking? Meals and coffee without them are like making love without orgasms (did I say that before?) But a second hand whiff comes close to satisfaction (porno thrills?). Love, see you soon, Lee

From: MaryJo: Re: fantasies

Can't wait to walk in pink turds of the gods.   Prescott is beginning to remind me of Lancaster PA. Find something quiet and environmentally pleasant and lots of things come in to ruin it. About the moving. Sounds interesting. I know you have always been high after your visits there to CA. Well if that is where you feel good then you should do it. There will lots of good cheap food and transport and culture. There are still quite a few years before the oceans rise. (I am a bit morose about the future of the planet)
Yes, of course I remember Alison, a very strong character - It is a shame she had to leave so soon. The biggest sadness though - and this is a bit selfish - is that I want more time with folks I love - like you. Taking tableaus of my friends. I have Omar on Monday - delightful, artful, articulate 7th grader who

CANNOT remember anything. What a challenge. I was showing him some memory tricks and he turned to me and said - " Ms Oresti do you think I can weave these same memory boosters into my study tactics? " NOW TELL ME is he gorgeous or what.??? Too bad he can't find his way out of a paper bag - I hope I can help in these few weeks. Hugs Mary Jo

Darling MaryJo All that matters, isn't it, being with those we love. That's all I'm aiming for. Bye, and love you, Lee

From Esther: Sent: Dec 29,

Hello dear Leebelle!
Hope your visit with Adam was all and more than you hoped for. I wish I could just do a quick hop and have one of your hugs! Today is a bit of a "Day".... Helga's death is hard....and Steven so wants to go also.....Where, oh where, can I get beyond the suffering and sense again the joy in life? I know that the "cracks" are where the light comes in....but some days it feels just too hard to go on. And here I am yammering on to you - who has so much more to bear in other ways! Much love and huge hugs, Esther

Hey darling,
Yes, some foundation should pay me $50,000 a year to go round hugging people. Don't need a voice, and I'm so often stunned by how few folk know how to really do it! Well - I have plenty of arm room for you, just my arms are rather far away. The pain of separation is terrible isn't it (I haven't forgotten) - like being skewered over and over? God I remember how deep into the flesh it goes. I will pray for some easement down the road. (Must say, friends brought a gorgeous Aussie architect, 68, for a cuppa recently and we chortled and chortled and he's the first to cross my threshold who said: "Now this house I could live in, built to the Golden Mean I'd guess, and you've got Judy Cassab's paintings, etc etc etc." But he passed on through. Maybe if I had been built to the golden mean he might have been tempted to stay?) It was such a reminder that so much of my soul lies like a stagnant underground pond - never mind the body - because no one here has heard of Judy Cassab. But then I go down the hill and get hugs from Addison - 22, covered in tattoos - and realize I don't want to be with another old fart - one (myself) is quite enough to put up with.
So you hang in there. Here's a little poem written (or maybe quoted?) by a 6th grader after 911 - I'll try to make a copy of the picture Devon also drew:

> *"When you come to the end of all light*
> *and stand at the edge of darkness, faith*
> *is knowing that you will either be given*
> *something solid to stand on in the darkness*
> *or...you will be taught to fly."*

When did Helga die? I didn't know, only that it had sounded pretty close.
Great for her, grim for poor old Stephen. I will write soon. That's the third
death of friends of mine in the past six weeks. Hugs, Lee

From: Ann: Subject: "Sisters"

Thank you friend! That piece moved me to tears. I will treasure it forever! It
felt so good to be included in your sister "list!" Well Lee - May the New Year
bring health and wealth for us all! We can only hope and pray that somewhere
on the face of the earth a bit of peace will begin to shine forth. Today they did
away with Saddam at 6am eastern time. What is he feeling and seeing now
about himself I wonder? Take care and write about Adam's visit. I'm sure you
had a fulfilling time with him. Love, Ann

Dear Ann,
Well, I just wrote you a long letter, pressed a button and whole thing
disappeared. I'll try again. Computer Adam gave me is too sensitive. I need
a coarser version as befits my character! OF COURSE you are one of my
fave sisters, always will be, and I miss you.
Adam and I had a glorious 3 days, bless his big heart. He had to fly back
through Christmas night to work on 26th. Hates his job, can't sleep when he
represents corrupt companies but does beautifully after working on a case
against Rumsfeld! Tomorrow - New Year's Day I have to begin some
writing. I'm really backed into a corner now with that. Do keep me in touch
with your doings, and undoings and all that seem to accompany us as we
move onward and upward again!!! Love Lee

From Sheila: December

Dearest Lee,
Re-rereading your October letter, and then the card and the two email letters
gave me such a vivid sense of the reality of your daily struggle, with the pain
and humour and courage and the despair and, I think, the underlying theme of
curiosity – where does this all lead to? What is it for? Anyway, it's a death-
and-rebirth journey, which is the only kind worth undertaking. My friends are
all saying "there's a lot of Pluto around" and they are probably right. Hard to
accept, though, when it comes to the planet, and – as I've been reading in my
newspaper – the polar bears, now threatened with imminent extinction. That
makes me want to call out STOP! Let's go back to the way we were And the
same with your voice, and those wonderful all-night talk-ins we all used to
enjoy in your parents' flat.
But we have to be where we are and not where we were, so I'm glad to know
that where you are is on the way to a functioning voice (as you put it) more or
less in time for Easter. A different voice, too, extended by its dip into the
unconscious.

In therapy, as you well know, you meet your client's story with what it evokes in you of your own – and healing is engendered in that meeting. In our discourse, your loss of voice matches my loss of balance, which in the last three months has suddenly escalated (14 falls since the beginning of September, most of them on a pavement). It is as though, after years of occasionally falling, I had become programmed to fall. Walking to the local Sainsbury's to buy a newspaper was like dragging a terrified child, or forcing a stubborn horse. I say 'was' because I do deeply sense that the pattern is changing and will eventually give way to something else, but there are still days when I can only inch myself along at a snail's pace, always with a stick. That's the story. Medical tests (a 'Tilt Test' – sounds like jousting) at the local hospital reveal nothing abnormal (one more to come in January, to check blood pressure) and I have been signed off by the NHS Professor of Neurology at Charing Cross, who found he could offer no help. Nothing left to turn to but imagination, together with a marvellous Jungian book by Donald Kalsched (NY analyst) *"The Inner World of Trauma"* which is all about the wounds of early childhood and the need to dismantle defensive structures which may have become a prison to the child still lost in them. Once I began to adopt that idea – perhaps two months ago – I felt I was moving in the right direction with a sense of "getting warmer" to guide me. Much learning was required, many false trails had to be abandoned. One important thing I learned is that you can't make that journey of rescue without, at a certain point, being stripped of absolutely everything you know, psychologically, spiritually, intellectually, so that you become as vulnerable and as defenseless as the inner child you are trying to reach. You come without hope and without power to a place without light and without meaning. I think that is hell! All that's left is a gritty determination: "If a part of me has to live in this state, I'd better get her out of it." I do now feel a response, with a sense of a journey back to the light of day. It seems to me that this sad child (and I did have an appallingly loveless childhood) had taken over legs and particularly feet, perhaps in protest against having to walk on an earth that seemed so unwelcoming. As a toddler, I used to lean out of my nursery window and listen to the music of the spheres. Who'd want to stay on earth after that?! So that's where I am – I think, on the way back and I think, with the prospect of beginning to walk a little more safely and without that gripping terror that made it tempting simply to stay at home. And if I had a computer – as I intend to have very soon – I might have become a successful recluse! By the way, I make absolutely no comparison between my childhood and yours: the common factor is 'loss' and the journey it forces us to take. Synchronicity comes into this too: scaffolding all around, bangs and thumps and clashes, all part of what our landlord calls "Major Works" - and meanwhile, 'major works' for me on the inner structures. Perhaps timing is significant in another way: I shall be 80 on Saturday, and the Jung Club is – amazingly arranging a tea party in my honor. This is rare and special – the last one I can remember was for Laurens van der Post when he was 80. I almost dare to hope that the return journey is meant to belong with the start of a new chapter in a new decade – but nothing can be taken for granted in the world of the psyche, as you and I both know!

Marvelous about Adam's exams, he'll make such a good contribution to his profession. You mention John le Carre – did I ever tell you that he once interviewed me for a secretarial job at MI5 in the 1950's? He was David Cornwell then, looking for junior spies. He didn't choose me! I like his books. He is one of today's real voices, like Michael Frayn and Alan Bennet and Jonathan Miller.

This is not the letter I intended to write, so forgive me for what may seem an irrelevant excursion. It comes with a big hug, lots of love for Christmas and for recovery. Perhaps email in 2007. Sheila

Dearest Sheila,

You said towards the end of your marvelous letter: "this isn't what I intended to write about," but how glad I am that you did, so powerfully and poignantly. I suddenly saw you, not as a child, but now, standing at your window, with all that scaffolding hiding the sky and trees, and hearing the music of the spheres. What an utterly extraordinary memory! I knew your childhood was sad and loveless, but that image captured it as nothing you have ever shared has ever done. Anyhow, with all your incredible descriptions of your/all our journeys to the place of no light, I just felt when that scaffolding is taken down, the Major Works will be accomplished, maybe then you can rest a little for all the work you have done, also on behalf of so many of us.

I also realized our correspondence is and has been the richest I have had with anyone in this life. (I guess because so many correspondences.) I was sorting stuff, and came across stacks and stacks of your letters, each one marvelous. You should have a biographer set up for when you cross. I find myself wishing David could join our conversations sometimes, he would be very enthralled and excited I think at all the insights you have. And I'm sure he'd be fascinated by my voice thing. (Well, of course, somewhere he *is* listening!)

I can hardly believe you are 80. (I seem to remember attending a party for Laurens van der Post with a bunch of Jungians - maybe his 80th? Good company, eh?)

This thing with your legs, my voice, makes me think back to childhood when we came down, and now we are going up again. Steiner says the gift of aging and illness is that we learn how the body is made as a preparation for creating one ourselves, out of the word, the larynx, in future evolution. And also that the three great human capacities:1) uprightness/walking, 2) speech, and 3) memory/self-consciousness emerge out of our relationship with the three hierarchies: angels/memory: archangels/speech, and archai (time spirits, primal beginnings) for walking. And if we could see spiritually as each child struggles to gain a foothold and walk on the earth we would know the particular relationship he or she had to the Archai before birth. Wish I could find the exact pages in whichever lecture. Has a lot to do, too, with our inadequacies in the realm of love. So I wonder what you and I might be forging for the next one as you totter and fall, and I can't sound forth? Didn't

Oliver Sachs write about someone needing to direct every muscle consciously in order to take a step in **The Man Who Mistook His Wife For a Hat?** I'm mailing a book to you. It was a lifesaver for me, by a storyteller who lost his voice. Just very lovely, I found. I'm going to start writing on Monday. New Year's Day, seems appropriate? These letters will be part of what I want to declare to the world - which may not want to hear! So very much love, and hopes that the Major Works will clear a new, beautiful horizons for you. Lee

From: Dawn: Dec 25, 2006

Dearest Lee, It is always so wonderful to receive your uniquely humourous and serious reports on both your own health and the health of the nation. There really can be nothing like them in the annals of English literature. I am so glad there has been some improvement in the state of your larynx and trust that it is continuing. I want to wish you a beautiful if quieter than usual Christmas and Holy Nights and send you all my love and blessings for this and a wonderful new year. Perhaps you are by now on your social security so I just want to warn you about too much excess and tell you that Patricia and I are still looking forward to a visit from you sometime in the next couple of years. So don't go squandering all your wealth.

I have not much to report. I am still in my chrysalis state and feel sort of paralyzed at the idea of saying anything much about myself since who I thought I was for so many years seems to have disappeared and who I am is still emerging. But hopefully by the time you come I will have achieved enough definition for you to be able to see me at the airport and come home with me. I have been in bed for the last month here at Patricia's with a very virulent form of throat and chest infection. I am still not well and spent Christmas Day in bed. If I am not significantly better by the end of the week I am going to start with antibiotics and just knock this thing on the head as they say because I have to fly to England on the 4th and start teaching on the 8th. That will be interesting. Who will it be that will teach? I have no idea but find myself looking forward to finding out. lots of love, Dawn.

Dearest Dawn,
Of course I'm coming. I have a jar with about 17 pennies in it already!!! And Adam and I were talking about it when he was here for the past 3 days. And I meant to write when Pat told me about your poor old larynxes. I'm so sorry. You have to use yours. Probably better if I just shut up!! But you can't teach a dog old tricks and although I love the solitude bit and don't mind being silent then, I seem utterly incapable of controlling my blabbing when I'm with others! (I think I've probably hit the halfway mark in recovery now. Another nine months might do it. I'd thought it would be like a pregnancy, but typically, I have to have an elephantine, rather than human gestation.) I do hope and hope yours recovers enough to teach. You know what I think of your gifts - they arise out of your sufferings, that's why/how they are so true and deep. I'll never forget crumpling on your floor, so "moved" by grief when

trying to sound forth Kathleen Raine. We must both be preparing for next time round, and spending more time together than we have been able to do in this life.

I forget so often I am living in a foreign country, speaking a foreign language, and really on the outskirts of whatever shreds of civilization the US has achieved so far. (Always remember Gandhi when he was asked: "What do you think of western civilization," and he replied: "It would be nice.")
Oh, I do hope England goes well, that you do what you really want to do there. It's awful, isn't it, to go into the abyss of unmaking and then to discover that there has been no real transformation! I was aware over a Christmas Eve dinner we always go to, that my croaking is no more succinct or meaningful than it was before surgery, just this infinitely awful tonelessness has replaced my deliciously raspy, smoke laden sound!! Lee

CHAPTER TEN. LA SCALA POSTPONED.

"Whatever you can do, or dream you can,
begin it..... Begin it now."
Goethe.

Well, I finally have my back to the wall. Can't work or travel. Nothing for it but to begin writing and what better time, I tell myself, than the first of a New Year.

January 2007 also begins to reveal glimmers of change. Not transformation, just little flickers of new awareness. One is, obviously, the fact that this ordeal is going to take way more time than I had thought or hoped. Another is that it may well have opened me to the conviction that I need to leave Arizona. And last, but not least, I begin the long, slow inner wrestling that may lead to my decision not to sue the surgeon. I have had lots of legal advice. There is always a case to be made. I still wake many mornings filled with rage. My life as it has been was effectively destroyed in a casual and, perhaps, unnecessary fashion. I continue to hear from others who have either endured or avoided similar ordeals: all very cold comfort, alas. How could I have been so idiotic? How could my surgeon have been so uninformative? Yet, as I watch or read the news, I have to begin to wonder if I want to add to the conflicts, adversarial consciousness, which characterize our times. Even if I tell myself I don't, I still have a long long way to go to close the gap between an action I may not take, and feelings I have far from laid to rest! As often as I can, I put the whole kit and caboodle on the back burner, and begin to gather the emails that will form the basis of what? Another book, maybe? I also begin my "habit forming" rituals that have got me writing in the past: half an hour a day for the first week, an hour the second and so on, in the hope that when a month has passed I have got hooked. I continue my walks, my therapies, my monastic existence, now passed in front of a roaring woodstove as temperatures plummet in my mountain retreat.

Current correspondence of course continues. Nancy sends the following:

Subject: Fwd: Exercise for seniors

This was tough for me at first.
I came across this exercise suggested for seniors, to build muscle strength in the arms and shoulders. It seems fairly easy, so I thought I'd pass it on. The article suggests doing it three days a week.
Begin by standing on a comfortable surface, where you have plenty of room at each side. With a 5-lb. potato sack in each hand, extend your arms straight out from your sides, and hold them there as long as you can.
Try to reach a full minute, and then relax. Each day, you'll find that you can hold this position for just a bit longer.
After a couple of weeks, move up to 10-lb. potato sacks.

Then 50-lb. potato sacks; then eventually try to get to where you can lift a 100-lb. potato sack in each hand and hold your arms straight for a full minute.
Once you feel confident at that level, put a potato in each sack!

Going to try to call soon. Love, Nancy

Dearest Nancy,
I LOVE it! The potato sacks! I'm still not talking on phone, alas. Sorry about that. I'll be in touch soon, as I won't come till it doesn't strain voice too much. Love you, Lee

I then, naturally, need to forward this to my friends. I am also sent another group letter by someone on Senior Sex, which includes the following tips:

1. Write down the name of the guy in your bed in case you forget who he is.
2. You may light candles but don't forget to blow them all out as soon as you start undressing.

It is quite amazing what one can find to do instead of knuckling down to the creative act! I clean house, make chicken soup, bring in firewood, anything to avoid that moment of sitting down and working - on what? Do I have another book in me? And might it be better in than out? On the other hand I am increasingly appalled by my unproductive lifestyle and that somehow spurs me on, at least for my initial half hour a day. One of the most interesting discoveries of these months is that without a voice I seem to have lost most of my actual being, never mind the "doing" part. (This seems illustrated in one way by the fact that I find it next to impossible to type a Capital letter "I". It invariably comes out in lower casing, i.e. "i". Even that can slow down the literary input.)   There's a general sense of implosion, a deep withdrawal from the surrounding world, at least the human one. I still feel called out by birds, skies, rocks and whispering trees. But any other engagements seem beyond me, and, alas, the engagement with any possibly developing inner life is the hardest of all. I know there are lots of amazing silent contributors to the life of the world. This could well be the seed of a desert monastic epiphany. But I suspect not, and at this point I think I am more likely due for some Sloth of the Year Award. A verse of a May Sarton poem comes to inspire me, as her poetry so often does.

> *"Silence, a membrane. Somehow I must get through*
> *Into the universe where stars still flock,*
> *To the rich world not empty but wide open,*
> *Where soul quietly breathes and is at home."*

And letters keep me from the black holes.

From: Steph, Jan 5: Subject: Checking In.

Hi! Thinking about you right now. How is the cord healing process (if not progress!) coming along? I ask in a _pal_ context; not a workshop context! Mainly, are you at least pain free?

The week with my brother was the best I've spent with him since he married his current wife. Then it was all systems go, with work, Christmas stuff (which for a while there I just wanted to cancel!), and the continuing chaos from the house building. Jana chose pretty wild colors for the inside of the house, which we are painting now. There is sort of an Easter egg effect, with every room a different and fairly wild color. Not the light & bright white of her boring old parents' home. The architect thinks it's all terrible. At some point last week I turned 63 and yes, have thought about "retirement." But don't really know how to do it, financially or practically. I'd be real happy to cut back, but wonder how in the hell to bow out in stages, when almost everything I do is connected to the whole picture? Write when you can & feel like it. I do so hope things are better for you! But write even if they are not. Mucho love and a happier 2007, Steph

Dearest Steph,

Well, I think we are clairvoyant, certainly joined at some kind of spiritual hip. My thinking of you had been increasing in intensity so that today was the day I planned to write, check in with you, say how much I was missing you - and voila, here you come!!

House building does sound hell. Hard to picture it - a multicolored blot between you and the mountains? Well, I guess, I hope, I'll see it soon enough. Briefly, the cords are improving. I have a small, unreliable, whine now. This trip will be my debut, coming out. May also be a swansong!!!

So glad you had a great trip with your brother, sounds marvelous and isn't it just, when we suddenly have special days with a family member that are often quite unexpected. I wish you lived on the mainland, more precisely in northern California. I am so tempted to return there. I just want to end my days tottering hand in hand along beaches with those I love.

Well, 63!! When is your birthday? We must be close (Mine 27 Dec). It is an extraordinary challenge for you, I can see that. I am really retired now from the point of view of earning anything to speak of (now I can't speak), and my $129 a month social security doesn't stretch far. Backed tight in my corner now, and started to write this week (an hour a day of balderdash until something maybe begins to emerge.) I'll put house on market in spring. I don't even know if I should or want to stay here. My spirit/soul kin are elsewhere. We can discuss both our futures. Many hugs, Lee

From: Teri Jan 19, 2007

Dear Lee, How is your voice? The last I heard from you, you were experimenting with croaking. No I think it went further than that. I believe you had found a good speech therapist and were making progress. Can you update me?

We are doing well. Last night we experienced a winter storm, an Orcan, which did quite a bit of damage nationwide. The winds in the mountains gusted to 198 kilometers an hour. Mostly though they raged at about 125 kilometers per hours during the most intense time. I saw pictures from England. It was worse there.

John is feeling well and working quite a bit. He is fully integrated into his old community and he and the priest who is now there like each other and compliment each other well. His sermons are full of hope and joy. He is teaching prayer and meditation, and has made opportunity out of what first appeared to be a quality of life threat. He has renewed his interest in Christian healing, something he laid aside when he became a Christian Community priest and has found a way back to it, without falling into a naïve form of faith, not that there is anything wrong with that! Grace upon grace, I tell you.

I returned to my work at *Musikseminar* but will not stay long. I became very independent in Arizona and won a self confidence that I will not surrender. It's great being 56! I'm beginning to tell it like it is.

How is it there in Prescott? How is Joan? Sharon? My English is becoming stiff and my German isn't much better, but I try. Have you gotten snow? How is your health? So much I want to know. I am seeing Marion in Feb. You already know that. We are going to stay in Delft in a cute hotel. I can't wait to see my friend. I miss her terribly. At the end of this month I am flying to Miami to meet my children for a long weekend. What I most look forward to is just being silly with them. Good old American superficial silliness.

I plan on coming to Arizona sometime in April...I hope. Maybe I could sing with some folks in Prescott and then stay with you a night. Dear Lee, I hope your voice is improving, I really do. I can't wait to hear from you.

Much love to you in this new year. I wish you health, a loud healthy voice so I can hear your famous laugh again...this time you will record it and send to me, so that when I have had enough of these sober northern Germans I can just play a recorded loop of you laughing. Your cackle could cure the world.
Love Teri

Dearest Teri,

Oh, how wonderful to hear from and about you, and THAT YOU MAY COME TO ARIZONA IN APRIL? I'll ask Joan about singing. I haven't used phone in 9 months, I go nowhere except to the park to walk, so I am very out of touch.

Oh, Teri, I too would like to hear my throaty laugh again - no such luck yet. (Hearing my old voice inside my head makes me so so sad.)

According to one voice pundit, who said "don't quote me", so I'm quoting him, I was "butchered"! I think my surgeon is an excellent generalist, who may have lacked the years of experience in this particular delicate procedure. Of course it is vastly improved from when I went to Marion in August and could only whisper. I can make sound - with no tone, no musicality, nothing that I associate with a true human voice. This week everything decided to hurt again, which is so weird and infuriating because it has nothing to do with whether I use it or not. Anyhow, as you may surmise, I'm in a bit of a January, winter, slump. - from which I will doubtless recover! I have behaved SO well, done all I was told, so WHY are my acoustics worse this month than 2 months ago? Not fair, eh? But maybe that's the lesson. Life isn't. It isn't for the poor Iraqis. It isn't for the people in Darfur. It isn't for anyone who finds themselves faced with an irreversible handicap, like my young friend Drew McPherson who jumped in American River last June and is paralyzed. So that's my situation. Really backed into a corner now, so have begun to write. Well, I am also going to send you a nice little exercise program, and when you have read that you will understand what I mean when I say "I'm lifting the sacks, just haven't put in the potatoes yet".

Yes, I saw the storms - it's incredible how the earth is heaving in protest? I'm so so saddened by it all. Even sending Bush and Cheney to Gitmo isn't going to turn this all around. But you would be proud of your people, roused now like a beast. And the satire is wonderful. After the proposed "troop surge", the Colbert Report (after Daily Show) had this, more or less, to say:

"Well, I'm proud of my Commander in Chief proposing a "Surge", so much sexier than a troop 'increase' (that's for the Democrat wimps), more like 'surging between some woman's thighs'. But, Mr. President, 20,000 isn't nearly enough. Nor is 50,000 as McCain suggests. Nor, really, is 100,000. What I suggest is 300 million Americans - that's every man, woman and child, - are sent to Iraq. Then you've solved the Homeland Security problem. Well, wait a minute, we must obviously exclude gays, but we know we don't need to protect them..... but that still allows us to send, say 200 million.."!!!!

(By the way, I noticed Condi Rice used the words 'troop augmentation" - the whole thing reads like ads for viagra, penis enhancement, doesn't it. If it wasn't so tragic, it would be hilariously pathetic.) Oh, Teri, I'd better stop. I am so glad John is happy. I am so glad Marion is coming to play with you. I am so glad you are coming here. Just let me know and I will put lovely flannel sheets on the bed. Can't wait. Miss you, love to you both, Lee

Dear Lee,
It was so good to hear from you but not good to hear of your ongoing dilemma. My God what did that doctor do to you? As for your regression, I can only say that frequently in voice training, a student makes a breakthrough and then suffers a physical (soul-caused) setback. This can be intense and cause despair. I experienced that during my voice recovery. And I know of countless cases of the same. In your case, you have raw cords, your poor babies! God, you need to proceed slowly and carefully. You can imagine the ideal voice and speak in your mind, for instance a poem, a lovely, inspiring, healing poem. Naturally your vocal cords will take the correct positions, sympathetically function as if you were actually speaking, but it can have such a strong etheric effect that it could work right into your physical condition and then maybe you would bleed. Try it and see what happens.

Mostly it is healing, because you are dealing with the etheric realm. But you are in such a delicate condition, that you need to be careful.

Love, I am ashamed to say that while in Arizona, I was so lonely and felt so isolated that I ended up becoming a HGTV addict. (Home and Garden). I kept watching renovations of old damaged houses into wonderful functional homes (wow, a therapist could really have a holiday with that one) and designer's challenges. 3 designers bid on a renovation or garden design and only 1 wins the job. Of course, I could usually choose the one the people would choose, because I am such a good anthroposophist I have become a little clairvoyant. I even watched reruns. Oy vay.

I too am really upset about the war in Iraq. It is horrible. It is so interesting here, the way the Europeans see so clearly what is going on there. But things hopefully will change with the new congress. I saw as I came home tonight that 100 people died today. I added it up and realized that if a hundred people in our village died per day that in 15 days our village wouldn't exist. That is sobering. It's true there is so much suffering in the world. I think if I saw just a fraction of what is going on, I would pass out. To think: Saddam was executed during the twelve holy nights. The whole thing was disgusting. I am so against the death penalty. The European Union won't allow any country who exercises the death penalty in.

Okay, I don't want to write about those things anymore. I want to concentrate on the good, the beautiful and true. I believe in this trinity and I believe that when just one person strives after these realities the world can be healed. It sounds so naïve and simple. But I believe it. I remember when I was doing gospel music, a priest friend and activist wanted me to become more political because my music was known and I had a national reputation. I had the feeling that that was not my task. I think he lost a little respect for me, but after finding Steiner I felt supported in my conviction. When I do my art for the right reasons, its fruit is a protest against inequity, its fruit shows the shadow, and so on. Therefore I stay in my art world, but with my eyes open and I allow these things to pierce my heart so that my conscience is honed and my intentions are purified.

I became very depressed over the Christmas holiday. I am I believe still in my third moon node and I am going through the eye of the needle. Right now my head is sticking out on the other side, but my ass is so big I can't get it through! I am trying to eat less....Well, actually instead of eating lots of fat I am rubbing more Weleda lavender oil on my thighs. I think it's working. I am not as stuck as I was. This move threw me for a loop! And John's tumor was really a wake up call.

I want to do a work and I want to serve the spiritual world. I want to work on the picture of the human being, to be a witness in this world. I've been thinking a lot lately of what it means to be a real witness. John and I have been having discussions about the Priest as witness. The one who accompanies others by witnessing and confirming their human struggle, their natural tendency to strive, their struggle with their destinies... Ah, Lee, life is good. Grace upon grace I tell you. Our sickness is our healing. But still I am so moved by your struggle, your pain, your desperation. I stand with you in this time. Please write back, because I love hearing from you. Love Teri

Dearest Teri,
Thank you! Seems you step in with comforting and empowering words just when I've hit rock bottom. This now the second time, with imagining the sounding of poems, which I did and will continue to do. It was heartbreaking when I realized I could not, might never, quote a poem again. And I have a bad case of Soggy Bottom Blues since the no smokes, think I'll try the lavender oil, God knows no-one else is paying my thighs any attention!!. Anyhow, I am so grateful. Maybe, if this thing is ever over - I'm told my voice will always be weaker now - I will be grateful somewhere for the experience of learning how to create vocal cords, because they have to grow out of what movements I make don't they? *"Form is movement come to rest"!* And we would not have had these mighty, transforming exchanges ourselves - you and I. Oh, how I wish I had known you were watching reruns of HGTV. Maybe I'd better try that as an alternative to my reruns of **Without a Trace.** As a "recovering psychotherapist" myself, yes, it's pretty obvious, you trying to restore a crumbling soul, and I trying to find a lost person!
As far as the wider world and its terrible suffering, I just sometimes ask the Christ to give me the pain that I, Lee, can bear. It gets very acute, almost body dissolving, but after 15-20 minutes I feel it lifted off me. As you see I have a ways to go.
(I met a young women once in a wheelchair, and after my workshop she asked if she could share something with me. We went out under the stars and she said: "I've never told anyone else, but 4 years ago I was so overwhelmed by the suffering in the world I asked the Christ to let me carry some of it so someone else might not have to. And the following day I had my car accident that left me paralyzed.")!
You have your art as a healing, I know. Michael Thomas (SF Symphony conductor) once spoke of "the underlying ache of all great music", I guess connecting us with the spiritual world, the painful reminder of how far we have fallen? I remember a storyteller once saying we must live and work *"inter canem et lupum"*: (between the dog and the wolf), where the firelight fades into the dark, and lean towards the light and create beauty. That's what you do for and with us.
No, I'm not particularly political. My first protests were vigils (I must have been around 15/16) outside prisons in England the night before a hanging, and we did feel that helped end death penalty. Yes, this country is utterly barbaric still. (Interesting how the Pro Lifers have no problem with Death Penalty!) I think as I do my **Women in Black** every Friday, 1hr silent vigil for peace, how I've come full circle. I do love a good protest march, though. The solidarity of folk when one gets desperate. And the songs! And I've been an Amnesty letter writer for 20 years, since they began. So interesting to see my son taking up all this and much much more.
Your description of your art is what I experience from you and it, anytime I listen. It is wonderful, pierces our souls. Just because (or maybe because) I

can't join in, I can listen better. An amazing novel **Riddley Walker** by Russell Hoban, written in phonetic English, a parable of 200 years after a nuclear holocaust, all written language lost, has as its chief character The Lissener, whose task is to "lissen to the silents" as a way of saving the world from the World Owl who is trying to eat silences, and thereby destroy the earth.

In a way, I'm not surprised, though saddened, by the depression you went, may still be going through. Is it grief? You have to balance moon (John) and Sun (work) karma is one thing. And we are always homeless now, unable to quite slot into either culture, the one we left, the one we embraced. I'm so glad John has found his place back in Germany. Can be quite rare to do that. And you are surely in the stream that can never stay, rest at the center of a community - and that carries its own particular pain? You are one of the blood corpuscles that travels in and out of the heart, enabling it to beat. Old Kings at the center. Heroes and Fools (that's me) going out to periphery, and bringing renewing forces back. Now, girl, I mustn't take more of your time. Just THIS! PLEASE COME FOR THREE NIGHTS IN APRIL. Book a flight, keep singing, love you, Lee.

From: MaryJo Subject: Exercise for seniors

What a hoot. Love the exercise. Well I have good news and bad news - or maybe just the facts. I have decided that Rob and I will come to AZ in Dec for Christmas next year. However, I can not make up my mind regarding April. June feels better. Joan sent me a photo of Adam and her baby grandson. How sweet they looked. Hugs Mary Jo

You know, my darling, I think April is too soon for me. Sorry to be so repellent. That's how I am these days: very depressed, very scared, and get anxiety attacks that close voice off at thought of needing to converse, just want to dig a big hole, crawl in, have some kindly friend put earth over top, who maybe comes and digs me out a year later. Also going through bouts of flaming jealousy as others are "so appreciated for doing such wonderful work in your place" etc. Hope you understand. Love, Lee

My dear Lee , I am so sorry you have to go through this. So here I am thinking of you and wondering what could I say that could be truly supportive? Except to say that I love you dearly and I recognize your need to pull in and hunker down so intensively. Life has changed so much for you that I guess the new processes you are experiencing will show up in all kinds of ways. About your jealousy. YOU CAN NEVER be matched You are the queen of biography. It runs in your veins. Every group has been ecstatic working with you because you can go with the flow so incredibly. That is not learned. It is a gift and a talent that has arisen from practice and dedication. I bet that even after we all cross over you will be pointing out the "milestones" and saying something like "Mary Jo watch out - look over there ---- Jupiter is trying to talk to you." Be well and as happy as you can. Did you get the men's bathroom email? Your loving friend, Mary J

My darling,
When I read your letter I wanted you here now, so we could hug and go for a long walk together. And as soon as we can I will let you know and we can make merry and I'm sure chirophonetics is just the job. And thank you thank you for your words about me and that I'm not totally irreplaceable. I tell you, probably the only good thing to come out of this ordeal will be that it might be easier to die. I seem to have had to let go of just about everything and everyone I hold most dear and that I consider made and makes me who I am. OH, I LOVE YOU AND WILL BE SO HAPPY WHEN WE CAN BE TOGETHER AGAIN. Lee (No men's room email..?)

From Signe: Subject: Exercise for seniors

This is perfect!! Just my style. And I unfortunately do have the dreaded osteoporosis -- or is this just the latest fad word for an aging body? Can't write much now. January is turning out to be very full already, even in retirement. And always complicated by Linda's situation, which now I think is very near the end. We'll head up there tomorrow. We may put in an offer on a house in Brooklyn today ... seems pretty good -- and is surprisingly big for the city – two bedrooms and a big finished room in the basement. So come along!! It's a good walk to where Adam is living. I hope you are continuing to have ever more voice. Happy New Year! Love, Signe

Dearest Signe,
First, I will be thinking of you all, Linda and Bob, and do please if/when you have time, keep me posted. Sorry about the osteoporosis. I think Americans suffer mainly from SDS "Surplus Diagnoses Syndrome". 100 years ago we wouldn't know what we'd got, or we'd be dead!!! Hope it doesn't hurt. That's all I worry about, not good with pain. Yes, we are definitely moving into a "chronologically gifted" phase. I think you will LOVE being in the city. I think cities are for "our age dear". (Did I ever tell you a friend's description of the 3 ages of man? **The Young, Our Age Dear**, and **Simply Wonderful**. I'm heading towards **Simply Wonderful**.) Much love, Lee

To: Adam Day Re: Nothing in particular

Darling Adam,
I'm sending a mini care package today assuming you haven't been fired yet. Do hope your boxes arrived safely? Do you have copies of emails you sent me, I seem to have lost a lot of them? I forgot to say how much I enjoyed Margaret Attwood. The chief character says she was never interested in keeping a journal because she knew what she would say in it, and it was so much more interesting to hear from someone else (viz your letters to me)!! Love you, Mum

Dear Mum,

I am completely swamped right now, but will definitely look out the emails. I think some may have been lost forever, but I give you full license to invent them as you choose fit!

Glad you liked the Attwood. I'm most of the way through **March** and it's very good. I didn't realize at first, but it's a retelling of Alcott's **Little Women**, but much more grisly. I think my aversion to US history sometimes makes me forget what a feat it was to win the civil war. Quite amazing to think how recently this country had slavery institutionalized, and how many Americans supported it.

I've taken on a lot more work on this Rumsfeld case. Doing my regular grind gets me so tired, but as soon as I turn to this human rights work I feel awake again. I'm hoping that I'll get to keep this on the side as long as I'm at Curtis-- it makes all the difference.

And I did not get fired. I had my review two days ago and the partner said that I had had some difficulty hitting the nail on the head with my memos, but had a good attitude and that I would improve with practice. So I'm in the clear for now. It is absolutely frigid here this week. I could feel little bits of ice near my eyes on my walk to the subway this morning. Not to fear, I have good woolies, gloves, hats, etc... and I'm not afraid to ruin my business attire by wearing them. Have you seen the new Idi Amin movie: **The Last King of Scotland**. I'm going to see it this weekend. Also, **Thank You For Smoking** is hilarious and very well done. Back to the document review. Lots of love, A

Darling Adam,

Don't worry about the emails until you have time. As you once told me, everything I attributed to you was pure fantasy anyway. Yes, I saw it was frigid (it's zero to 20 here now, and I wondered about wearing underwater goggles, or those goggles welders use? Sure Curtis would be very impressed if you showed up in those.) Glad you didn't get fired, though it must be a misery doing that kind of work. So I, too, hope you can keep on the Rumsfeld case. And find other ways of restoring yourself - good literature, food, art, guitar? And friendship!

Glad you are enjoying **March** (or, by now enjoyed it). Yes, I wonder so much if every nation has to go through all its stages of development, no way of short circuiting any, and the US is still at a fairly fledgling stage. This latest move is atrocious isn't it. I suppose Bush has nothing left to lose now, so his only weapon is "history will vindicate me, the God King!" Tragic. Well, you haven't time for my blather. I now assume the boxes reached you? I do hope so, and your room is happily lined with books. I had voice setbacks this month. Nothing to worry about, just part of my Job's patience journey, I guess. Gotta drink another 5 galls water daily (not very tempting in subzero temps, rather wish Pinot Noir had been prescribed) and learn to breathe like an opera singer so I put no stress on cords. Keep warmish, love you, Mum

From: Judith: Subject: Exercise for seniors

I don't have potato sacks! But I do do a little gentle yoga most days, and some not-at-all-gentle yoga once a week, so will that do? What do you do to keep energy levels up? Rather dreary January weather here, but Jon has just arrived for a few days' rest and recuperation, and is at this very moment making custard to go with our rhubarb crumble. I'm very glad to have him here! (Can you get rhubarb in Arizona?) Lots of love, Judy

Dear Judith, Not much rhubarb in Arizona. Gosh how I remember the crumbles you would make for **Momo's**!!! Well, since I became disabled, I walk a lot. Not much else to do and I've basically been running away from myself for past nine months because I still crave the smokes so badly. I've begun to try to write, but more along the lines of laying out the potato sacks, no potatoes in any yet. It is honestly hard to think when you don't speak. Well, at long long last we got a little snow yesterday, so soon, when it gets light I shall go and walk in it and smell it. There is NOTHING to compare to the smell of snow or rain in the desert - it is amazing. Definitely not like Wales or Shropshire. Much love. Lee

From: Adam Day

Dear Mum,
Got your stress package yesterday, thank you!. I took about five drops of that stuff and was out like a light all night. It could have been the drops, it could have been the fact that I had worked 15 hours straight, but who am I to say what causes and effects are? I think it was the drops though.
Had an interesting email today: a friend of a friend is looking for a young lawyer to go to Cambodia and train Cambodian lawyers in impact litigation (mostly human rights, land ownership stuff). I have tentatively thrown my CV into the mix, just to see. Back to my memos. Hope your voice is doing well. I read somewhere that when one reads and writes, one's larynx actually moves slightly along with the words. Maybe your writing a book will be all the exercise it needs to get back in shape. Lots of love and thank you again for the package, A

Darling Adam,
SO happy to hear about the drops. I am in middle of reading a pretty astonishing book **Left To Tell**, by Immaculee Ilibagiza, sole survivor in her family in the Rwandan holocaust. She now lives on Long Island and works at UN. Yes, it is very fascinating about the cords moving sympathetically. When you speak to me, my cords imitate your words etc. Keep warm, it looks pretty nippy where you are. Love you, Mum

Drew McPherson's Holiday Greeting

Dear family and friends, Merry Christmas and a Happy New Year to you all. I apologize for not writing sooner but I have been busy with the holiday season, as I'm sure you all have been as well. Besides visiting with family and friends, I have been busy trying to keep up with my therapies as usual. Between mat work and weight lifting as well as standing up in my standing frame one hour a day I manage to find time to do my visualization and weekly visits to Dr Zhu's acupuncture in San Jose. My strength is gradually increasing as is my upper body functioning. I have gained vertical control of my arms allowing me to turn lights on and off in the house. This holiday season has presented me with a new and enjoyable challenge of tearing open letters and wrapped presents with my teeth, and the therapeutic exercise of picking up cookies and grandma's fudge; the perfect ending to every holiday meal. I have mustered up a bit of new fervor for the New Year and have put in my application to Project Walk, a rehab program based in southern California. It is a rigorous exercise program intending to support recovery. You can check it out online if you are interested. I am also signing up for an adaptive weight training class at American River College (our local community college) allowing me access to essential equipment to further develop my strength and mobility, not to mention the opportunity to get out of the house and meet new people in a variety of situations. In addition to this I am going to UCD rehabilitation center for an evaluation and possibly some outpatient therapy as was requested by the Shriners' rehab program because they do not do outpatient therapy. I am going to be even more busy, but its good. I wanted to let you know that my parents have set up an account in my honor through the NTAF, National Transplant Assistance Fund which manages donations for people with catastrophic injuries. The purpose of this fund is to assist me in my recovery; the work I am committed to doing, the equipment I am going to need to accomplish my goal as well as the therapies which we believe are beneficial to my recovery. It is a 501C3 and donations can be sent in my honor. Thanks a million for all of your support. I once again invite anyone who is willing or interested to come pay us a visit and help out with exercises. As mom acknowledges, it is a great workout; she doesn't need to go to the gym. There may be cookies too. Andrew McPherson

Hey, my dearest Myra,
It was so wonderful to get Drew's letter and the photos (tho' you look almost transparent and I so wanted to take you in my arms, and rock you!) I've written snail mail. This boring little request I am making, however , to put us in the bcc box for group emails. That way we don't get sent dozens of ads for penis enlargement etc. First thing in the morning seeing up close and personal pics of enlarged penises is not my fave thing! I think of you all almost all the time. I love you all all of the time! May 2007 bring much healing. Lee

Certainly dear Lee, Thanks for the advice,. I am such a slug at this e mail business anyway and I certainly am past my prime at caring about enlarged penises. I feel a bit transparent and do feel like I only exist in the arms of my angels; I spend lots of my time crying when I am not caring for Drew which is most of my waking hours. It isn't that I don't want to do it or even feel honored at times to be able to be with him but it is just so all consuming and when people like you tap into my heart the flood gates open in overwhelm. My house looks like it was hit by a cyclone and my sanguine or ADHD tendencies are working overtime these days. Oh well it must be good preparation for something. My love to you. I hope to send my own letter soon to all but in the evenings when I am done about 11 p.m. I just head for the barn and almost always fall asleep before my head nestles into the pillow. Myra

Oh, my friend, I knew it was like that for you, even without your photo, and I wish my arms were longer and stronger and I could enfold you in them and rock you to sleep. Just know there is someone trying to hold you as best she can because of all the great souls I've been allowed to meet, you are one of the greatest. I've imagined so often how it might be when the adrenalin runs out, when even your community turn towards other tragedies. I once asked a friend, whose daughter I've known and loved since she was five, so for 30 years, was spending year after year in mental hospitals, what he thought he forging through the experience. He said, "just the tenacity to get up each morning and face another day of no change" (well, I think he probably put it a little more poetically). And I asked: "Is that ALL!!" Even the angelic hierarchies don't have to use bodies to keep our show on the road, and don't even know what it must feel like as you crawl into your bed each night. Now you just let me know what, if anything, I can do for you, please, other than to keep loving you and I couldn't stop that ever. Lee

From: Lee Sturgeon Day
Sent: Jan 16, 2007
Subject: La Scala Postponed

Dear Friends,
I promised I wouldn't send another group email. This is to my Northern Californian friends only (do you know you represent 20% of my global email address list? What does that mean I wonder?)
Anyway, I know I had spoken of coming this spring, after I cancelled the fall, and, alas, I will have to postpone again. I'm still a long way from being healed. I had thought, optimistically, that nine months was an appropriate time to gestate and give birth to a new voice. Now, I suspect, as a very slow developer, I'm looking at the time frame for pregnant elephants. My therapist is still hopeful, but this last visit and home movie revealed cords as still raw in places, and my acoustics - well, you truly don't want to hear them.

Now I'm being taught to breathe like opera singers, so I don't stress them.
Alas, it won't mean I can ever sing!!! So La Scala definitely for next lifetime.
I'm still hopeful I'll be able to pay you a visit next fall. Nothing left for me
but to hunker in and write - darn it! I realized there was absolutely no point
in coming unless I could lift the phone, make a date and either walk a beach
or sit in Simple Pleasures coffee house and have a conversation without
stress. I miss each and every one of you hugely. So please just stay where
you are, and wait for me!!!! And I wish that 2007 can bring all kinds of good
events, even miracles, to all of you, and to the world. Much love, Lee

From: Lalla

Dearest Lee:

Happy New Year! News of you from Meg made me very happy, hearing
that your spirits are as high as can be and that your voice is fairly fine,
considering that it encourages people to speak more softly and listen more
keenly. Such a service to humanity!
We had Karen and Paul and other friends with us on Christmas Eve and, for
the first time in ten years, we found ourselves sharing our traditional
Christmas celebration. It was very special, and made me realize that I have to
stretch more to make gatherings happen! Karen and Paul are wonderful
people, and no wonder your friends! I finally saw their couch and it might
actually be better than mine! Anyway, it is too bad that I won't see you this
spring, and I look forward to your visit in the fall. Lots of love, Lalla & Co.

Thanks, my friend, and let's have one of your wonderful Italian festivals
when I come, please!! Meg told me about the gathering, and the thought of
being with you all again someday inspires and comforts me (had a big relapse
this month, all the pain back again, darn it, but this too will pass.) Love Lee

From: My dear Doctor Friend

Dear Lee It's possible that all of us do not have the voice that we had in high
school. But you have the best excuse for not opening at La Scala in our
present life time. Meg is on her round the world trip, as you probably know.
We here at home in sunny, cold San Francisco, are trying to do without
Saturday night Indian food and an **Inspector Poirot** movie, watched with
Zeke barking at passers by. In a word you know how it is to miss her. I am
getting ready to visit my son in northern Florida in March. Love, DDF.

So January draws to a close, marking nine months since my operation. I had
so hoped that "gestation" period would have brought forth the birth of a new
voice. But, as I mention somewhere, I seem to have moved into a non-human

category. My voice resembles something from the animal kingdom, so quite probably my recovery is going to imitate some large slow birthing mammal. I hope it isn't a false pregnancy. Some days it is truly hard not to despair. This seems to be the month for a poem (Mary Oliver's **In Blackwater Woods**) that captures this whole horrible business of loosening from what one has cherished and taken for granted for so long.

> *To live in this world*
> *You must be able to do three things:*
> *To love what is mortal;*
> *To hold it*
> *against your bones, knowing*
> *your own life depends on it;*
> *and when the time comes*
> *to let it go*
> *to let it go.*

CHAPTER ELEVEN. LENTEN JOURNEY.

"Only the curious
have, if they live, a tale
worth telling at all...
And what he has to tell
On each return from hell
is this: that dying is what the living do,
that dying is what the loving do
and that dead dogs are those who do not know
that hell is where, to live, they have to go."
Alistair Reid.

February is a classic dark month. Lent invariably begins in it. Although our weather is better than most – Adam claims the liquid in his eyeballs freezes on the way to the subway – it is colder than usual and no rain or snow. We can't even water frozen ground This is so hard on plants, trees and shrubs, and we'll see that soon enough in whatever passes for Spring. In the nine years that I've lived here I can really feel the earth dying, all its vitality draining away. So, too, this year is mine!

I'm probably depressed. If I were someone who went to doctors, I'm sure that would be the diagnosis. In my twenties, after a particularly brutal series of losses and betrayals, I simply went out and bought large bars of chocolate and burrowed under the bedcovers, only emerging over a 6 month period to go to work, come home, eat and fall asleep again. In retrospect, that was undoubtably clinical depression. Similarly in the year after I emigrated here and was abjectly miserable, (with what I think were legitimate good reasons) and within a hair's breadth of anorexia – weighing around 80lbs – I'm sure I would have been diagnosed depressive then. On both occasions time worked its wonders. I'm sure it will now too. This period falls short of the previous ones, in misery ratings, or I'm just more adept at living through such times. I daren't buy chocolate because my hips and thighs are expanding in alarming directions and I always bear in mind that, slender as I may appear to a fairly obese population I did have one great aunt who grew too fat to fit in a train!

As we know, depression is anger turned inwards. I can sense that quite frequently. I think it would be far easier if I had been told to be utterly silent, not to use my voice at all. There is a deep pull in me to that place of silence, a great longing not to speak for a long long time. It is why I love the **Taize** services so much, and my quiet home, and my times communing with creatures born without sound. But at least three times a day I have to use this useless voice of mine. Everytime I do the exercises, I am pulled outward again, but without even the benefit of decent sound. It is also good to exercise my cords within reason when I am walking with my doggy friends. It's a bit like longing to sleep and being jerked awake over and over again,.

Stuck in my burrow, I can't even pull branches and leaves over my head and hibernate this winter through.

I'm also sickeningly aware that there have been no changes, no epiphanies. When I converse I am the same old blatherer. So this suffering so far has been for naught. Just plain old pain, physical and emotional. At least so far. At a time when I would love to meet the best in myself, all I can find is the worst!!! Oh, how classic can you get!

This is the month I try to accept the slow pace of recovery and battle through to a decision not to sue my surgeon, even though there are many dark nights when I feel he deserves that, and I deserve some compensation. Yes, a good lenten experience I'm sure, to wrestle with inner demons, and to feel so often how puny and inadequate my spiritual biceps are!

The final straw, too, is that I cannot tolerate the idea of even my best beloved of friends coming to offer solace, or company or whatever else they would bring. Like some mangy old lion trapped in its cage, I don't want anyone entering it, sharing my meat and then leaving again. I can't leave. I can't rejoin the world. Also, more understandably, what is the point of friends coming when we can't converse? I have enough on my plate taking care of myself. And yet, without them, I have this huge sense of loss. This extends to a real loss of self. It is interesting that we use the expression "to have a voice" to mean a lot more than being physically heard. Our voice stands for our real space on earth, our true being, our human and spiritual entitlement and reality. Without a physical voice I feel I am vanishing. This is ridiculous! Many exist who never speak. One of my favorite weekly encounters is with a young deaf mute man in the meat department of our local health food store. He is the only person I know in town with whom I feel true compatibility. He clearly and magnificently exists. His smile can set me up for a week. But this is my experience right now. And I certainly haven't reached the smiling stage yet. Oh, I know that great quotation that we need to "lose oneself to find oneself", but I've only got as far as the lost part, and found nothing, no-one yet.

So, all in all, February signals a time of dreary struggle. But, in true British fashion, I soldier on, immensely fortified by my correspondence, initially from my beloved friend Sheila in London. She has always known about dark times, and met them with unparalleled courage and integrity.

Sunday 28th January, from Sheila

Dearest Lee,

Two surprise packages – first your letter on the back of the poem: **"Let This Be the Year":** I'd never heard of Paula Sullivan and liked the poem. It's good to be reminded about "gratitude for the body" when mine has been behaving so oddly. And I was truly delighted to hear that you had read my heart poem to your group, and that it had been well received. A migrating bird landing safely! For that, I felt real gratitude.

And then, next day, that marvellous little book! **(The Beggar King and The Secret of Happiness)** It has become my favourite bedtime reading, and I'm now half way through it (and resisting the temptation to cheat by peeping at the ending – did he regain his voice? I'll just have to wait.) But I do want to know about your voice – where it is, how it is, how you are? I'm anyway glad you chose this brave and funny book to bring me another take on 'loss', which could at the same time be a marginal note on your own.

I hope you've had a satisfying Christmas. I think you said Adam would be with you this year? And then your birthday and the start of a personal new year. I had decided that my 80th birthday would slip past without any fuss, but with no prompting on my part the Jung Club arranged a tea party for the people I knew best – perhaps twenty, or a few more. I think I may already have given you an account of this party? It remains a warm and cheering memory, (including the chocolate cake with eight twisty candles,) in the middle of a season of quite extraordinary stress and complexity. If becoming 80 has to be seen as a rite of passage, then maybe it needed to be accompanied by the massive rebuilding works in our square, the noise and dust, the frequent intrusions – though workmen are always polite – and the sheer unpredictability of the various stages of the work. That's the outer environment (and it will continue like this at least until April/Easter). And the inner one isn't much better, though I do struggle to hold on to the idea that all this is meaningful and is somehow necessary. But I don't always manage it! Added to this, I now have to pay about Seventeen Hundred Pounds per quarter for the next three years – it feels like robbery, but is actually perfectly legal. However the very worst is that, having had a massive number of falls in the autumn, I have now developed a kind of neurotic terror of walking on pavements – a terror that lives in my legs rather than in my head, making it very difficult to walk much further than the local corner shop and the bus stop, and only that far at snail's pace. There are lots of good and helpful factors – above all, the patience and kindness of friends, and my ability to use the subsidised taxi scheme for disabled people; this enables me to go to the odd theatre or lecture or longer distance shopping and I'm grateful for it. I sometimes feel like, and perhaps I am, a nut case! Either that, or someone going through a mammoth ordeal which will ultimately lead to a rebirth. Well, take your pick!

Deep down I do feel that there will be a change for the better, not yet perceptible. I feel that I'm clearing up a lifetime of unfinished business, and perhaps unpaid debts. There's a strong feeling that the traumas of early childhood are playing a big part, and that to make a serviceable map of the journey one would need to consult **Dante, Blake** and **Goethe (Faust)**. I simply cling to what Papa Jung had to say (and there's a lot of that), and to watch out for helpful ideas and images that sometimes come my way.

I went with Mary Ormond (a Jungian friend) to see a play at the National Theatre last week, based on "The Waves", one of Virginia Woolf's last novels and directed by Katie Mitchell, one of our brightest and most imaginative young stage directors. Very interesting stagecraft – Needless to say, there were frequent glimpses of a beach (St. Ives?) at different times of day, beautifully timed to accompany special moments in the story. And beneath the stream of consciousness a sense of the underlying destiny, a death that could not be ignored or avoided (I mean V.W's death). I do like the way that theatre in London has shaken itself into new ways of telling stories, sometimes more than one at once, and new ways of bringing together the art of acting and the craft of managing theatrical happenings. I would love to be able to take you to something like this, and discuss it afterwards: a treat not possible... I'm enclosing an obituary of one of my longstanding heroes, Abbe Pierre: perhaps I see in him the human face of Catholicism. He's worth knowing about, in case you don't already. Many thanks for the book, a most welcome birthday present. Big hug. Lots of love. Sheila

Dearest Sheila,
I was in the middle of re reading letters of yours when your latest came. I truly am awed by our "shared space". So glad you liked the book, lovely I thought, and not just for us voiceless ones. In any challenge we have, so to speak, (Oh, God, the puns) lost our voice, haven't we!
This was to say how much I am hoping and hoping you get a little steadier on your pins. After all the inner major works, you deserve to be able to put on a Chariots of Fire dash!!! There's a TV ad for baby food running a lot here, shows a toddler trying to walk and falling down a lot. The slogan is: "*Solid Food for a Wobbly World*", and I invariably think of you whenever it comes on. Ever thought it's the world that's wobbling, not you, my friend? The earth was supposed to shift on its axis last year. Maybe that's the problem!! I am really enjoying the Planet book, I tend to dip in to it, then something else, then go back to it. It seems to suit that. So I've just finished Margaret Attwood's **Alias Grace** (golly, is she a good writer) and a moving account **Left to Tell** by a Rwandan women, who survived the genocide, hiding with seven other women in a bathroom 3 by 4 ft for three months!!
Oh, I do wish you had access to therapeutic eurythmy. I'm sure it would be just the job for the wobbles. I am doing it for the voice, obviously. One of my self-imposed therapies is to imagine I am speaking a poem in a poetic voice, while I go for my walks, and the enclosed by Philip Larkin was a choice two days ago. I thought you'd like it! He used to visit John B and I quite frequently. John would say: "The gloomiest poet in the world is coming to lunch today." He had a point, didn't he? Having hit rock bottom recently, I am now just sitting at the bottom (much more comfortably) wondering if I'll ever have the energy to try to clamber out again. Yesterday was a breakthrough when I realized: "Hey, I'll always have bouts of pain", we always do after a major injury, which the surgery definitely was, never mind the chunk of pipeline they needed to insert down my throat. It was a huge relief not to feel I was failing every time it hurt.
I so agree with the task of accepting the wound, getting to the place where "suffering becomes privilege". I don't think either of us need to elaborate on the cost of all that, the integrity and the battles along the way. What was interesting recently was the memory of what Helen Bessemer would call the "shared collusion" between the surgeon and myself. I simply cannot tell you how often and how strongly I asked what could go wrong – over and over I

gave him the opportunity to tell me, to warn me – right to the few minutes before I was given the "lethal injection" and he is standing over me in his blue scrubs.   It's as if I knew intuitively that if he performed the surgery this could be the consequence and I was giving him the opportunity to warn me, and he couldn't. In one of our later sessions, I mentioned this to him. "I wish I had known this might have happened." To which he responded: "Well, then, maybe you wouldn't have had the surgery."

"Not good for business?" I asked rather tartly. He said he meant that my polyps might have been hiding a deeper problem (i.e. cancer) but the lovely doctor in San Francisco had assured me it didn't. All water under the bridge now, of course. Do you remember our friend James Hillman on the bond between Betrayer and Betrayed?

I'm going to leave you, with thanks for your last letter, the lovely cutting about the French Abbe, and go and do my own version of Major Works (putting putty round my window frames and repainting, to ready my house for sale next month.) Much love, Lee

Next, Please.

Always too eager for the future, we
Pick up bad habits of expectancy.
Something is always approaching; every day
Till then, we say.
Watching from a bluff the tiny, clear,
Sparkling armada of promises draw near.
How slow they are! And how much time they waste,
Refusing to make haste!
Yet still they leave us holding wretched stalks
Of disappointment, for, though nothing balks
Each big approach, leaning with brass work prinked,
Each rope distinct,
Flagged, and the figurehead with golden tits
Arching our way, it never anchors, it's
No sooner present than it turns to past.
Right to the last
We think each one will heave to and unload
All good into our lives, all we are owed
For waiting so devoutly and so long.
But we are wrong:
Only one ship is seeking us, a black-
Sailed unfamiliar, towing at her back
A huge and birdless silence. In her wake
No waters breed or break.

Philip Larkin

Subject: Germany sues CIA

Darling Adam,
Worth a quick glance if you hadn't seen this. Love Mum

I hadn't, thanks. Germany is also getting in on the suing Rumsfeld thing. I have decided what is going to help me sleep best is making beeswax animals with Stefan and Chenta's son Cyris, so I've ordered some beeswax. Apparently, he can name all the different kinds of horses (within reason), so when he gets back from Hawaii, we're going to make them. I'm going to swing by a bookstore tomorrow. Any recommendations? Love you, A

Darling Adam,
Beeswax is just the job, specially with Cyris!! Take the Avena Sativa too, though! Well, if you haven't read **Poisonwood Bible**, you'd better, if you may go to Congo. Way her best (Kingsolver) but you probably already did? I have been hugely enjoying Margaret Attwood, since you reminded me with **The Blind Assassin**. Reading **Alias Grace** by her at the moment. Also **Left to Tell** (Rwandan genocide/ Immaculee Ilibagiza). You might find it too prayerful, but hey, if prayer works!! She works for UN now in N.York. Love you, Mum

Adam next called and left a message on my phone to tell me a friend of his, Uma, had come for a visit to New York with her fiancé and had had an aneurysm and stroke and was in a coma. He asked me to "do my thing": intercessory prayers and suchlike. I promise I will, while also sending him some Trader Joe's organic dark French truffles for Valentine's Day.

From: Adam Day: Feb 14, 2007 7:22 AM

Thanks Mum. You and Uma are my Valentines for this year. She got a pretty bad result on her latest cat scan, so we'll just keep praying

Will do (keep praying). Keep warm. Love Mum

He leaves me another message reporting Uma's progress.

Darling Adam,
I did want to know about Uma, and thank you for that phone call. Tell everyone too to watch out for their dreams (Erik etc). I remember so clearly when Crystal Rose at Detroit Waldorf School was in a coma for I think around 3 months, her mother dreamed that Crystal came and said she was missing the party, and wanted to be there. Then her mother knew she really wanted to pull through and rejoin everyone on this side. Hope your eyeballs haven't frozen yet. Love. Mum

To: Signe: Subject: What news of Linda?

Dearest Signe,
How is Linda? You felt this last time was her crossing moment, but maybe
she's doing Hungarian dances again? I do think of you all a lot!! Read in ole
RS that if you suffer pain you are beautiful next lifetime. Isn't Linda as
beautiful as anyone can get already??
Thought you'd like to know that Adam has solved his insomnia. Told me he
had ordered beeswax and would go over and make beeswax animals with
Cyris, was sure that would do it. Oh, I forwarded info on Stefan's movie* to
everyone I know in Austin. Thinking about coming to Brooklyn in June even
if I still have (which is highly likely) a terrible voice. It actually has gotten
worse this month as strange nodules grew over scar tissue and create "double"
sounds (how's that!!! Can't hide my double any more - as if I thought I ever
could!) Love you, and love to your family, Lee
***Arranged** (which later won the Brooklyn Film Festival).

Hi Lee,
We just came home from Gt Barrington and Linda is still going (relatively)
strong! It's a strange limbo life we all lead these days. And to complicate
things, we have just signed contracts on two houses: one in Brooklyn and one
in Gt Barrington! Neither is at all grand, but we hope they will suit us. The
Brooklyn one has two rental apartments. It's a few blocks from Stefan and
Chenta, close to all subways, and an easy walk to Acorn. Are we crazy to be
doing this? It sometimes feels overwhelming, but is also very exciting. Ah
sanguinity! We will move to Brooklyn in mid April, and Gt Barrington at the
end of April. But how do we pack up this place? Stefan and Chenta's baby is
due in mid-June so we will be there then. Do you need a place to stay? A
double voice sounds very interesting ... does it mean talking half as much? Or
does the double part say all the things the first one holds back on? I don't
mean to be flippant, and I do hope it's sorting itself out. I won't care if we
write notes to each other -- it will just be fun to see you. And I'm still waiting
to see your fine son. Love, Signe

Dear Signe,
Oh, Lord what a journey Linda is leading you all, including herself. I am so
thrilled you have a house in Brooklyn. How astonishing our kids are all so
close and now you too. I told Adam I would come and visit in June or July,
so I'll see you then for sure.. No, I can stay with Adam. We've had a lovely
system over the past years, where I sleep in his bed, and he sleeps on the floor
at my feet, bless him. Much love to all, Lee

*Did I mention Francie yet? One of three British friends going back almost
half a century. We shared her house in London, on Lettice Street (Parson's
Green), in our early twenties. Later she moved to Suffolk, a
Master/"Mistress" Gardener. I will type in some of her later letters, seem to
have mislaid earlier ones from this year. Looking for them, I have been*

rereading those she sent years ago. It astonishes me that we see each other so seldom – haven't for over a decade now – and yet the soul connection is so deep and strong. Every time I see her distinctive handwriting my heart expands very quietly and gratefully. Francie must be one of the deepest, truest, finest souls to grace my life.

Darling Francie,

Thanks so much for your letter. Yes, I agree, if we'd known then what we know now, maybe we would have said, hey, let's not come to earth!!! Actually, the only potential good thing to come out of all this is that I think it might make it easier for me to die – I seem to have had to let go of every thing, person, place, that made me who I thought I was. Sometimes afflicted by raging jealousy as life goes on merrily without me.

I'm thinking I'm at the halfway mark now, and hope to get to San Francisco by next fall sometime (so I would love to see Giles if he is there, and has email). I'm an optimist. Some days I'm a pessimist as in : "A pessimist is a well-informed optimist"!

My beloved Adam would certainly keep me in my old age, he is one of the most amazing, tender hearted souls I've ever met. I'll include a photo!! However he absolutely hates his job, working for corrupt corporations (which is where the money is of course) and can't sleep at night. He's got a sideline preparing a brief to sue Rumsfeld and when he works on that he sleeps like a baby. He's going to try to stick it for a year, pay off some of his student loans, and is putting resumes in to the UN as he'd like a job in Sudan, Congo or Cambodia.

The birds I feed? Morning (mourning?) doves, finches, tanagers, western bluebirds, and I did once hold a wounded Ruby-crowned Kinglet in the palm of my hand. The peregrines and bald headed eagles are a little large for my feeders, but I see them, and sometimes the pure white freshwater pelicans. How's that?

Well, I may enclose a very gloomy poem by Philip Larkin that I found this morning. One of my self-chosen therapies is to imagine me speaking poems – the cords will move sympathetically. But maybe I shouldn't do this one? Better go, I have a couple of garden projects, trimming old stuff away – so lovely to be able to be out in early Feb in 65 degrees and smelling the sap rising. Much much love, Lee

Darling Lee,

Thank you for your letter, photo of Adam (I never expected he would have such a strong featured face, and so handsome!) and for the very gloom inspiring poem by Larkin – actually I rather like it. I will of course give Giles your email address when he gets back (I'm not sure he is email oriented but my friends constantly surprise with their uptodatedness.) I am also inspired by my friends' fortitude in the face of physical and emotional disasters - how do you manage to have no bitterness? – and their mental resilience, not retreating to a safe place and leaving the world to get on without them. I am only heard when pushed into a brick wall and I come out shouting (quite interesting getting angry in one's 60's, blood pressure soars, and I feel like throwing in the towel) but stand my ground as I never did before, and refuse to kow tow to indifference, lack of care, thoughtlessness, and failure to ask forgiveness. Why don't people in the church ask for forgiveness – it seems to be a basic principle of being a Christian? I tried it out with an old friend and she said it was fear of losing face – *balderdash!* (I hope you are enjoying my idiomatic/quaint use of English? When did you last hear someone saying *balderdash?*)

I am so so sorry that you feel you have to let go of everything you thought you were. When I retired from the plant business, I felt v. adrift, but came through not to be someone else but to use my talents (ha ha) to be with people and make them laugh and to hear them and to allow *some* people to see my vulnerability, sadness and failures – large chunks of me and my life. So maybe a new direction, unexpected, will be thrown at you. I find so many middle-aged women fill their lives with busyness. They don't see or want to see new opportunities. A bereaved male friend says his life is pointless without his deceased wife, and he races around being busy and gets no fulfillment from the jobs he does. I find although I am nursing a bruised heart, I am glad (not a word I use much!) I know I still have a heart.

I do hope your voice (physical and emotional) comes back soon. You are much in my thoughts which you probably find difficult to relate to as it has taken me a month to answer your letter – apologies. I love getting your letters and I do appreciate you and your warmth, love and friendship and your humour, humanity, empathy, support and forgiveness – you are valued.

I loved your descriptions of your birds – it's like seeing and listening to Bill Oddy's bird film of Central America. The world is full of beautiful things one person takes for granted and another is inspired by its beauty and rarity – like my trying to describe to a four year old that apples have to grow on an apple tree, and you first have flowers etc…watching her face trying to absorb this amazing piece of information was a delight and a reminder of how good and vulnerable children's visions of the world around us are. I gave several people for Christmas fossils and they said how inspired they were by them. Perhaps that is why I am so wrapped up in my life drawing – the body is so beautiful and can make extraordinary shapes.

You must be proud of Adam's integrity and moral stand. I do hope he gets the job for the UN which would use his talents to the full, and keep him secure – Congo doesn't sound a "safe" bet, but then nor does Cambodia or Sudan – nor for that matter is London - strange to see armed police in London, but it doesn't stop the day tripper, like me, or the commuter. Must stop waffling on this quiet Sunday evening. This comes – even though you probably wish I'd typed it – with very much love and a big hug, Francie.

From: Jackie, Subject: Good to hear from you

Hello Lee: I was thinking about you this morning and so was surprised and happy to hear from you this evening! In a nutshell I will tell you what's up. The LifeWays program I operate from my house is full (licensed for 8) and it has brought many, many young families into my life. The local Waldorf initiative school is failing and so those dear souls are ringing my phone for help on thinking through what might happen to keep the community together and provide a kindergarten. for the little ones. Meanwhile, a group of parents with school age children is meeting with me to form a Waldorf home schooling cooperative. All of this activity has really picked up since Christmas. It is amazing how pushing against limits causes people and ideals to emerge. That's all I can say about it for now except that I am very happy and feel that I am meeting my destiny group and work. The weather, warm in January, frigid in February, has broken again and a warmth can actually be felt in the afternoon. Snow is melting, our chickens stay out of their hen house more often, birds are calling, the children are eager to play, play, play outside. I am so sorry that your voice is still not OK. I can hear you speaking in my head and I miss you and your voice. I wish you'd tell me more about your journey (diamond in the doughnut?). Let's renew our friendship via email until something better comes along. Yours with much warmth, Jackie

Dearest Jackie, Hurrah - thought I'd lost you for ever. I wonder what happened that my Christmas card was returned And how lovely that you were thinking of me. I am also so happy (well sad to hear about other initiatives weakening or failing) to hear that you have found your new destiny, which means all around you can find theirs through you. And I can now carry you and your group in my thoughts. This seems to be the major work for me these days - thoughts and prayers. It has been, and still is, a pretty arduous journey. Try not using the phone for 10 months (while living alone!) The surgeon really carved me up me, so I'm having to regrow my cords. This is the first month (I'm holding my breath) with barely any pain. (No you'd have to ask your son in law what I meant with diamonds in doughnuts, it is a picture that comes up when I'm tested for sound.) I had 5 months aphonic (no sound) followed by 5 months dysphonic (horrible sound) and last month I added another challenge but I've forgotten the name, that means 2 horrible sounds simultaneously! Like you, I hear my voice in my head. Unimaginably painful, actually! A friend emailed yesterday saying (so sweetly): "*This almost amounts to a world tragedy! You, Lee, are the one person I know who could read the phone book and make it sound like poetry*". Not any more. Actually, I think the 3 potential positives are, or will/might be: 1) I've given work to others, and it was probably their turn now; 2) that surgeon is never going to carve anyone else up with quite the same aplomb and 3) it may be easier for me to die. It is always remarkable to lose what matters most isn't it. Please keep in touch, I am so happy to have found you, but of course you were never really lost! Keep warm, love, Lee

*   *   *

In the next couple of weeks I perk up considerably as I begin arranging trips. One is to Sacramento to stay with my beloved Rosemary for our Biography Group day again. I have said little or nothing of her, and have included few emails, since we confined most of these to practical arrangements and caught up when I stayed with her which is as frequently as I can manage and she can bear! I treasure her friendship as deeply as anyone's. We go back over 20 years, first meeting in England (she herself is from South Africa.) Whenever I arrive at her little home I feel like some beaten up traveller finding a hut in the forest, doorway open, and a gentle, welcoming soul awaiting me. A true Rosicrucian healer, and such a kindred spirit! Emails fly back and forth madly, and Esther, who can no longer join our group as she has returned to Vancouver, picks these up....

From: Esther: Re: Biography Group

 Dear Lee!!
Wow!...All this lovely back and forth! I am glad that you all chose a date...and I would die to come! (I know that is a little dramatic.....but I have to cope with this grey malaise somehow! I am now going to THREE diff. kinds of " Therapy"!..) I certainly will if I can, and I would love to do the eurythmy if I do!, Esther

Darling Esther, I knew it was improbable that you could make it, tho' glorious if you can. Now, girl, you will get through this grim Lenten phase. You have already done wonders. Lent passes. And Easter does come. P.S. I'm sending you my therapeutic advice under separate cover, as I understand snail mail letters are read and emails only skimmed. Hugs, Lee

24 Feb (Snail Mail letter)

Darling Esther,
First I love you.
Second, here's advice from a few wise folk, including your friend, the recovering psychotherapist – ME!!

1. From James Hillman (best psychologist on this continent, I think!!)
*"People make the mistake of thinking they have problems and are always trying to solve them. **Being human IS the problem.** We just have to learn how to bear that!"*

2. From Steiner: *"Those who suffer in this lifetime will be particularly beautiful physically in the next life."*! So, don't you want to be a Beauty Queen or King next time around?

3. From Lee Sturgeon Day!
Don't take anyone's advice, least of all mine!
a) You have suffered depression, grief, anxiety etc etc now for 56 years. And you are still here. That is an incredible accomplishment. It has also shaped who you are, what you bring to the world. You wouldn't be you

without all that. (Another Hillman quote: "garbage is also fertilizer". Don't ever forget that.)

b) Having survived 56 years, chances are you will survive another 40 or so. You are already over the halfway mark, on the home stretch in fact!

c) You may very well continue to suffer. That's OK too. If you've survived this long, none of the same can destroy you now – you have resources that you didn't before.

d) so, what's the worst that can happen? Some good times, some bad times?

e) So any time you feel miserable, feel miserable and then go walk by the water or do eurythmy so you balance misery with maybe a little joy.

f) Anytime you miss B., go down by the waterside and see if there are any gorgeous fishermen about - if you can't find anyone to fantasize about, rent a good movie with a very sexy hero! (I prefer that myself, because I can turn off the TV and go to bed and fart alone!!!)

g) Write down the things you want to do before you die, and see how soon you can do a few of them. Buying new underwear was one thing on my list. Now I have to do a load of laundry without including a Kleenex.

That's it. Sorry I seem to have lost the letter I was sent about the daffodils, lots of pictures of fields of daffodils, planted by a lady "ONE BULB AT A TIME" for 40 years. So, you have 40 years. Enjoy planting! Love you, Lee

Marjan is a Dutch psychologist, whose doctoral thesis was on Forgiveness. She drew significantly from the Truth and Reconciliation work in S. Africa. We met as colleagues in a training program in San Francisco under the auspices of Dr. Robert Gorter, and have corresponded since. She had told me she needed back surgery.

Dear Marjan, Do please let me know whenever your surgery is scheduled, so I can be thinking of you, praying for you. I would never have gone ahead with mine if I had known then what I know now! Although my son would like me to sue (and who can blame him) for "failure to warn"/inform at all of these possible consequences, I think - and you'll appreciate this, with all your work - that I have to struggle through to *Ubuntu*, and have a kind of truth and reconciliation experience with my surgeon. There is just too much hatred in the world. Go well, I often think of you, love, Lee

Dear Lee,
Happy birthday! I wish you a much better health and a wonderful voice in your new year. Truth, reconciliation & forgiveness take a lot of time! A friend of mine who submitted an article on his study on compassion was told that his research was too much pro criminals and idealistic...... We try. My surgery is planned coming Monday (was called today); I will be admitted tomorrow (!), but probably will be able to be home through the weekend. And then back to the hospital Sunday night. More after surgery. Hope you are doing well. Love, Marjan

Dear Marjan,
TODAY IS THE DAY I AM SENDING THE FORCE AS YOU LIE
UNDER THE KNIFE. JUST SO YOU KNOW. Love, Lee

Dear Lee,
Thank you! Surgery itself went well, but there were complications: bleeding
that caused blood clot that pinched the nerves for four days. Then another
surgery in the middle of the night to remove that. Lots of pain and loss of
feeling in legs. Doctors say it will be better, but that it will take months.
Yesterday I moved from the hospital to another place (temporarily) to recover
a little more before going home. Can sit a little now and walk a little with a
walker. More later. Love, Marjan

Oh, my dear, dear friend, That puts my silly voice situation in perspective.
It sounds utterly grueling, and I will continue to think of you and pray for you,
and wonder why we have both been disabled in this way so soon after we
met? What is the spiritual world wanting of us? Or what do the counter
forces NOT want from us - at least for now? Please keep me in touch with
the process (even when it's not "progress"). Love, Lee

Dear Lee,
One of my American friends said: "*you must have pissed off the Gods....!*"
Joking, of course, but still, we never know what really is the meaning of such
experiences. Maybe later. Any decision about suing or forgiveness? Actually,
I believe you could do both...... I think of you too. Love, Marjan

Dear Marjan,
No, you've pleased the gods, they can use your suffering, and you will be
even more beautiful next lifetime (just read about suffering transmuting into
physical beauty next time round!!!) You're right, I probably could do both -
sue and forgive. What about your surgeon?? Doesn't sound nice at all.
Much love, heal well, Lee

To: Marietta
My dearest friend and only Valentine this year!!! Oh what a lovely card, and
I'm returning the message this way, (* I sent her a few organic french truffles
from Trader Joes) as I fear the dozen red roses etc would probably get lost in
a snowdrift. I'll try something snail mail soon. I still think we should all move
somewhere closer to each other and not too rainy when our houses have sold.
Will put mine on market next month, but it will take a long time, not many
appreciate that it is built to the golden mean, and painted with earth from the
Hopi lands, they'd rather state of the art bathrooms and architecture that looks
like an upscale penitentiary! So much love, and thanks again, I could hardly
believe it when your card arrived. Spring will come!! Meanwhile hugs, Lee

Dearest (SWEET) Lee----Thank you for this forward and THANK YOU for
those luscious truffles!! They arrived just in the right moment (in the nick of

time, as it were) and wow, you can't just have ONE. No no. Well, I'm glad you shared some or I wouldn't be sleeping for a week. Yum!.......and thanks for thinking of me in such a sweet, 'supportive' way. I think I can get through, now. Re: your friend Pamela's initiative....you turn out to be a real hub (center) of people's creative ideas and inspirations, it seems. And you know who needs to have the information. If one thinks about networking, you may be the great 'switchboard operator' in the U.S.! Don't you think, sometimes? Marietta

To Myra McPherson Feb 20th:

Darling Myra (and Drew...and Mic and....Todd of course),
I discovered I had flight credit I needed to use so, guess what, despite still sounding like a distant (sometimes two distant and dissonant) factory hooter hooting through fog and wire wool, I have booked to come to Sacramento 11-18 April, to stay with Rosemary, have our little bio group meeting on Sun 15th, and we may have a little outing on Saturday AND: hoping and hoping to visit with you. I know you have a schedule to beat the band, but PLEASE please find time for me! Love you, think of you always, Lee

Dear Lee,
It would be wonderful seeing you even if we can only do form drawing together. Drew is quite good at it. It is far away and our schedule will probably change between here and there because U.C. Davis will end, so we will be home more. Yeah evenings are often open and weekends. We go to San Jose on Wednesdays now. All is well. Mic, Drew and I are off to Project Walk in Carlsbad, Southern California for a week of intensive therapy and some time at the beach. I look forward to it as a vacation. We just got a Toyota van with a ramp so Drew can drive his power chair into it and off we go. That will definitely make life easier.
I am doing better, have more help and can breathe a little easier sometimes. I am even planning a weekend away to take a workshop with Dennis Klocek on the Black Madonna. Seems like a appropriate workshop for me at the moment. Wanting to spend time looking at my biography -- things just are too interesting when viewed from an anthroposophical perspective. Perhaps we can do some work together. I recall beginning that once long long ago when first you came to Fair Oaks. Whenever that was. Love to you my dear friend. Will see you in April. I look forward to it. Myra

Good, my darling.
Have a great time in S. Calif and I will get in touch nearer time. Let's do bio work any time you fancy. Funny, I thought about Dennis and Black Madonna. Then I thought, hey - I have the Madonnas in my life - you and Rosemary! So I'm choosing to be with you both instead Love to you all, big hug to Drew - I hope his arms are very strong to give me a hug when I come, God how I've missed him and you!! Lee

From: Salemla: Subject: how are you?

Dearest Lee, you have been in my thoughts and heart a lot recently. How are you doing? I was without email for a couple of months while in transition. So delicious that you will be here soon. Our homes are virtually complete...a little worse for the wear as a result of the earthquake...we are still discovering new small damage...but the big picture is delicious. I am so grateful to be here overlooking this earth so deeply in need of care. It is also wonderful to be living in rhythm with the sun, turning phones etc.., off at night and waking with such gratitude to the sun for keeping the oat milk cool!

Otherwise I continue to heal this body...as you do yours.. Quite a process, *n'est ce pas?*! It demands as I am sure you experience, a lot of courage at times. I feel all of us carrying such body challenges are forging new relationships to and concepts of health, and ultimately new physical forms more capable of reflecting Christ Self. But I really don't know why we all had to make it quite so difficult! Much, much love. S

Darling Sukie,
How lovely to hear from you. I had just begun writing back and forth to Kona, Laura etc and had been thinking of you strongly. Sounds wonderful, cooling the oat milk and being without a phone at night. (Not that anyone phones me anymore, entering 11th month of no phone use!!!!) Well, I plod on. Lots of setbacks. I have to go to the surgeon again in a couple of weeks. He just pokes and prods, and fishes down my throat and makes knowing noises because he doesn't know, then just raises his hands and says : "Well, I guess you are one of the unlucky ones." Indeed, I am, for letting him near me! But, as you say, we are probably forging all kinds of awareness and soul strengths for the future.
By the way, do you remember those glorious big bouncy balls with horns that you and Bill used to bound about on. Don't suppose you remember what they were called. They probably don't make them any more. I went on line yesterday to try to track one down for Sophia (not much good if they aren't in/deflatable) as it seems she needs activities to exhaust her! That's what Laura tells me. So, I should be with you right after your birthday! (Don't imagine you want a bouncy ball too?) Much love, Lee

Dearest Lee,
My heart is so touched by what you are going through... I will write more when I am not trying to save my energy in preparation for Sophia's birthday party - tomorrow. Laura has invited around 29 children and they all come with parents in tow!
The reason for this brief response is just to let you know that Sophia has one of those large bouncy balls with horns. I had forgotten Bill and I had them. Anyway she doesn't seem to use it much... lots of love, s

Here are words from someone - a whole family - who ARE REALLY
SUFFERING, and which put my little glitches in perspective!!

Greetings everyone.

I can't believe it has just been the 6 month anniversary of Drew's
accident. I cannot begin to express in words what lives in my heart
today from this life experience; 6 months of experiencing love and
support which has carried me through the shock, disbelief, pain,
anguish, sorrow, grief, gratitude, exhaustion, questioning, and
surrender. There have been so many days that I know in the marrow
of my bones that I only do what I do because of each of you and the
spiritual worlds which surrounds all of us. It is as if an invisible web of
love enfolds Drew Mic, Todd, and me and carries us through the days
and nights. This experience has truly brought to light the love and
support that exists in this world; what humanity is striving for-
community of life. I often feel like I am living a fairy tale and have at
least 13 fairy God mothers and fathers taking care of me and my family.
Perhaps that is truly what is happening. People ask me how we are all
doing. A short synopsis. Drew, who in the world of his injury know him
as Andrew, is growing stronger and more capable every day. He
currently has a wonderful experienced physical therapist at UC Davis
rehabilitation outpatient clinic who works with him twice a week. It is
a privilege to be able to witness how the two of them work -together.
He is also participating in a research project with a wonderful man
Nils using a FES bicycle to determine if using such equipment effect
lung capacity and oxygenation of the blood. Drew get hooked up and
plugged in twice to three times a week and bicycles at 45rpm for 20—
30- minutes. This is one of the pieces of equipment that Christopher
Reeves used to maintain his health as long as he was able to. Two days
a week Drew goes to American River College for an adaptive PE class in
weight training. The college has the largest disabilities program in the
state and has fantastic machines for him to work out on. So he goes
with his brother one day a week and a friend the other who help to set
him up for his own personalized exercise program. And if that isn't
enough one day a week we journey to San Jose to see Dr Zhu for neuro
acupuncture and physical therapy. And to top it off Inge Ring comes
once a week to do some spatial work with Drew that is based on the
therapeutic special dynamics work of Jaimen McMillan who we were
privileged to have come work with Drew for 3 days in early December.
He is truly a master in his field and I am definitely committed to
integrating the spatial work into the therapeutic paradigm. The weeks
are full. In his spare time we do mat work at home and use the
standing frame for a minimum of 1 hour several times a week. He is
working really hard!!!

Drew has several young people besides us who are attending to him; Ruth and Robin and Rosemary. Their support is invaluable. Almost as invaluable as my fairy god mother Pati who lovingly prepares nourishing breakfasts for us several days a week and goes shopping for me and cleans up the kitchen after I have so often demolished it and on and on and on. We have three fairy god mothers who do our laundry. I put it out on the porch dirty and it disappears and comes back clean. Thank you.

Mic returned to work ¾ time in December. We are adjusting to his absence and appreciate his willingness to still get up in the middle of the night to care for Drew after putting in 10 hours at the office. What a committed father! Mics' brother Scott, two years his junior, died tragically in a house fire on January 13th. An example of how amazing our support is, we had two gourmet lunches prepared and set out on an elegantly set table for our family after his brother's funeral.

Todd is living in two worlds; finishing his degree in community studies at UCSC, volunteering for a sustainable coffee organization CAN, running their farmers market booth once a week and writing his final thesis this quarter and coming home about 3 days a week to support his brother in his therapy and us in the aspects of care giving which we share. He has been and continues to be our tap root and for this I am truly grateful.

I am slowing learning how to allocate jobs, prioritize and breathe. This is truly a life experience that encompasses every aspect of community life. Some days it is a bigger challenge than I feel up to and yet I can say that it is all becoming easier. What once took us three hours to do we can now do in 1 hour.

There are times where I feel I am running a business. We are coming to define some of our needs and beginning to prioritize them. We are looking into an accessible van into which Drew could drive his power chair. This is a major expense; used vans range from $20-30,000 and new vans up to $50,000. We are also going to need to do some modification to our home, purchase specific rehab equipment and pay for alternative medical treatments and medicines; acupuncture and anthroposophical physicians. I so appreciate you being there for us. In the meantime be good to yourselves and those in community with you and know that this gesture is what will bring healing to this world. In sincere gratitude for the loving warmth that we share. Myra

If this isn't a deep Lenten experience I don't know what would be one? It certainly puts my little setbacks in perspective, and I try to be slightly less self piteous as I read and commit to heart Myra's words.

CHAPTER TWELVE. FORWARD MARCH.

"Just as we take a train to go to a city, we take death to go to a star."
Vincent van Gogh

This is the month I begin inching forward; making real travel plans, rather than the virtual globetrotting I have indulged in over the past year: checking flight prices to distant lands and imagining I might get to one someday. Apart from my trip to Portland, I've been nowhere. And here is not where I want, any longer, to be. So with joy, I correspond with my Hawaiian group, my Californian friends, and am so excited I can hardly think straight. Then I learn of others who are really moving forward into quite other territory.

From: Signe: Subject: sad news

Dear Lee,
I am writing with such sad and shocking news -- Judy Laury has just died. A few hours ago. Chenta and Stefan and Cy are here with us because Chenta is in a course at the college, and Dmitri called with the news. Apparently she was found peacefully on her couch. She seems to have died in her sleep. No cause yet known. Chenta is of course devastated. And trying to figure what to do at such a great distance. They will go back within a day or so -- they just returned from Maui a week ago tomorrow. It's hard, with Chenta six months pregnant. I had hoped that Karen might have some advice of what Judy might have wanted in a service, and general Hawaii knowledge, but she is now on a flight to England. Did you ever speak of such things with Judy? Of course, I want to go to Maui too, but I can't now. Linda really is on the very edge. I am trusting that Judy will help her across. I must go now. More later. Love, Signe

I responded to Signe several times before beginning to beat the drums.

Darling Adam,
Sorry to be in your hair again but I thought you would want to know this, knowing and loving Chenta (and Dmitri) as you do. Love, Mum

Hey Mum,
I just heard when I went to the laundromat (where Dmitri's wife works) this morning. How are you doing with this? I know she was a good friend of yours and you were going to see her on your trip to Hawaii. All I can do from this end is send my love to you and her kids, and I'll offer to do anything Stefan and Chenta need over here. Uma is undergoing a shunt operation today, which is a permanent tube running from her brain to her stomach, to drain fluid. We thought she wasn't going to need it, and everyone was hit a little hard yesterday when the doctors said she would. I now have her fiance staying with me and stayed up fairly late talking with him last night. The hope is to get her back to California via a med-evac flight. I don't know if

you're going to Hawaii for the funeral, but please send my love to everyone. Most especially, send my love to you! A

Darling Adam,
Nothing you need to do, you are doing it all. Tell Uma's fiance that Archie (my godson) had a draining shunt for years, very successful. Oh, god, the suffering. Hope you can get more rest soon, though. I'm fine, don't worry about me, love you, Mum

Dearest Chenta,
I am so so so sad, shocked, and sorry to hear of Judy crossing so swiftly, without giving you time to say goodbye, except during your recent visit. I can understand how utterly devastating this must feel. Typical of your Mom though, just to quietly and courageously take this step. She was such a remarkable soul, I am so grateful to have been able to spend some really "up close and personal" times with her, and just sad that I hadn't seen her over the past 4-5 years since my own family moved to the Big Island. I have such treasured memories of staying with her, right from her pick up at the airport, my room deliciously awaiting me, her second car at my disposal, and being able to go off and enjoy the beach while she plugged in all that awful car stuff till who knows what hours at night. I was able to occasionally cook supper for us (bagels seemed to be all she had time to prepare, oh and all that delicious juiced melon!) Just sometimes, she would take a break and we could watch a movie together, or have a conversation before we probably both fell asleep in our respective chairs or couches.
The only way I can make any sense of this is that I always felt your mother was a stupendously large, creative, soul with a huge heart and all the impulses this world needs, but not enough people got to experience this. And now they can, for she will surely be pouring those amazing influences down over a much wider sphere (and of course even more strongly able to support you, Stefan and your family.) When my Mum died I was utterly awed at how close she was (and still is) and I don't know how many times I call on her to support or protect Adam. She always does.
I think the spiritual world and its inhabitants are very ruthless these days, they have to be, there's too much at stake and I can only look at it in this light, that Judy was needed – her warmth of heart, her courage, her compassion, her insights etc. I'm truly sorry that you have to let go of her as a physical presence but I know she's right with you.
We had some pretty "woo woo" (as Adam calls it) conversations, as you might imagine as fellow anthros. One of our last was around her question of what happens to souls who love animals. Well, ole Rudolf says the animal kingdom is the first we enter after death. I do have to imagine a lot of very grateful felines awaiting her, don't you?
So, my heart is with you, (and Dimitri and Stefan of course). And I hope to see you this summer, when I'm planning a brief visit to Adam. I gather there's no way I could see him without you all – he apparently has quite a thing with Cyris. We are all looking forward to the next family member who

may have arrived by the time I get to NY. So very very much love. As I told Signe, I just wish my arms were a lot longer so I could give you a big hug. Lee

While awaiting Chenta's baby (so often a child comes soon after a death in the family), we have a wedding announcement between Kim, Adam's closest friend, and the lovely Moroccan Meryam!

From: Kim-Fredrik : Subject: Friday, the 15th of June

After an arduous search, Meryam and I have finally found a location – and a date – for our impending wedding at which we request the pleasure of your company. The event will be held in Paris on the evening of Friday the 15th of June. Please let me know if I can be of any assistance with making travel arrangements or anything else. Best, Kim

Dear Kim (and Meryam)

How I wish I could celebrate your wedding with you - but I will be sending all good thoughts for a smashing time, and hope to see you again before too long. I was so glad you could be there for Adam's graduation, and I could meet you, Meryam, even though speechless. Kim, I think Adam told me you love fiction too?? I just finished **Maps for Lost Lovers,** Nadeem Aslam, and both **Swallows Over Kabul** and **The Attack**, by Yasmina Khadra (pseudonym of an Algerian army officer who took a woman's name to avoid military censorship.) I'm into a hefty Muslim writers phase. (Oh, and nonfiction: Diane Rehm's **Finding My Voice** - thought it might help me find mine again. Didn't know she was Lebanese! I've always admired her.) Much love, Lee,

Hi Lee,
We would have loved to have you there! The experience would have fit so well with your current literary consumption, as well.
I'm just finishing **The Sea** by John Banville - Adam's recommendation. Magnificent. No, not the right word. I need something indicating equal brilliance, but more subtly so. He is a master of language; makes me love English even more than I already do.
I will look into the books you mention. I haven't heard of them. But via Adam, I've already received many an excellent tip from you! On your current theme, I'm sure you've read **Naguib Mahfooz**? I know you love to find contemporary gems, but much of his work seems even more relevant now than when he wrote it. And I'm sure you didn't miss **Map of Love** by Ahdaf Soueif a few years ago. After reading that and **Mahfooz's** Cairo Trilogy, I fell in love with turn of last century Cairo. For Islam, that city and that time were also particularly dynamic. Much of the good and the bad that we see today were born in that city at that time as classical scholars and

young activists tried to reconcile the colonial experience with their history and find their place in the modern world.

I've been reading updates on your health passed along from my mum. I was very happy to hear that there is some progress, however slight! Not sure if you will be around, but we will be in SF and Sac in early May. Otherwise I hope we can see you somewhere else soon! Much love, Kim and Meryam

Dear Kim,

Oh great!!! Another rare reader!! Try Banville's **The Book of Evidence** next!!! He is superb, isn't he!! Some days I think I'm remaining on the earth just to read good books! And that's good enough. Indeed, I loved **Map of Love**. Let's pass these back and forth, please, if you can continue to humor an old woman! Cairo trilogy, yes, also more recently **The Inheritance**, Palestinian woman, forgotten her name. No, I won't alas be in SF in May, I'm scootling (is that how you spell it- cross between scooting and scuttling?) through for a couple of nights in April. BUT I just put house on market (deadest market in 25 years here) because I'm ready to stop being a householder even if I never get to be a yogi, and I'm thinking about a 1 room apt in Berkeley. I miss "my people" too much here. Oh, I am so happy for you both having found each other. Just find a good one for Adam please!!!! Much love to you both, Lee

From Marjan
I am not sure what to do with my surgeon; right now I am just getting angrier. I have a follow-up meeting with him April 4. Next week I will see the rehab doc again, see what he has to say this time (he was a bit shocked by what happened). Not much news really; things are going very slowly. Not an awful lot of change. Today finally sunshine after many rainy days; rain again tomorrow. Good day to file my taxes.....How is your healing ? Love, Marjan

Dear Marjan, Oh, I am outraged on your behalf!! I'll never forget the look on my voice rehab guy's face when he first got a glimpse of my vocal cords. Darn it, we should be together, then you could scream and howl for me and I could stamp and kick for you!! And those guys are probably merrily carving up others before going off to play golf!! I have to see mine next week, he generally prods my Adam's apple incredibly hard, then says, "does that hurt", and I say, "what do you expect?" and he turns his back with a judicious murmur and writes something illegible in his notes, and tells me to come again in another three months. I think we should both have a free consult with our beloved doc Robert. I just have these wonderful memories of the three of us walking down the street to the coffee shop, and you could walk and I could talk, and we need to know from him the deep esoteric significance of what has been perpetrated. Yours is far worse than mine, my pain is almost over, just feel as if I'm being strangled sometimes. I send you love, and hope that Easter brings a little resurrection to you. Lee

From: Dianna

Dear Lee, Finally realized that I had been using a wrong email address for
you. Hope this finds you recovering well. How is the voice? Are you still
thinking of moving? Walli has been ill. Pleurisy. I didn't know what that was
until recently. It seems its quite serious. She's been down with it for a couple
of months now. Count down here. Lawyers continue to suck the life out of
my finances. Like being a hamster on a wheel sometimes. Have been more
involved with peace activities. Would love to go to DC on the 17th. A
friend's husband just optioned for a film, the book which supposes a trial of
Bush and Gang. I hope he gets it going FAST. I can't understand why my
beloved dems are so chickensh*t about going for impeachment.

Kyle, I hear through the grapevine, is still planning to go to Mongolia next
school year. No official program - just a teacher who wants Kyle to do her
research, I suspect.

All in all, doing ok here - next moon node coming up in about a month. Have
been feeling it for several months now. It's either that or I'm just plain nuts!
My friend, Astrid, has begun speaking on the AA circuit. I'm very proud of
her. She has used her experiences and her study and WORK with
anthroposophy to go deeper than any other AA work I've seen. Last week, a
man asked her if she'd be willing to speak in "the hood". She said, "If you
drive." She spoke to a crowd of 75 black men and women waiting to get into
a shelter called skid row. Two people asked if she would be their sponsor.
(She's already got 8 sponsees). Hugs, love and all that's good.   Dianna

Dearest Dianna,
How wonderful to hear from you. I often sit around reading old emails (way
of getting writing) and am perpetually awed by the friendships I have. So
sorry to hear about Walli. I'll write her today. And bully for Astrid - she's a
great gal and I so enjoyed meeting her. Well, voice comes and goes - it was
two steps forward, one back, for several months, then an awful one step
forward, three back, and I'm now moving forward again, I think and hope.
House goes on market on 21st (first day of spring, I decided), but that market
is dead as a dodo here too, despite fact that Denzel Washington, Sean
Connery, Angelina Jolie, Dick Cheney, Dan Quayle (does that cover the
professional, political bases?) seem to have bought property here. So, I will
bury my St. Joseph and say my prayer (you know that technique don't you)
and hope for the best, which would be a decent price within next 6 months.
I think I really should move to Berkeley. But who knows what I can afford.
Two friends, my age, dropped dead without warning in past two months, so it
would be pretty silly wouldn't it if I kept squirreling away my nuts rather than
spending them now. Why don't you join me there? I looked into co- housing
there yesterday on line, but backed off rather rapidly when I saw photos of

darling folk, all under thirty, under dressed, under washed, with lots of underarm hair, kiddies, chickens, bongo drums, and thought that wasn't for me any longer. Hey, couldn't we have fun, maybe do things, not sure what, but something other than propping up walls and plugging leaks. Be very very vigilant through Holy Week, when we can get forces for whole future destiny, after the confusion and depression that often runs through Lent.

No, I won't go to Washington, but we'll do our bit on 24th here. I think impeachment is too good for this gang (my son is working on a brief suing Rumsfeld, and those are the only days he can sleep at night – 'sleep of the just'?). Documentary **Road to Guantanemo** is about his clients. I just think a couple of months for that lot to be incarcerated there would begin to satisfy me - lovely picture of them each in their little wire cages, chained hands and feet to ground in orange jump suits, shaved heads, black blindfolds, while groups of Marines yell at them from a safe distance behind their riot gear..... I'm glad the Germans are suing the CIA for torture etc. Oh, I'd better not get too riled up. Just try to sell your house, move to Berkeley with me. Couldn't we HAVE A BLAST!!! Aren't we ready for some real colleagueship and connections now? When I booked flight to S.F. I got so excited I almost began to levitate, so that told me something about not being in the right place any longer. Go well, much much love, Lee

Dear Lee,

Loved getting your letter, too. Had I mentioned that I was looking into co-housing. A lot of different kinds around now. It would be so nice to have a small community of reliable neighbors and to have one or two who share a spiritual path. Even more wonderful to live near someone like you who has so much to share. First thing has to be pulling this place out of harm's way with that evil business with the crooked lawyer. But that takes backseat to concerns about friends.

If Walli hasn't told you, she's in quite a serious way. She's been diagnosed as having ovarian cancer and cancer cells have been found in the lung area as well. I'm sending you her e-mail to me. She sounds quite positive and I can't help but adhere to her wish to be held in the most positive light. If anyone could have worthwhile advice for her at this time, I would think it would be you. I'll keep you posted. Big hug tonight. Love, Dianna

Dear Dianna,

First to you, SH*T SH*T SH*T about Walli and I'll have to go and have a howl outside in a bit. Takes your breath away, doesn't it. And if the angels take her, they are (as I was once told) a ruthless bunch, and have to take so many whom they can use fruitfully. Only way I can think of the worst. Now, I'm going to write her and think of the best. I just sent her a card. Thanks for keeping me in the loop - please continue. Much love, keep in touch, Lee

Walli is a strong and lovely German woman, married to a Czech, Joseph. They met in South Africa, married and lived there for several year, before coming to Nevada. They have a remarkable 8yr old son, Janni, and have hosted workshops of mine in a small community just south of Reno over several years.

Dearest Walli,
I am going to be sending you the biggest force this old fart can muster- and even with a voice that sounds like a distant foghorn bleating through wire wool I am going to tell the spiritual world we NEED HER THIS SIDE, so stop messing with her! And, just let me know what else? I'm a little league pro as you know. You must also know how many defeat this beast, and if anyone can, it's an old battleaxe in disguise, because you aren't really, you are just a knight with lots of courage, with a lot of people praying for you. You probably have no energy to write, or anything, Dianna will keep me in the loop, but just so you know, I'm here, day and night. Time to lay down your arms and let us put ours around you. Love you, Lee
* Walli's full name means Battleaxe!!

Walli and I correspond for the next month or so, and I treasure these letters but won't include them here, then Dianna takes over and keeps me in touch with Walli's journey towards her star. She dies in June. I fly up to Reno, arriving a night too late to say goodbye, but in time for Dianna and I to do the honors - a three day vigil in the Prach's small home, and small community. This deserves a book itself - the joys and challenges, the hilarious, painful and deep experiences such a great soul can bestow upon those left behind.

To: various friends
Subject: Fw: the luck o' the Irish to you!

Well, I'm mainly bog Irish and never celebrate St. Patrick's so why not for the first time in this way. Nice story, if true - you never know with us Irish - love Lee

IRISH LUCK

His name was Fleming, and he was a poor Scottish farmer. One day, while trying to make a living for his family, he heard a cry for help coming from a nearby bog. He dropped his tools and ran to the bog. There, mired to his waist in black muck, was a terrified boy, screaming and struggling to free himself. Farmer Fleming saved the lad from what could have been a slow and terrifying death.
The next day, a fancy carriage pulled up to the Scotsman's sparse surroundings. An elegantly dressed nobleman stepped out and introduced himself as the father of the boy Farmer Fleming had saved.
"I want to repay you," said the nobleman. "You saved my son's life."

*"No, I can't accept payment for what I did," the Scottish farmer replied
waving off the offer. At that moment, the farmer's own son came to the door of
the family hovel.*
"Is that your son?" the nobleman asked.
"Yes," the farmer replied proudly.
*"I'll make you a deal." Said the nobleman. "Let me provide him with the
level of education my own son will enjoy. If the lad is anything like his father,
he'll no doubt grow to be a man we will both will be proud of." And that he
did.*
*Farmer Fleming's son attended the very best schools and in time, graduated
from St. Mary's Hospital Medical School in London, and went on to become
known throughout the world as the noted Sir Alexander Fleming, the
discoverer of Penicillin.*
*Years afterward, the same nobleman's son who was saved from the bog was
stricken with pneumonia. What saved his life this time? Penicillin.*
*The name of the nobleman? Lord Randolph Churchill .. His son's name?
Sir Winston Churchill. Someone once said: What goes around comes around.*

Work like you don't need the money.
Love like you've never been hurt.
Dance like nobody's watching.
Sing like nobody's listening.
Live like it's Heaven on Earth.

From: Lalla : Subject: The luck o' the Irish.

Hi Lee:
I want to take this opportunity to send some love back!!!! I am thinking of
you and wishing to hear how things are proceeding with your voice and your
general health. I heard from Karen that you might at some point actually
"move to this part of the country"! That would be terrific.
I want you to know that there is a very interesting building that some friends
are wanting to give up, which would be great for communal living, something
like an "anthroposophic center of applied wisdom". I thought maybe you and
Meg might want to team up to start a new anthroposophic denomination,
something offering "best movies" night, "chatting with angels" night, "just
plain telling funny stories" night..... and what not. Anyway, you can come see
it... or just have a laugh! I shall add that some parents have requested a
Biography Workshop specifically with Lee Sturgeon-Day. Karen told me you
would like to pass for the fall, but know that you are in many hearts... I will
tell you our news some other time. We are plodding along fine and it's .as
good as it gets, and much better than that on the good days! Lots of love,
Lalla, with Paolo and company

Dearest Lalla,
Well, that sounds interesting, wonder if we could pop past it when I'm with
Karen 16th/17th April. I was thinking of a 1 room apt in Berkeley. Though

my voice still sounds terrible, we are getting hopeful. I have to learn to use cords in quite conscious ways now. I decided good poetry would do the trick, so I chose **Dante** and **Rilke** last week!!!! If *they* don't do it, who will??? All I DO know is I need to spend more time with those I love. Like you, Lee.

From: Signe

Dear Lee, I assume that you have heard about Linda's death early on Saturday morning. I am only just now back home. She went very peacefully in her sleep. Bob and I had been with her all through the preceding day and evening. In the end she was ready to go, without fear or regret. I am thankful for this. Now I feel her free from the burdens of her body and soul. We had a small funeral on Tuesday -- I spoke and the Christian Community priest gave a lovely eulogy, and there was the fiddle music she wanted. On Sunday the 25th (her 65th birthday) we will have a memorial at the community center -- hopefully a real celebration of her life with the hundreds of people who love her for all her wackiness, her kindness and her vulnerabilities. It's such a strange time for our family, with this coming so close after Judy's death. I should be packing since we leave this house on April 9. But I have little will for anything today. I guess it will come. I hope things are well with you. Love, Signe

Dearest Signe,
Thank you so so much for letting me know, no, I didn't. Some time, at your non-leisure if you could send me Bob's address so I can write. It sounds so good, though, the peacefulness and acceptance. What a trooper. But what a lot for you, with Judy too. I've lost so many so suddenly it is extraordinary. I will now include Linda in my reading to the "so-called dead" - optional attendance. And you in my heart and thoughts, because you will need time, won't you, to really grief as well as celebrate, and you are the last of the line too, in your family (I mean first don't I?) and I think that's something.
But how striking all these moves to as it were complement these huge transitions, and before Easter, so you are all set for a future with Linda and Judy really supporting you from the other side.
Well, I need to dash to attend to the needs of the living. I will see you in June in Brooklyn. Well, we all need at least one laugh a day, so this is what Esther Chase sent me this morning: *A couple give birth to a baby boy who has no brain. Surgeon tells them he's needing to transplant one. "Trouble is," says surgeon, "the male brains are very pricey, they run around $5000, whereas you can get a female brain for as little as $200." " So, why's that?" asks the couple. "Well, the female brains have been used already!* Love you, Lee

Dear Mum
Don't you think it's strange that a story called "Luck 'o the Irish" is about two Scotsmen? I have my first weekend off in about three months! My Rumsfeld

brief is done and I'm going to relax and read the new book you sent me! I may not have a chance to get at the chocolates, my roommate appears to be even more addicted to them than me. Uma walked today, with the help of a rail, but she walked. That's a pretty big step from two weeks ago, when she was almost comatose. I'm going to leave work before my luck of the Irish runs out and I get a weekend assignment. Love you, A

Darling Adam,
Well, you're the only person who picked that one up (Scots/Irish bit). Enjoy book. And I am thrilled to hear about Uma. Guess what - my luck of the Irish wish was directed to her! Sometime in next 2-3 weeks shall I pick up a flight? I wondered about say 20-27 June? Chenta might might have had her baby, Chris and Signe will have moved in, and there between other trips. (By the way Linda, Signe's sister died too a week ago, she had been very sick for ages). Grab a few chocs, and enjoy weekend. Love you, Mum

Another month passes. Suzanne Bishop, Judy Laury, Linda Norris, (all my age), and two other friends from Detroit, Eve Hardie and Ralph Marinelli, then dear fighter Alison Greene, (age 30) have all gone to their stars in the past 3 months. Walli follows in June. What grace to have known each and every one of these extraordinary souls. Now I will have to develop the new, different and sometimes even more intimate relationships we can create with those on the other side.

-

CHAPTER THIRTEEN. FINALE

*"There are people on a parallel way. We do not see them often, or even think
of them often, but it is precious to us that they are sharing the world.
Something about how they have accepted their lives, or how the sunlight
happens to them, helps us to hold the strange enigmatic days in line for our
own living.*
*Here is a smoke signal, unmistakable, but unobtrusive...we are following what
comes, going through the world, knowing each other, building our little fires."*
William Stafford.

It is almost time to conclude this chronicle. My continuing correspondence
will remain unpublished, just close to my heart. Smoke signals....yes, indeed!
Amazing to think a year has passed since this story began. Easter is on its way
too. There is always a rising of hope along with rising sap, yet not born of the
natural world.

I signed off with my surgeon a couple of weeks before our anniversary
proper. A pretty sad encounter, actually. Adam was right. I was the "Whore
of Babylon". I know the best method of defence is attack and his was swift
and vicious. Only when I think he was convinced he had won: "game, set
and match" (I had forgotten he wanted to be a tennis champion) did he
simmer down, turn on the charm, assure me I would never be forgotten, invite
me to visit them in times to come. I think not. Karma, as I told him, will
have to take care of all we could not. *Surgeon v. Sturgeon* was not how I
hoped it would end. I understand well the pressures, the terror of lawsuits
etc., but an honest admission that the severity of a surgery he deemed
appropriate could lead to my condition would have gone a long way to heal
our connection. Maybe someone else will benefit down the road. I drive
back to Suzanne's struggling not to want to sue all over again. I guess this
letting go, which I thought I had done, is never fully accomplished. It takes
little to make my gorge rise all over again. Part of what I am going to need to
learn to accept is my own failure to discover all this beforehand and to rely on
an "expert" who may not have been quite so expert after all. (A few months
later I learn they have almost abandoned my procedure in British hospitals,
preferring less invasive approaches.) "Mustn't dwell," I exhort myself (as
most Brits do, only then to dwell ferociously thereafter.) It is, alas, the only
relationship over this past year that has deteriorated rather than flourished.

Now I am preparing to go forth, still with an appalling sound that passes for a
voice. But there's sound, at least. It is neither as strong, nor as human, as the
one I brought to surgery, even allowing for the gravelly huskiness of a long
term smoker. That at least had some range of motion, some tone. I could
quote poetry. Heck, I could even sing with the tenors and bass! I doubt I'll
ever sing again. I would love to be able to speak a poem, to speak with
feeling, rather than the monotonous rasp that resembles a wire brush being

dragged across the bottom of a steel saucepan. At good times, its pale whispery whine reminds me of a 10 yr old girl at school, whose arm I savagely bit because I couldn't stand the sound of her. Maybe *that* old karma is now coming to roost!!

Since it is obvious what I have lost, because along with a voice goes my spoken work, my travels it allowed and paid for, and all the visits with my friends, then I must look at what has been gained!!!
The world has had a break from me, my blathering. That's not insignificant! We forget, so often, that our lives are lived for others, not ourselves. Here and there friends have taken over "my" work, and been much appreciated. We all have different gifts, and all need to be displayed!
I have had a small experience of what it feels like to have a permanent disability - to wake each morning to this remembrance. Even now, a year and a half after surgery, I notice I make small whimpers throughout the day, "testing, testing" to see if I can. And how small this loss is compared with the young returning from war zones, with Drew and thousands of others looking ahead to a life without some limb or faculty.
Since I really cannot hope to work again orally, I wonder: is this how it is to be laid off? This feeling of being utterly useless, of no value to anyone or anything? How many millions face this, with the far greater added agony of not being able to support themselves and others? Will it increase my capacity for empathy? I hope so.
And I have learned, yet again, that I have the most amazing friends and am nothing without them. They have supported and cherished me with devotion and great goodwill. They never gave up on me, even when I felt like giving up on myself. What more, really, can any of us ask for? I didn't need convincing that friendship is the most important factor in my life. But it still astonishes to have this reaffirmed so powerfully through this time. Maybe the best way of trying to bring this chronicle- at least in print - to some sort of conclusion, is to share a few of my favorite exchanges from Easter through to the time I am writing this. Do they tell me who I am? Or are friends expressing who *they* are in some essential way?

New to these pages, is my friend Peter, who sent me this Easter poem and followed it with almost a poem a day through the next months. That's quite a treat to wake up to each morning.

EASTER, 2007

*Morning cabochon of dew at a single
leaf's center, reverent radiant reminder,
there are gods still all around us,
still at work on us: inhaled god for one
whose branch blooms in the blood,
killed god for another the blowing one*

passing from warmth to air to light,
though always a portion gets left behind
becoming the hindrance the certain weight
slowing down what wants to hurry on.

So am I lost because I go across the fields
of feeling in all directions at once
out into the hills frantic to find again
my lost thinking how its depravity began
the drunk divinity of each particular thing
leaves ranged as faces lifting their flowers
past the shame that binds them here
to arrive at my desire again
here where the body began
where you, heart, were being planned
to feel yourself in each thing
outside yourself in each thing
hovering inside yourself again.

There is my son's continuing career. I feel proud of him, and of being counted in such distinguished company as these other friends of his.

From: **Adam Day**
Sent: Jul 16, 2007 2:51 PM
To: Ashish Bhatia , Rodrigo Ordóñez , Zinaida Miller , Lee Sturgeon Day,
Marisa Arpels Ian Johnstone, Rahul Chandran, Michael Lieberman, Jane
Kembabazi, Shree Nadarajah , Erika Lopez , Niki Ganz Moss , Gillian Cull ,
heather ryan , Kim-Fredrik Schneider , Laura Sitea, Kevin Moss , "Gupta,
Roman - Paramount", John P Gohring , Rene Betancourt, Kenny Kupers

Subject: Decision Time
Friends, Family, People Who Have Watched Me in Despair at My Job for the Last Ten Months,

First, thank you all for putting up with me over the last year. I have been unreliable, grouchy, selfish, and depressed. Also, thank you for talking with me about my life, giving suggestions, and/or just being one of my friends. I honestly would not have made it through the last year without you.
I have to give a special thanks to Zina, to whom I owe the rest of this email.
Human Rights Watch would like me to start work for them in August on a consultancy position for their International Justice Program. The pay: low.
The benefits: none. The work: three days a week minimum, but probably moving quickly to overloaded. The time period: two months with a basically guaranteed renewal up to six months, maybe up to a year. I know, it sounds too good to be true: I will make 1/13 of my current salary, I will have very

little job security, and I'll have to pay my law school debts with money stolen from my roommate's laundry quarters.

The only twinge I have is that, through the relentless efforts of several Fletcher alums and faculty, I have an interview at UN DPKO set up for the end of July. But I think I have to take this opportunity, get out of the firm while I'm still sane, and then work on getting into the UN in 2008. Is it the right decision to take this HRW job? I have slightly less than 24 hours to decide and inside I'm screaming "yes," but I don't want to make a bad decision just because I hate where I am right now. I'd love to hear what all of you have to say, pros, cons, etc... Lots of love, A

Darling Adam,
Go for it!!!! Where is it? I'll help you any way I can. Love Mum

Thanks Mum,
It's here in New York. In the Empire State building! I am going to go for it. I'll survive, I have some money put away. I feel like my heart is finally beating at the right rate again. Love you, A.

From My Dear Doctor Friend: May 22nd

Dear Lee,
So good to hear from you. I didn't know that you were planning to come back to the Bay area. I would like to spend some time with you before we are "gathered." Why don't you think of renting something near me in the Mission? It would be a lot easier than spending all that precious time on the Bart before *The Gathering*. Then you could work with Dr. B. easily. And you could walk to my office for your ear acupuncture treatment. Today there is S.F. opera in the park across the street from me. When I hear them singing their arias I am going to picture you up there singing all those high notes that you could never have reached with the voice you used to have.

Well I have to say that I'm thrilled that you are coming back home to California. Your digs will be smaller, but here's where it's all happening. The richness of the arts in this city is so much more important than square footage. I feel like I live in paradise. Welcome to paradise. Love DDF

Dear DDF,
I think I may be suffering from terminal excitement at thought of moving closer to you all. We may yet enjoy The Rapture together, being "*gathered*" on a high note, holding hands!!! Love Lee

From Sheila: 31 March
Dearest Lee, I love your letters, rich with anecdotes and fragments of story, and I enjoy re-reading them just before writing to you, always finding something I had forgotten or overlooked.

I like the Larkin poem, and thank you for it. "A huge and birdless silence" - I seem to know just what that sounds like! Here's a poem for you, given me recently by a new friend, Jean Mason (retired psychiatrist with a strong interest in Jung).

(Here is an excerpt from it: **Spring Wedding**, by Andrew Motion.)

> *I.................found the Spring*
> *Had honoured all its promises to start*
> *Disclosing how the principles of earth*
> *Can make a common purpose with the heart.*
> *The heart which slips and sidles like a stream*
> *Weighed down by winter-wreckage near its source*
> *But given time, and come the clearing rain,*
> *Breaks loose to revel in its proper course.*

So, Easter comes round again, yet another wedding anniversary. (Sheila is referring to my wedding on Holy Saturday,) yet another descent into hell, yet another resurrection. I'd love to think that this year's immersion in the ancient rituals will bring you the joy of finding a new voice (or better, the renewing of your old voice.) But I know that for both of us, the real task is to accept whatever comes and find the gift within it.

Perhaps my Giotto card (I've had it ages, waiting for the right moment) is timely for you, this Easter? I do feel sure that initiation can require a betrayal, and that it is up to us, sometimes, to spot this and name it for what it is. This is what you are doing, I think, when you describe the extraordinary run up to your operation, and also the experience of your Dutch friend. Forgiveness is at the heart of it. But there is something else - the recognition that at times we, and other people, may be required to play the part of the betrayer in order to bring about a necessary result, one that couldn't be reached by any other means. And at those moments, we probably don't have a choice. A Wobbly World indeed! But leading to another state, unimaginably steady..........

The real exchange between us is a greeting based on an unquenchable friendship and a profound respect for eath other's essence. That's love, isn't it? Sheila.

Oh, yes, dearest Sheila, what an unquenchable friendship we have. That is love indeed!

December 8th
Dear Mum,
I hope you're feeling better. I'm so excited you're coming out in only a couple of weeks! The job hunt is over. I still have an interview set up with the mission in Congo, but I know I'm going to accept the offer I got yesterday. UNAMID (the acronym you will have to get used to, which stands for United

Nations African Union Hybrid Mission in Darfur) has offered me a position in Darfur for one year. This is exactly what I was hoping to get out of my current job at the UN and I'm going to accept it. I'm very excited - nervous - but very excited.

What this means: (1) I will deploy in early January, (2) I will be living in a city called Al Fasher, (3) I will be a political affairs officer, (4) I will not be in danger, but I will be very careful, (5) I will be gone for at least one year, but I get five days off every six weeks (for Wendy trips, or for meeting you in exotic locales), (6) I will learn arabic and get a good tan.

It's all very exciting and happening very quickly. I'm going to start getting prepared for the big move now, so that by the time you get here I won't be too frantic. But I'll probably be fairly frantic. When you're back home and feeling better, let's have a chat and catch up. Lots of love, Adam.

Exchange with Teri on her brief visit to the States in November when we hoped to hang out in Phoenix airport for a few hours and my car died and my body felt as if it were about to die too.

Darling Teri,
You may get this before you call, but I've decided to stay put here. I obviously had, or am having, some kind of virus that afflicts head and tummy. I am so so sad to have different cords and they can't speak foreign languages any more, and they can't sing happy birthday and they can't speak poetry, and they can't say healing words in healing ways, and there's no chuckle, just a chicken squawk, and I just have to face that that may be as good as it gets, but I guess it's better than no sound at all. Losing what we love is always hard, isn't it. I know one must always be hopeful, but one definition of a pessimist is "a well informed optimist", so I'm not going to live with illusion either. Love you, and so sad, but no good coming if I feel this lousy. Bad case of *Grief and Grumbles*, which sounds like an English pudding. Maybe one better than *Toad in the Hole?* Lee

Hi Lee,
I understand and I am also sorry. Listen Lee, I know you are grieving and I really really can sympathise with you and I am so sorry for your loss. But you have also been gifted with a new voice which is not a whine at all. You sound vulnerable and quite beautiful. Of course your old voice was wonderful. But what is your task now? You are right, your voice could heal others. Maybe you have a new task with your new voice. Think of all the writers who search for a voice and can't find their own. You have had two voices. I see this - perhaps in a slightly perverse way (the spiritual world has a wicked sense of humor) - as a new chance. Perhaps you need to do something very very different? Hold strong. Love Teri

Darling Teri,
Thank you again for wonderful words. I KNOW I won't get my old voice back, I KNOW! But I still find it so hard to accept that, specially when I

listen to Vanessa Redgrave or Joan Plowright speaking in my old timbre. But since there's absolutely nothing I can do, I just have to go plodding along. Enough! As you say I have raised a beautiful son, what more can anyone achieve on the earth?

Here's an extract of Doris Lessing's nobel prize speech (you once sent me a quote of hers.) Also a letter from my son, so you know what's happening in our lives. I don't know if I have any "new work". I have never come through an ordeal transformed and with new impulses. So I must accept that too. Hey, maybe I'm here on this continent to balance the Born Agains? Everything here is about leaving the old behind, and never suffering again, and becoming utterly different. So I just have to honor this journey, not feel dismayed when you and others hope for "new words" or "new directions". And I will try not to be such a *Toad in the Hole* so often. Accepting that no one may ever hear my cackle again won't be easy. though! Now I'd better get back to my other Terri (Kosmicki) who will - in my son's words - begin fluffing my aura in hopes of turning this bugaboo around. Love you, Lee

From: Teri : Sent: Dec 19.

I'm so sorry for prodding the way I did. I forget that the greatest spiritual task is to live well, to *be* well. And my God, you are absolutely right. Someone has to balance those Born Agains, or at the least the people who remain Born Again. Nothing wrong with being Born Again, but then one must grow up, no?
I think that your friends often prod you to find a new task, is because we are all in absolute awe of your abilities. You are loved and it seems that you have friends who hover over you like Jewish mothers. Oy! Keep fluffing your aura. It's gorgeous. Love Teri

If I don't stop somewhere, I never will. We are approaching the second anniversay of my surgery. Maybe by the third I will be able to produce my cackle, even if never again the voice I used to have. Adam is now in Darfur, my incredible friends continue to keep me abreast of their lives (now isn't that a wonderful expression "abreast"?) and to show interest and support in mine. I'm still in Prescott in a totally collapsed housing market, but planning all kinds of wonderful adventures in future- to France (my brother's house there) next Christmas to meet Adam and Wendy - his love - and my family, to Australia still, and maybe now Africa? The main lesson I've learned this year is to spend as much time with those I love as I possibly can before I'm "Gathered" and probably afterwards too! Perhaps the best way I know of ending this little chronicle is a poem sent by yet another friend, Joseph. It doesn't get better or truer than this, I think.

FRIEND BY FRIEND

Who is my mother,
Who my father,
When I am being created
Friend by friend?
I don't remember who I was without you.
We have been tending sacred fires
For a long time
We are wanderers, drawn by the light
Of those fires.
Surrounded by darkness,
Emerging out of darkness,
We enter into the sacred ceremony
Of each other's life.
We sing, we dance,
Humbled by the power
Of each other's presence
We pray.
We become prayers for each other.
We sing praises to each other.
And breath by breath, thought by thought,
Touch by touch,
Music rises between us.

What I was, I am no longer.
Shaking with hope, yielding to your hands
I stand trembling before you.

Joseph Rubano